# Fighting
# Violent Crime
# in America

# Fighting Violent Crime in America

※

*Ronald S. Lauder*

**DODD, MEAD & COMPANY**
*New York*

Grateful acknowledgment is made to the Community Research Center, University of Illinois, for permission to quote from the address of Andrew Vachss in Chapter 4. The author is grateful to Mr. Vachss for helping edit his address for use in this book. Acknowledgment is also made to CBS, Inc. for making available a transcript of "Murder Teenage Style," *CBS Reports*, September 3, 1981, and for granting permission for its use in Chapter 4.

No part of this book may be reproduced in any form
without permission in writing from the publisher.
Published by Dodd, Mead & Company, Inc.
79 Madison Avenue, New York, N.Y. 10016
Distributed in Canada by
McClelland and Stewart Limited, Toronto
Manufactured in the United States of America
First Edition


*Library of Congress Cataloging in Publication Data*

Lauder, Ronald S.
  Fighting violent crime in America

  Bibliography: p.
  Includes index.
  1. Violent crimes—United States—Prevention.
2. Information storage and retrieval systems—Criminal
justice, Administration of—United States.   3. Prisons—
United States—Overcrowding—Prevention.   4. Criminal
justice personnel—Training of—United States.   I. Title.
HV7431.L38   1985      364.4        84-21249
ISBN 0-396-08495-8

# WILDERMUTH

The fear of crime is making all of us part of the greatest prison population in history—self-made prisons formed when we place bars on our windows, double locks on our doors, alarm systems throughout our homes and guard dogs outside our entrances. This fear, if allowed to go unchecked, will empty the cities, destroy the American sense of friendliness and community and lead to vigilantes.

> —WILLIAM CAHALAN, prosecuting
> attorney, Wayne County, Michigan.

With ready-made opinions one cannot judge crime. Its philosophy is a little more complicated than people think.

> —FEODOR DOSTOEVSKI (1821–1881)
> *Prison Life in Siberia*

※

# Contents

# Acknowledgments

F<small>OR</small> their editorial help and other
contributions, I want to thank Thomas Otwell, Joan Braunstein, Natalie Lang, Jerry Gross, Cynthia Buckley, Lisa Cannon, Natalie Neviaser, and Judith Howell.

For generously providing me with material (and leaving it to me to decide how to use it), I am grateful to, among others: the President's Task Force on Victims of Crime; the United States Senate Subcommittees on Juvenile Justice, and on Criminal Law; the United States House of Representatives Subcommittees on Criminal Justice; on Crime; and on Courts, Civil Liberties, and Administration of Justice; the Federal Bureau of Investigation, and particularly Assistant Director Roger Young and William Baker; the Police Foundation, and Thomas Brady; the Justice Department Office of Juvenile Justice and Delinquency Prevention, and William Modseleski; the Advertising Council; Dr. Jerome Miller; Andrew Vachss; Janet Dinsmore; Professor Alfred Blumstein; the Rand Corporation; Figgie International, Inc., and Mark Murphy; the House of Umoja, and Sister Falaka Fattah; the Justice Department Bureau of Justice Statistics; the Montgomery County (Maryland) Department of Public Libraries, particularly the Four Corners branch, and Evelyn Whitaker and Mary Conover; the Jaycees; the Salvation Army, and Jordan Rothbart; the National Youth Work Alliance, and Robbie Callaway; Robert Woodson of the National Center for Neighborhood Enterprise; Talbert House, and Janet Patterson; the Police Departments of Hartford, Garland, Texas, Detroit, Houston, and Washington, D.C.; the Florida Governor's Office, and John Newman; the New York Mayor's Office, and Kevin Frawley; the Washington Post; the Washington Times; the Shelby County Violent Offenders Project, and Michael Whittaker; the National Institute of Education, and Dr. Oliver Moles; the Texas Crime Prevention Institute, and Leland Wood; the Safer Foundation; the American Enterprise Institute; The Brookings Institution; the Prison Fellowship; the National Council on Crime and Juvenile Delinquency; the Federal Bureau of Prisons, and Emile Aun; the Census Bureau; Ira Lowe; the International Association of Chiefs of Police; G. Patriok Gallagher of the Florida Department of Law Enforcement; M. S. Knowles; the National Center on Child Abuse and neglect; the National Institute of Mental Health, and Thomas Lalley of the Center for Studies of Crime and Delinquency; the United States Chamber of Commerce; the American Civil Liberties Union; *Corrections* and *Police* magazines, and Olos Pitts; the National Association of Manufacturers: the New York Chamber of Commerce and Industry; CBS, Inc., and Francesca Beale; "CBS Reports," and "60 Minutes"; the South East Secure Treatment Unit, West Chester, Pennsylvania, and Fred McNeal; the Phoenix Institute and its SoJourn Project; Betty Southard Murphy; Ingrid Annibale: Richard Bast; the staff of Representative Barbara Mikulski; Jack Anderson; Environments for Human Services, and Byrn Anderson; the United States Conference of Mayors; the National Criminal Justice Reference Service; the National Institute of Justice; the Washington Legal Foundation; Elan and Sharon Terry; the Library of Congress; Senator Orrin Hatch and Nancy Taylor; the State's Attorney's Office, Montgomery County, Maryland, and Stephen Savage; the American Correctional Association, and Diana Travisono.

   I am also grateful to the victims, police, prosecutors, federal law enforcement officials, and many others, including the criminals, who helped with this book with the understanding that they would not be quoted by name. I have used random initials or personal pronouns to shield their identities.

*Ronald S. Lauder*

*Author's Note*

In the text, notes, and bibliography, I have generally used writers' and speakers' positions as of the time they made their statements. My purpose: To give their words the proper official context. When I have departed from standard annotation and bibliography style, it has been to make reference books easier to locate and notes easier to key into the text. Both notes and bibliography are lengthy, but not all-inclusive. I have cut them slightly in the interests of conciseness.

# Fighting
# Violent Crime
# in America

※

# Introduction

Criminologists, sociologists, and penologists have written books on violent crime. So have prosecutors and public defenders. Victims have had their say. Even criminals have told us about vicious lawbreaking. All of them bring to their writing special insights.

But to my knowledge, no businessman has ever researched violent crime specifically to come up with answers based on business practices and old-fashioned entrepreneurial common sense.

True, businessmen have written—and ably—about white-collar crime. That is what they perceive as affecting them most closely. They have abandoned violent crime to the experts. But to paraphrase parallel adages about generals and diplomats, perhaps violent crime is too important to leave to the professionals.

Suppose, I thought, I wrote a book suggesting how business practices could solve crime problems, not through endless studies, debate, panels, seminars, multimillion dollar grants, but through often simple, though sometimes complex methods.

Some crime experts might find this a quixotic approach. And in some ways, they might be right. But what I know bone-deep, as sure as I know my name and the operations of our family company, is that many of my ideas will work. When they do, lives will be saved, injuries will be averted.

I do not think for a moment that I can restructure the criminal system or make our cities entirely safe from criminals. But if the business principles I recommend do work, then our children, our

*1*

parents, our employees will be statistically safer. "Statistically," of course, is the hitch.

One of the people I spoke with in preparing this book said, "Sure, why not write it? It'll be worth it if all you save are four or five lives."

His thoughts are accurate; his figures, skewed: It will be worth it if out of my labors, *one* life is saved.

To make my point about this business approach quickly and I hope unarguably: All successful corporations are predicated on the idea of finding solutions. They survive only if they are cost-efficient and if, year after year, they produce perceptible results. Obvious as these premises are, the crime-fighting establishment does not pass muster on any of them.

Here are just a few examples:

• Using techniques developed by business, several cities have programmed computers with information on violent career criminals. When any arrest is made, the computer can be queried to see whether the suspect is one of these prize catches: a habitually vicious felon. The answer is almost instantaneous. If it is yes, the arresting officer gets from the computer the suspect's arrest record, his previous victims, his modus operandi, his accomplices, his hangouts, the areas where he has been active, and so on. Instead of closing a single case, the police may be able to close dozens. In addition, the prosecutors can be alerted to begin an all-out effort to lock this criminal up for a long, long time. But the monkey wrench in all this is that—unlike parallels in the business world—these brilliant systems are allowed to corrode because of lack of funding, poorly trained operators, bureaucratic bickering, and the like.

• In several areas, again using business principles, a single computer incorporates crime data not just from the main city but from outlying jurisdictions.[1] No more than a criminal nickname or a clothing description can signal the alert for a dozen previously uncoordinated police forces. If the clue clicks in another jurisdiction, then a name or names are put on the network making possible apprehension of a malefactor. Before, he would have remained at large. The FBI has a setup that permits similar cooperation on a nationwide basis. But despite these examples, no more than ten percent of all police computers are geared for this kind of work. Such foot dragging would be unthinkable in any competitive industry.

• Cost accounting, a business sine qua non, is almost nonexistent in many law-enforcement systems. As just one such example of financial inefficiency, local governments simply do not understand that it takes far less money for police to catch and jail the violent criminal than it does for health and rehabilitation agencies to treat his victims. Decades ago industry learned it was cheaper to buy a hard hat or metal-toed shoes than it was to pay sick leave, doctors' bills, civil court judgments, and lawyers' fees.

• A well-run commercial distributor knows where all his trucks are at any given time. Urgent orders can be filled by trucks already on the road. The savings are enormous. Police computers could achieve the same kind of on-the-road efficiency, not just with patrol cars, but with scooter officers, foot patrolmen, even police auxiliaries. What a boon for scheduling and crime response! Yet most police systems designed to do this basic kind of pinpointing are primitive and unmonitored.

• Industrial plants have built-in electronic warning systems to cut down on injuries. Why not something similar for street police? Shouldn't an officer know if he is responding to a call at an address from which four violence reports have emanated in the last couple of months? It is easy to store such information in a dispatcher's computer.[2] Relatedly, shouldn't dispatchers have on hand continually changing "priority lists" so that a highly trained officer is not responding to a week-old burglary report while an urgent rape alert is understaffed?

• Business inventories are often so tightly monitored that at any moment a company can tell what is in stock where. Why not the same kind of system for, say, cells? There is a national scarcity of prison beds, but one in a maximum security penitentiary in State X may be occupied by a check forger while, in State Y, there is no secure cell for a violent robber.[3] A "cell bank" could easily be set up on an interstate basis, with the state that transfers the prisoner paying the fee to the receiving state. There are legal problems, but there are also many legal, businesslike solutions.

In addition to explicit problems and solutions, there is the matter of changing ways of looking at things. Sometimes the business view, while seeming hard-boiled, is actually more honest and just than traditional sociological attitudes.

Most people, for example, including many anticrime workers, are not aware that high technology research has produced a "model" by which we can predict who is most likely to become a violent criminal.

Thousands of interviews, scanned and collated, show that this habitually violent criminal has a juvenile record of awesome violence, abuses drugs or alcohol or both, has nervous symptoms, is hostile and remorseless, and has a very limited or twisted sense of right and wrong.[4]

Industry takes such things into account when we hire. Yet, in sentencing, judges often ignore the probability that such a person will be out on the street unreformed and ready to commit more mayhem. Why not use a computer "model" to give the worst criminal a longer sentence than those outside the model? He should, of course, have some way of proving that the miracle has occurred and he is rehabilitated. Some combination of testing, lie detector examinations, prison work, and social record could be used. But in the absence of rehabilitation, why could he not be "incapacitated"—that is, kept off the street longer than the ordinary criminal?

Collaterally, criminal research is not far from being able to predict which children are most likely to grow up to be violent criminals. It is based on a complicated weighing of factors: whether the child was abused, his environment, his parents' and even grandparents' criminality, his responses to psychological and other tests.

I certainly do not advocate locking these children up. But I do advocate strong family counseling, school supervision, and community involvement for these kids with a high potential for violent crime. Twenty years ago, such focusing of resources was attempted. In nine out of ten cases, one study showed, the results were no better than if nothing had been done.[5] Now, however, research has narrowed the difference between what will work and what will not. Money saved by turning these children away from crime—in terms of victims' medical bills, death payments, property loss, and so on—is almost incalculable.

Part of the problem with fighting crime, as anyone will discover who reads the literature of law enforcement, is that its academicians, with few exceptions, use so much jargon that they are almost incomprehensible. Even when they have incisive things to say, things that should stimulate the reader with possibilities, the language is dense, dull.

A corporation with something important to say employs a competent outside writer or uses one on the company staff whose job it is to make "business-speak" easy for everyone to understand. Why, when governments, foundations, and other institutions spend treasure troves for studies, do they not spend the extra few dollars and pay someone to interpret useful but abstruse findings into simple English?

In a way, this despecializing of criminal lore is at the heart of what I am trying to do in this book. If the nonbusinessman will only pause a moment and think about how he would run a company *if* he had one, he will see what I mean.

He would surmise that businesses make many costly failures, that the product that booms in Belgium may fail in Portugal but fly in Chicago. And he would be right.

But he would also find that we try to learn from such mistakes. He would see the logic of applying business procedures to law enforcement. Here are the kind of elementary applications that are easy to understand:

By studying the demographics, the health system, and the traditions of an area, the physical and psychological characteristics of potential buyers, and the advertising language that appeals to most people in general, and by programming all these things into a computer, an executive can get a good idea of what will sell where and what will not. I believe the same kind of detailed assessments can be used in fighting specific types of crime.

By tracking inventories, returns, and sales volume at midweek, at weekend, at Christmas, and in summer (for sun-related items, for example), a businessman can cut deeply into costs and keep in the black. Why can't we do similar tracking for crime-fighting equipment and personnel, hardware for jails and prisons, standard clerical supplies, even office space? It's certainly not being done in any systematic or organized way now.

Businesses cannot survive if relations with employees, whether union or nonunion, aren't fairly amicable. We make much of employee promotions; we try to fire people with as much fairness and dignity as possible. But it takes work, hard work, and ingenuity to keep morale up. It doesn't just happen. I *know* that the lessons established private enterprises have to teach can make life better for our demoralized crime-fighting bureaucracy: the police, prosecutors, judges, parole and probation people, corrections officers. In fact, proven business and personnel management techniques can go a long way, I believe, toward making prisoners, parolees, and probationers a less volcanic element in our society.

By bringing more technology to production, by merging or streamlining duplicatory functions and facilities, by rapidly cutting items that are dead limbs and nourishing fresh ones, business can make quality products, advertise them and see an honest profit. Yet even my first week's reading on crime convinced me that the overlaps and the tattered inefficiencies in the criminal justice establishment would have made the disjointed Austro-Hungarian Empire look as efficient as Xerox.

By pricing, accounting, and other financial wizardry that was ivory tower stuff only a year or two ago, we can project income, then allocate it to short-term costs or to products a decade down the road.

It may be that businessmen take a particularly stern view of crime because it so often is directed at us or our companies. For instance, kidnapping insurance is a hot item now. Forty percent of American executives fear kidnapping and not without reason.[6] In the last decade, industry has paid out a quarter of a billion dollars in ransoms.

When we travel, we check out the windows of our hotels, the door locks. Most of us have burglar alarms in our homes. A third of us take different routes to work each day.

Crimes against business hurt all Americans. To pay for the television camera you see on entering a corporate office, we must charge more for our products. To meet the kidnapping and theft insurance bills, we must sell more dearly. But if we did not take these precautions, we would have to charge even more because of losses to crime. So it is not just local and federal taxes that are used to fight crime. It is the consumers' spending money. You, the ordinary American, are paying for crime, and through many different cashiers' windows.

All authors would probably prefer to have their work judged entirely on how well it does what it sets out to do. But readers don't generally agree. They want to know "who this guy is." Someone who is recommending, as I am, drastic changes in how we spend tax money and novel ways to look at as important a subject as crime, probably has an obligation to tell his reader who he is, to present his bona fides. Briefly, here are mine:

I am a husband and a father, a businessman, a civic activist, a government executive—a mix of personnae, just as most Americans are. Also, like most Americans, I was brought up to work hard, to believe in country and flag, those basic things that nowadays we admire almost with embarrassment.

For twenty years I have worked in all phases of the business that bears our family name. My employment has, by good luck, coincided with the boom in technology that began in the 1960s and is now a mainstay of American industry. Today, technology is the electronic, computerized, intricately programmed way of getting things done.

My education was at the Bronx High School of Science, the Wharton School of Finance and Commerce at the University of Pennsylvania, and the International School of Business in Brussels. At the Sorbonne, in Paris, I earned a degree in French literature.

I am tempted to romanticize myself and say that but for my family's firm I might have been a poet or a professor of French literature. But, while I love French writing and envy its precision, I have always been satisfied that my skills and inclinations lay in the world of management.

Nevertheless, at the Sorbonne I was intrigued by Baudelaire. Here was a man from a well-to-do family who never committed murder, probably never knew anyone who had, yet in *Martyr* and *The Murderer's Wine* seemed to write directly from inside a violent criminal's brain.[7] Only in *Crime and Punishment* did I ever read the equal of such insights, and Dostoevski, although he had indeed been imprisoned, had also never murdered.

My point is that one does not need to consort with criminals or commit murder to understand and write about violence. Through their technical skills, these two superb authors gave us early and lasting visions into the violent criminal's self-hate, alternating paranoia and guilt, and peculiarly detached sociopathy.

Crime can be examined in many ways. We look at it as individuals, as parents, as homeowners worried about physical security, as concerned citizens seeking ways to bring about legislative or judicial reforms.

It is as a businessman that I feel most competent to report, analyze, and recommend. Not that you will find this merely a "how-to" book. I hope you will see it as a voyage of discovery, a vista on crime. The gaps between what I once believed about crime and what I found out about it from the raw data and the specialized readings I undertook were almost incredible.

I was nonplussed to find that many of our cities do not even track and act on the late teen "bubble"—the group in a community's population that is responsible for a disproportionate amount of its crime and violence. Data analyses can show precisely when this "bubble" will burst on a city.[8] Law enforcement, job programs, social service agencies, and other community resources could be made aware of this potential for criminal behavior and could prepare to deal effectively with it. To use an analogy, if a modern corporation failed to make such a basic projection, the rest of us would sadly assume that it *wanted* to go bankrupt, that it had about as much will to live as a migrating lemming.

When things go wrong in business, we do not, as government does, ordinarily toss good money after bad. We name some tough-minded troubleshooter answerable only to the chief executive officer. The CEO backs his recommendations to fire, to hire, and to reform and helps him turn the situation around.

This kind of attitude should be taken in reforming the anticrime establishment. There, because the troubleshooter is too often playing politics, and the workers are civil servants, the problems are accurately assessed, but the reforms are never made. The drunks stay on the payroll but are shuffled around; the inept administrators are made consultants or given less responsible jobs or sometimes even kicked upstairs (their pay is almost never cut); the goof-offs are countenanced, their salaries paid at terrific waste to the taxpayer.

As a result, good workers are first infuriated, then demoralized. Small wonder go-getters rapidly turn into passive go-alongs. In business, although this may sound cold, we cannot afford that kind of inefficiency. We feel that not to fire incompetents is to insult those who *are* competent. In the long run, it makes for a happier, harder-working, fairer, and more stable shop.

Almost from pilgrim days Americans have believed that the criminals among us could be rehabilitated if we just tried hard enough. When that concept began to change a few years ago, it changed with a vengeance.

Now, two of every three Americans want to have murderers executed. Ninety percent want stringent, mandatory terms for all violent felons. Fifty percent even want sterilization for habitual criminals.[9]

Among businessmen, as I know from my associations with other company officials, the feeling is even stronger about punishment of criminals.

From reading hundreds of scholarly papers, law enforcement agency reports and studies, and dozens of books, I concluded that nothing important in crime is solved in one quick stroke. But the situtation does improve if the confluence of positive actions occurs at the right time, in the right city. You will find recommendations for making these beneficial confluences possible, for speeding up the time when action can be taken.

To me these discoveries have been fascinating. I share them because I feel that if we expect to act wisely against crime, we must know something about it, and not just from the media. I believe my research will help us to shortcut the tortuous, contradictory, and arcane paths that, at first, confuse.

My perspective is as a city dweller. But I have included findings on the spread of violence to smaller cities, even to rural areas. It is there that a businesslike approach can be most useful: dealing with crime is easiest before its corrosion is advanced.

In choosing anecdotes, I have tried to give my reader no solace in saying, "Oh, it couldn't happen here." An episode about twenty rural Virginia villagers tyrannizing an old woman in her clapboard home for months is removed only by distance from the hazards in New York City.[10] I have come to understand that all kinds of crime can happen here, there, everywhere.

The data and studies I have drawn on generally are from the 1980s. It is not that ground-breaking studies on criminal types from the 1950s were not useful, but only that their findings have been updated. The material on crime is mountainous. There are almost 50,000 entries under crime, criminology, and the like in the Library of Congress, not counting the legal and other specialized library adjuncts.

In some cases, I have purposely chosen data from the early seventies in preference to more recent works. Such a source as *Newsweek*'s "Justice on Trial" in 1971 has a freshness of discovery, a brilliance of writing that is unduplicable.[11] Its magic is *Newsweek*'s surprise and outrage in finding out that none of the midcentury promises of the criminological establishment were coming true. It is the de Tocqueville of our time on crime, tough and lucid. Much modern popular writing tends to be jaded.

By contrast with *Newsweek*, some of the scholarly studies are so difficult to read that at first "go" I was tempted to give up. One, by Dr. Dorothy Otnow Lewis, cites "choreiform movements" as one of many indicators of possible later criminology.[12] I could not find the word in my big *Random House Dictionary*. Finally, from its root— *choreia*, a dance, in ancient Greek—and a little medical help, I realized that "choreiform movements" meant jerky fingers.

When I deciphered Dr. Lewis' study, I realized that it was one of the most important works we have for understanding what early signs identify potential problem children. It may be, when all is said and done, that my best contribution in this book will be translating some of these works into ordinary English. In that regard, I hope the experts will forgive me for popularizing their findings and for citing knowledge that, as professionals, they have been aware of for some time. A major problem with violent crime is that basic research done by criminological pioneers never reaches the public.

In writing of violent crime, I have drawn limits. To do otherwise would make this book so general as to be useless. I have reluctantly omitted a crime I consider violent—at least in the passive-aggressive sense—drunken driving. I have also not dealt in depth with the violence of riots, sex offenses, terrorism, organized criminality, and police abuses. To have covered everything I would have had to write an encyclopedia of crime.[13]

In regard to nonviolent crime, by not writing about it I certainly do not wish to minimize it. Indeed, few crimes match in villainy the defrauding of the elderly. Arson, which has killed thousands in the past two decades and costs more than a billion dollars a year, is certainly a major crime threat. So is embezzlement, computer fraud, antitrust violations, narcotics, and commercial and international espionage.[14]

The crimes I felt needed emergency treatment are the violent street crimes. At first, I thought of dealing only with homicide, rape, robbery, assault—the main components of the FBI's violent crime definition.[15] But I read too many case histories of the two- or three-year-old whose arms were burned by his mother's male companion's cigarettes, whose mother was battered by the man, and who then—with all his systems of remorse shut down—grows up himself to be a violent predator.[16] So I devoted research to domestic violence, for it seems to have been experienced by many who became the most ferocious "wolf children."

Indeed, on the subject of the home life and social world of the young criminal, I find myself in substantial agreement with a man most of us businessmen regard as the classic "flaming liberal," former Attorney General Ramsey Clark. While he seems almost quaint in some of his mid-sixties antidotes to crime, I cannot fault him when he digs at the roots of violence:

> In every major city in the United States you will find that two-thirds of the arrests take place among only about two percent of the population. Where is that area in every city? Well, it's in the same place where infant mortality is four times higher than in the city as a whole; where the death rate is 25 percent higher; where life expectancy is ten years shorter; where common communicable diseases with the potential of physical and mental damage are six and eight and ten times more frequent; where alcoholism and drug addiction are prevalent to a degree far transcending that of the rest of the city; where education is poorest—the oldest school buildings, the most crowded and turbulent schoolrooms, the fewest certified teachers, the highest rate of dropouts; where the average formal schooling is four to six years less than for the city as a whole.[17]

When I seem to deal shortly with such things, it is not that I do not recognize their insidious nature. If this book proves to be of worth, I would like in my next one to apply business solutions to some of the ghastly problems Ramsey Clark addresses.

My belief that a business approach to violent crime was long overdue led me to write this book. However, I would be dishonest if I did not admit to a more personal reason, secondary but compelling.

Like all New Yorkers, I was aware that criminals stalked every borough of the city. I knew friends who had been robbed or assaulted. The daily ration of newspaper and television reports made it pretty clear that eventually all of us were likely to be touched one way or another. I was fatalistic about it.

I already knew that crime, at least indirectly, had reached into our neighborhood, our homes. Schoolchildren tell their parents how their teachers warn them to carry "mugger money"—a dollar, two, or three—so that if they are robbed they have something to give up.[18] The theory is that if the robber gets cash, he won't hurt the victim.

"They're learning fear," I thought when I first heard about it, learning that it was necessary to submit to extortion in order to keep from being hurt. They were, in effect, carrying their ransom money with them. Practical perhaps, but that kind of practicality in the city where I grew up and that I love?

A short time later, I got a much more immediate crash course in criminality. After the rear door of my mother's home was opened in response to a knock, a man disguised in a chauffeur's uniform barged in with a large revolver in his hand.[19] Two other men, both wearing ski masks, strode in behind.

My mother, who had just come home from work, ran up the stairs and locked her room. Two of the housebreakers went after her, broke down the bedroom door and demanded her jewelry.

My mother, maybe more plucky than wise, and even though the bandits' guns were in view, pushed an alarm button that set off bells and buzzers throughout the house. The men shoved what jewelry they found into a pillowcase, brushed everything valuable off mother's dresser on top of the jewelry, and bolted down the stairs.

The man downstairs joined them as they rushed out the back door. Within ten or fifteen minutes the police arrived, and the private alarm-answering agency came a tardy twenty minutes after that. Mother had already summoned me, and when I got there she was shaken, although she felt she had handled herself coolly.

When the initial excitement died down, more enduring feelings settled in: we were thankful that she was alive, but we felt a terrible helplessness, a sense that no matter how hard the police tried, neither she nor anyone else would ever feel protected again, even in our own home.

Only six months later, a young woman who worked as one of my administrative assistants was mugged on the way home.[20] I've tried to capture her painful story in the next chapter. I was determined not to accept this kind of daily hazard as a way of life. I was mad as hell, to paraphrase Peter Finch in *Network*, and I wasn't going to put up with it anymore, not without doing something about it.

It may be that I would have done this book without hearing about "mugger money," without my mother's robbery and my administrative assistant's victimization. But it was these things that got me reading up on violent crime in a purposeful way.

One final note in this introduction. If the reader has a right to know about some aspects of my personal life, he has an even greater right to know about my biases.

First of all, I believe in the Bill of Rights. I heartily agree that the rights of criminal and noncriminal alike must be protected. John Donne, in words quoted so often because they are so true, was absolutely right when he said, "No man is an island, . . ."[21] What happens to the defendant in a criminal case, in a certain sense, happens to you and to me.

But there is also the Declaration of Independence, with its promise of the right "to Life, Liberty and the Pursuit of Happiness." Without some kind of safety, without freedom from fear, we cannot enjoy those rights.

I know we must understand and seek answers to the mental and emotional horrors that fuel the violent person's destructive fires. But this book is more concerned with how to douse those fires before they burn down our civic house and how to help those already scarred by the violent predator's conflagrations. In short, I grieve for a criminal, but I fear him and I want him off the streets.

# One

✳

# Crime Today

F<small>ACTS</small>, hard data, are the lifeblood of every business. They are the first thing we businessmen look at in the morning when we check out the computer printouts on our companies' performances of the day before. The statistics are what we study when we intend to buy a property—whether it is an entire company or a new copier.

My first tendency in dealing with "crime today" was to begin immediately with the cold data of crime, just as I do with the numbers in my world of business. But I thought of how crime has touched my own life. I realized that while knowing and understanding the data of crime are indispensable, there must be a context for it. And that context is the intensely personal and—I am sorry to say—the everyday, firsthand effect that crime has on our lives. For if we haven't been hurt or robbed ourselves, then that has happened to a family member, an employee, a friend, a neighbor, or a business acquaintance.

Magazine and newspaper articles on violent crime often begin with a derelict doused with gasoline and burned to death, a high school girl gang-raped, a mass murder, an addict who ambushes police. Such things occur with alarming frequency.[1] And they make us afraid.

But violent crime in America today is generally far less lurid. To me the three cases that follow, all of them drawn from my personal knowledge, epitomize our fear. They also illustrate how we cope with

15

fear more realistically, I feel, than the shockers we read about in the newspapers or watch on television indicate.

---

*Case 1*: R.J., a serious, experienced administrative assistant in my office, is the kind of person who comes early, stays late, gives her work the time it needs, and then some.[2]

One day she came in piqued, not only at a pickpocket but at herself. The sneak thief had gotten $100 and a $45 wallet that she loved. Next time, she'd be more careful, she said.

And in a way she was.

On a Friday, work done, looking forward to a weekend in the country, she crossed a busy downtown street, and a man on a moped swerved toward her. He grabbed the shoulder strap of her bag, and with one hand on the handlebars, tried to wrench it from R.J.'s arm. However, R.J. is forty-two and strong.

This thief had a fight on his hands. R.J. screamed, struggled, and held on stubbornly to the strap. The moped, careening wildly, took off toward Fifth Avenue with R.J. in tow.

"There was no way I was going to release it willingly," she explained later. Bystanders, watching the courageous woman, screamed at her biker-assailant to let her go. But he roared on, dragging her a half-block before he gave up and sped away.

The velocity of the bike and the suddenness of the release catapulted R.J. onto her head and right side. As she hit cement, she had a vision of "my brains scattered all over the avenue." Then she blacked out.

When she came to, sympathetic pedestrians were picking her up and helping her to the curb. Within seconds, one of them brought an ice pack for her swollen face and head.

At the hospital she was treated for cuts, a concussion, and massive bruises up and down her right leg. Later, when she was able to tell me about it, the words came in a rush:

"Each time I think of it, I become absolutely infuriated to think someone would attempt to violate another human being. They don't know if someone is carrying five cents or five million. But it doesn't matter to these animals—which to me is what they are."

She feels lucky to be alive. And glad she fought back.

"I would do it all over again. I can't imagine anyone being so passive a person as to allow that violation without trying to defend themselves."

For a month, she had almost unbearable headaches. She was still troubled by them three months after the assault.

"My anger is as strong as ever," she said recently. She replays the whole trauma every time she goes past the same street corner. "It's something that will stay with me always."

---

*Case 2*: C.A. is twenty-eight, a hard-working radio engineer, capable, affable, and medium tough.[3] Coming home from the studio at 2 P.M. on a bright, cool day, he caught no more than a peripheral flash of motion and threw up his arm in the direction of the movement.

His instincts were good: a heavy, two-by-two club wielded by a husky thug caught him on the wrist, instantly shattering its bones. Crippled, he turned on his attacker even as two of the man's confederates, also twenty to thirty-three years old, moved in on him, lashing him with clubs.

"Hit him in his head," their leader urged.

C.A. covered up and refused to fall where he would be totally at the robbers' mercy. He spun like a top, trying to avoid the blows. His wrist was struck agonizingly again. One of the men grabbed at his rear pants pocket. But his wallet was hidden in his fleece-lined jacket.

When the hoodlums failed to find C.A.'s money, they took off at a brisk walk, then broke into a jog. Bystanders, who had been unwilling to help for fear of injury to themselves, approached the badly beaten engineer. It had all happened in less than a minute.

Conscientiously, C.A. went to his job. But the wrist was swollen and throbbing. Nasty hematomas had formed beneath the torn skin. At a hospital, he was X-rayed, and his arm was quickly put in a heavy cast.

Soon enough the bones and flesh were on the mend; his spirit remains raw, unhealed.

"They tried to hit my head, to get me subdued so they could do anything they wanted," he said. Or it may even be they tried to strike him down from behind so he could never identify them.

One thing is certain. If he had not raised his wrist and deflected the initial blow, he might have been killed. The largest of the robbers weighed 200 pounds; C.A. weighs 165.

"It's made me so bitter, so leery, so careful all the time," he continued. "But what can I do? The cops don't even call things like that a robbery. The chances of catching them are nil. And even if they were caught, what would they get? A year? Two years? I feel this rage: that something like that could happen to me! I never thought it would. But it did. It can happen to you, to anyone."

What would he like to see done to the attackers? C.A., a hard edge of hate to his voice that had not been there before the assault, said after a moment:

"I would like a solid oak baseball bat. I would like to get them at the end of a good piece of oak and begin on them. . . ."

---

*Case 3*: Mrs. H. is the white-haired widow of a successful middle-level businessman.[4] She is eighty-six, the mother of a friend. Her brown eyes are intelligent and expressive. She is, as her generation would say, very much possessed of her faculties.

In her quiet neighborhood of handsome but not sumptuous high rises, she has kept her health and buoyancy with a daily walk to her shopping center and a Sunday walk to church.

Even away from the center of town as she was, she was too cautious to walk out at night. A neighbor had been robbed on the street, another bound, beaten, and robbed in her apartment. A shopowner, almost as old as she, was beaten, his head permanently injured by a gang of marauding teenagers. Mrs. H. was both prudently brave and prudently fearful.

One afternoon, on the way down a familiar, tree-lined street near her home, she heard the drumbeat of feet. She thought it was a jogger thumping down the sidewalk and moved to let him pass. He drew nearer, and suddenly she felt herself jolted as she had never been before. The heavy body knocked against her cruelly and deliberately. Reflexively she clutched her purse.

But holding a purse against the onslaught of a young man is a futile gesture for a woman of 86, particularly one whose fingers are beginning to angle painfully askew from arthritis. The stocky youth was all over her for a moment, punching, pushing to get the purse, then smashing her to the ground with all his might.

She screamed at the robber as he fled with her pocketbook, and two men ran from a nearby house in pursuit. But he was gone. Next day, the purse turned up a mile and a half away in a trash can. The $20 in it was gone, the credit cards and the pictures of her grandchildren intact.

That, of course, is not the end of it, any more than it is for anyone who is a victim of violence. For weeks, Mrs. H. was at home recovering from her physical injuries. Even when she was able, she dared not go out. Her body had weathered eighty-six years of a good, busy, and useful life. Now it began to atrophy.

Her three sons urged her to get some exercise. A daughter-in-law took her for walks, but she remained timorous. Her oldest grandson, seeing the fear in this once keen old lady, cursed and told her how he longed to kill her assailant.

Now, months later, she ventures out alone again. She depends more on a cane, but gets about surprisingly well. Whenever she hears running feet, she panics. She is afraid and always will be. And she never walks down that same street, even in daylight, although the streets she does walk are no more—or less—safe than that one.

## A CRIME PANORAMA

What astonished me about the outrage against Mrs. H. was not that it happened, but that such cases are decreasing. Not rapidly, but measurably.[5] Another myth collapsed when I discovered that muggers like the one who attacked her are not all teenagers. At least half are over 21.[6]

These were just two of the misconceptions I had held about crime from casual conversations and from the media. By the time I had done a week or two's work, I realized with genuine wonder that my concept of crime—based on what I was seeing in the papers and on television—was about as accurate as a pre-Copernican's concept of the solar system.

For example, just in the matter of crime against the elderly, consider these other facts: the burglary wave against old people is actually a reverse wave.[7] In the mid-1970s, 551 households out of every 10,000 headed by people over sixty-five were burglarized annually. Recent figures show it's now 483. Still too many, but a sizable decrease.

To return again to the mid-1970s, 85 out of every 10,000 senior citizens were a victim of violent crime every year. Now it's 70 out of every 10,000, another substantial decrease. And only about 15 per 10,000 are victims of purse snatchings and muggings, the kind of small, vicious robberies we most often associate with the elderly. The majority of crimes against the aged are assaults of one kind or another, many by acquaintances or relatives.

Rape, the most dreaded crime and second only to murder in terms of violence, is about the same for elderly women as for the rest of the female population—10 cases per 10,000.[8] The least serious crime, petty and covert theft of personal goods, afflicts 200 of every 10,000 aged a year, far less than the 350 per 10,000 for the general population.

Across the board, the elderly who are victims of crimes are most often from the same groups victimized regardless of age: blacks, the poor, city dwellers.[9] But the aged have similarities that cut painfully across talk of color or wealth or locale. They are more enfeebled, more vulnerable, and therefore more fearful.

To measure the extent of crime in America, I picked a standard that may at first seem odd. Rather than draw my statistics from crimes against individuals, I chose to use households as the most meaningful measurement.[10] To me it seems logical: As with Mrs. H.'s family, as with my own, when crime touches one of our household members, in varying ways and degrees it touches all of us.

In America, we have 86 million family units. In any year, members of 24 million of them are victims of crimes. We are much more likely to have a robbery in the home this year than a heart attack, a rape more often than cancer, a violent crime more frequently than a fire.

Horrible? Right. Crime hits new highs? Wrong. The likelihood of a crime against your household is considerably less than it was in the late 1970s, if you are white. Crimes against whites are slowly decreasing; crimes against blacks are rising.

A member of a household is equally likely to be assaulted by an unarmed person whether the family is black or white. But black and Hispanic households are far more liable to be robbed or assaulted with guns, knives, or similar instruments. They are far more in danger of rape or burglary.

In terms of economic levels, the best available data show exactly the opposite of what I had believed to be true. Burglary, or housebreaking, breaking and entering—it is called by different names—is not mainly directed against the well-to-do. On the contrary, it touches far more homes with incomes around $8,000—at the poverty level. Minor pilferage, on the other hand, is twice as likely to hit a household making $25,000 a year or more. Predictably, the urban household is twice as often subject to robbery at gunpoint as one in the suburbs.

The members of the home most likely to be the victim of a violent crime are the males from twelve to twenty-five, except, of course, for rape. Divorced or never-married women are far more often harmed by criminals than married women. Unaccountably, widows are harmed least of all.

As would be expected, most violent crimes occur at night, although a large number do take place baldly in the daylight hours: a third of all rapes, two-fifths of robberies and nearly half the assaults.

In terms of injuries, fewer than 10 percent of those hurt need to go to the hospital. And of those who do go, only half have been wounded by a knife or gun or other weapon, or have a broken bone or internal damage.[11]

The gravest injuries—except for murder—are sustained by rape victims. Six percent are badly hurt and 36 percent suffer some physical injury or another. Although about a third of the robbery victims are also injured, only a small fraction are wounded seriously.[12]

Robbers armed with knives are more likely to cause injury to their victims than those with guns: they do so in a quarter of the cases. Hold-up men with clubs, beer bottles, or rocks are even more likely to wound—44 percent of the time. It may be some comfort to know that robbers armed with guns fire less than 15 percent of the time. But when they do, they only miss three times out of every 100 instances, and the results are frequently fatal.

In general, the home is a sanctuary from crime. While 20 percent of all rapes occur in the home, only 7 percent of robberies and 4 percent of assaults happen there. It is seldom the bogus salesman or repairman who talks his way in and commits rape. Most often it is a housebreaker who is surprised.

When burglars do hit, the family reports it only about 30 percent of the time. Rape victims fail to tell the police half the time. And those subjected to petty thievery keep quiet about it in 87 percent of the cases. Only when our cars are stolen do we almost invariably call the authorities.

In thinking about violent crime figures, it is important to remember that two-fifths of the offenses are committed by criminals known to the victims. It may be a neighbor, a relative, a schoolyard acquaintance.

But it is, with good reason, the stranger whom we regard as the most dangerous criminal threat. As a robber, he gets his loot 80 percent of the time. Who wants to talk back to a man with a gun? Those with knives "score" in 60 percent of their robbery attempts.

The number of murders was 19,310 in 1983, far fewer than traffic deaths. But looked at over a person's lifetime, 1 man of every 100 will be murdered; 1 woman out of every 323.[13] If you are a white man, the chance is 1 in 164 compared with 1 in 28 for blacks. For women, it is 1 in 450 for whites and 1 in 117 for blacks.

It may or may not relieve some of the nervousness to know that most murders result from domestic feuds or fights between acquaintances. As a result, police catch more than 75 percent of the killers.

In themselves, figures like these are interesting. But their real value comes in helping us to discriminate between when our fear is justified and when it is excessive and unhealthy.

To assess this fear, a corporate executive, Harry E. Figgie, Jr., whose company makes things as diverse as fire engines and fielders' gloves, commissioned a study. As fed up as I am by crime, Figgie also was determined to make some kind of contribution.

"Crime and fear of crime," he explained, "have, like a dark dye, permeated the fabric of American life. Yet the change has occurred so gradually, so insidiously, that society has accepted it."[14]

Optimistic, as most businessmen are optimistic, Figgie *refuses* to accept it. He points out that we pulled out of the Depression because we developed "a sense of common purpose and common challenge," and believes we can pull out of the crime mess as well.

What his researchers found is that 40 percent of Americans concretely fear they will be victims of violent crimes. Forty percent—with a good deal of overlap—also have vague, unsettling fears that they are "unsafe" in their day-to-day locales: their homes, shopping centers, neighborhoods, their workplaces.[15]

Fear of both kinds is infectious. When a person knows someone who has been a crime victim, that person's concrete fears double. And those already afflicted with troubles are those to whom the fear is most painful. The poorest; the divorced, separated, or widowed; the aging; the retired; the unemployed and part-time worker; the least-educated—these are the Americans most haunted by anxieties about their safety from criminals.[16]

Synthesizing it another way, when the specific fear of violent acts and this floating, oppressive fear are combined, the groups most distressed by it are blacks, women, and city dwellers. For urban inhabitants and blacks, there is a good deal of justification: they *are* the most victimized. But contrary to modern folklore, women are far less victimized by violent criminals than men.

Part of the excessive fear of women is based on panic over rape. The incidence of rape is minute. Fear of it is intense in 55 percent of women. Fear of homicide is widespread, but not epidemic. Seventeen percent of us fear we will be murdered—although as we have seen, the chances are remote.[17]

When crime strikes, it is sad to relate, most city dwellers expect no help from their neighbors, not even a call to police. They are dubious even about whether their neighbors are law-abiding. Only half the urban population believes "practically all" those living near them are within the law.

In smaller communities and in rural areas, the vast majority are convinced they live among law-abiding folk. Indeed, 75 percent of rural Americans—where fear is lowest—believe that neighbors would physically pitch in if they were attacked by criminals.

Responding to his fears, the urban resident has increasingly begun to take care of his own security. He locks his home and his car doors, even when the car is moving; he dresses plainly, to avoid attention, telephones to friends or relatives to say he has gotten home safely, skirts dangerous areas and passing groups of teenagers, stops delivery of papers when he is on vacation, and in the subway—when he must ride it at night—he keeps from behind columns and cringes near the turnstile, where he is most likely to be seen by others. Often, he buys a gun. The Figgie Report shows half of America's homes now own a firearm.[18]

These kinds of precautions are taken most often by those least victimized, the "resource-rich," in the jargon of the researchers. A Northwestern University study shows that the well-to-do most often become the "coproducers" of their own safety.[19] The poor tend to be passive in the face of crime, accepting it as still another penalty of urban life.

To get good crime protection, people are overwhelmingly willing to pay higher taxes. They also overwhelmingly trust the police, although the trust drops among the young, blacks, and those who know victims of crime.

Fear of crime is costing more than tax money. The precautions we have described often have dollar amounts attached. But there are other costs which are ignored or even unsuspected by the general public.

When a plant or company is moved out of a city or out of the United States because of crime, the costs are enormous in jobs; lost tax revenues to city, state, federal governments; and in money once spent by employees in the community. The moving expenses are all passed on to the customer. We are talking about billions.

Right now, three out of five companies have bought expensive physical security systems—floodlights, burglar alarms, and the like. Half also have purchased closed-circuit television monitors, and lights timed to go on and off at set intervals. A quarter have hired guards with guns. Forty percent have set up electronic employee identification card programs. Sixty percent have security specialists on staff, have paid for crisis-management studies and run anticrime educational courses for their personnel.[20]

Crime around the plants of 65 percent of the businessmen surveyed has gone up since 1980. Right now, the robbery *rate* for businesses is far higher than it is for private citizens. While it is true that 75 percent of all robberies are committed against individuals, the *rate* per 100,000 victims is 1,500 for companies compared to 150 for individuals.

Figgie probably speaks for everyone, businesses and private citizens alike, when he observes, "approximately one percent of the population is terrorizing the other 99 percent."

Just who, though, is this 1 percent?

Once again, the common belief turns out to be off the mark. Whites and blacks both think they are more likely to be attacked by blacks. Nationwide, the blacks are right, but the whites are wrong. The majority of violent criminals are white, by a three-to-two margin.[21]

Although blacks make up less than 15 percent of the population, they commit 76 percent of the violent crime against blacks. But contrary to many whites' opinions, blacks commit only 27 percent of the crime against whites. Almost all the rest is white victimization of whites.

This is not to say that on a *rate* basis, blacks do not commit an alarmingly disproportionate amount of crime. But the black crime rate has been decreasing lately. The white rate is climbing.

With all the concern about juvenile crime waves, I was not dumfounded to find that violent offenses by those under 18 have more than doubled since 1965. What set me back is that despite the hue and cry, juvenile crime is leveling off. After an explosion of juvenile crime in the late sixties and early seventies, the arrest rate for eighteen-and-unders has become more or less constant.

An interesting and unpublicized fact popped up while I was researching criminal ages: At the other end of the age spectrum from the juvenile is the violent senior citizen.[22] While juvenile crime has ballooned, violent crime by those over fifty-five has gone up 40 percent since 1965. In the early 1980s, the percentage of older men committing violent crimes has been overtaken by the percentage of violent offenders under 12.

With subteen criminals, the problem is youth gangs. Older members use the younger ones for dope running and even for robberies and shootings. They get the job done, and there is less chance of punishment if they get caught. Members of these gangs commit four times as many crimes as loners. And when they become adults, they commit five times as many violent crimes as men who never belonged to a youth gang.

In the past few years, researchers have come up with some pretty good predictions on who belongs in the tiny hard-core group who commit the great bulk of the crimes. One study shows 354 criminals committed 775,000 crimes over an 11-year period. Another shows these "career criminals" or "violent predators" committed 28 percent of all crimes, although they make up only 6 percent of the criminal population. Another shows this habitually violent man commits fifty times as many crimes as the "Sunday thief."[23]

From the studies, we are beginning to delineate this violent offender's face:

He is young—in his late teens or early twenties. He is unmarried and has a sorry work record. If he does not have a serious heroin and barbiturate history, then he has heavily used barbiturates in combination with alcohol. By "used" alcohol, I mean eight cans of beer a day, or seven glasses of wine, or ten ounces of hard liquor.[24]

As a child, he saw his mother beaten by the man in the house and was himself frequently and badly abused. He was a troublemaker in school, had learning difficulties, has a background of nervous disorders ranging from uncontrollably jerky fingers and very bad coordination to severe seizures. He has no religious ties.[25]

He got into violent crime during his early teens, was locked up in at least one reformatory, and had a long record of youth violence by the time he became an adult. Since then, he has one or more convictions for violent crime and he has already done adult "time."

Several of these elements may be present—epilepsy, agnosticism, learning disabilities, abuse as a child, even alcoholism—and a person may still be a useful, even a preeminent citizen. But the lawbreaker with *all* these experiences in his past who is convicted of still *another* violent crime is likely to be a habitual, even an unreformable, criminal. The knowledge we have of his predilection, and his background, it seems to me, should be used to decide who gets straight time. And the absence of such experiences in his background might be a consideration in who gets parole, bail, probation.

What has happened is this: scientific studies have made it possible for us to say one man is more likely to maim, rob, and kill than another. When we did not have this knowledge, we could not target the chronic offender. We had fixed rules, and the violent predator and milder criminal often suffered similar penalties. Doesn't society have the right to protect itself from this violent predator, now that we can identify him? I am not for an instant saying that he should not have every civil right and every Constitutional defense the law makes available to him.

What I *am* saying is that if the judge has substantial scientific evidence that this man is unusually vicious and irremediably violence-prone, and so long as the sentence does not exceed that provided by statute, then the guilty criminal should be put away for a longer time in order to protect society for that period.

This is an iffy matter that makes the Constitutionalist in me squirm. But the reality of hardcore, repeat offenders being out on the street makes me squirm even more.

We in the cities serviced by fiercely competing television stations and newspapers—each eager for listener or reader—get an unrelenting dose of crime and violence. Every crime seems a mass murder. We come to think crime is worse than it is. The truth is bad enough.

Violent crime in cities over 50,000 is three times worse than in smaller cities or in the suburbs and six times worse than in rural counties. At present, it is fairly stable in rural areas and is growing faster in the suburbs and small cities than it is in the big cities.[26]

But it may be worth considering what we have to build on. For one thing, *rates* of violent crime, of youth crime, of urban crime, of crime against the elderly, as we have seen, are leveling off or decreasing. For another, the most crime-prone group of all—those between 15 and 25—is getting proportionally smaller. By 1989, it will make up only 14.7 percent of the citizenry.[27]

We are also finding ingenious precautions and community steps we can take against crime. Historically, it is the coming together of these diverse, positive actions— such as what I have already suggested and will later elaborate on—that have ended crime waves.

In the 1700s in London, crime lords bribed judges while gin and lax enforcement turned entire sections of the city into centers of drunkenness, robbery, child abuse, and prostitution. Police dared not to venture into these areas, and citizens barricaded themselves in at night. London was the crime scandal of Europe.

The hundreds of public hangings (eighteen of every twenty who went to the gallows were under twenty-one) and the grisly prisons (in one, 350 starved to death) did nothing to cut the crime rate.

What appears to have halted the wave was the fortuitous coming together of judicial reform, the professionalizing of police, the hanging of a number of crime leaders, and the famous Licensing Act of 1751, which controlled gin sales.

In the 1980s, we should not have to trust to chance. We are far better equipped to discover what works and what doesn't.

Throughout crime's long history, judges and jailors have been as closely linked as supply and demand. Perhaps alone among the elements of the violent crime process, judges and the courts have been well-defined by the media.[28]

The courts, blessedly, are open to our inspection. They are subject to frequent and often thorough media coverage. We are aware of their corruption, their politics, their traditions, and their limits. And we, who could change things most, do almost nothing.

The judges, prosecutors, legal defenders, parole officers, and probation officers who might do something from inside to reform seem too demoralized, too beset by papers and people to find a way out of the debris. The courts are like a moribund man in a hospital: he is kept alive by tubes, acted upon because he is no longer able to act for himself. When there is room in the prisons, the judges send men there. When there is no room, the dangerous are often cut loose on the streets. There is no equity in sentences, only variances in the direction of leniency or punitiveness. A violent man goes free in one court; a petty criminal goes to prison in another.

Mandatory sentences, set up to force no-parole sentences for certain crimes, supposedly make for consistent sentences. But the "system"—although it is different from any system I have ever seen—finds its ways of getting around the sentences, switching charges as nimbly as a con man switches peas under the shells.[29]

Whether the courts like it or not, there is a strong feeling among the citizenry for stricter punitive action against criminals. Our leaders ignore such feelings at risk. We are working our way toward fixed, retributive terms for the violent; it is only a matter of finding a way to make the sentences work, to find the necessary escape hatch for the one prisoner in a hundred who wants to change his ways.

How do businessmen feel about such matters? Nine out of ten businessmen want the death penalty, a greater percentage than the general public. More of us want the violent in jail on no-parole sentences than private citizens do. And three-quarters of the business executives favor wiretappings compared with only one-fifth of the public (I would approve them only in the most extreme cases).

What everyone agrees on is that the courts are chaotic. Some of the problems are, in fact, insoluble. We cannot wipe out overcrowding; we can only ease it. We cannot guarantee equal punishment for the same crime. We can only encourage lenient and strict judges to draw closer to compromise. The list of what we *can't* do goes on and on.

But what we *can* do is also enormous. We can realize that many problems are caused by inertia, the idea that things must be done the way they were ten, fifty, a hundred years ago. The roster of companies that perished because they believed that would fill a city telephone book.

Through modern business approaches, some of which I outline in Chapters 3, 6, and 8, we can bring a great deal more fairness and efficiency to the courts. For example, we can treat court staff and even judges with the impartial standards that good business brings to its employee relations. We can promote those who achieve, and retire or discharge those who are laggardly. We can, as a company would its product line, thoroughly reevaluate parole, probation, sentencing practices, court calendars, and the physical process of getting a prisoner from cell block to courtroom. We can give our admirably public court system an admirable public airing.

Unlike the courts, the prisons are as hidden from us as we are from their inmates. Television and the papers leap from one prison riot to another. Only rarely do we look honestly at the inmates; only rarely do they look honestly at society. As a result, we have never really developed realistic, consistent expectations about what we expect the prisons to do.[30]

For centuries, we nurtured the Quaker dream of rehabilitation.[31] Now, by a ratio of eight out of ten, we realize that the prisons are not getting criminals rehabilitated. Most of us rightly feel that the *means* of rehabilitation should be put at prisoners' disposal.[32] Those who want to can take advantage of work programs, studies, and the like. But it is not the state's job to enforce attendance. The state's job is to punish the criminal for his violent crime and to lock him up for a just term so he can't hurt anyone else.[33]

This "tough" attitude, which most Americans seem to share with me, has sent the prison population to (and for a change, the words are accurately used) "record highs." At this writing, the population of jails and prisons has soared far over 700,000 and we are still counting.[34]

An ingenious opponent of further prison construction, William Nagel, has posited a mythical city called Prisonia with a population made up of all the people in our jails and prisons.

It would be larger than Pittsburgh, San Francisco, Washington, D.C., Milwaukee, Cleveland, Boston, or many other cities. Soon, it will have more people than seven of our states. Move Prisonia to a deserted island, make it an independent country, and it will have a larger population than twenty-four members of the United Nations.

Prisonia is mythical. But the prison population is not. America is bursting with prisoners. Over half the one-man cells are too small; 90 percent of the two-man cells are too small. To uncrowd them means $40,000 per bed in a "cheap" minimum- or medium-security facility, up to an average $125,000 in a maximum-security institution. We are already paying $1 billion a year for correctional construction.[35]

It is no exaggeration to say that if any other nation would take our prisoners, we could subsidize our prisoners there in luxury, give the host nation a bonus, and still come out with a fine profit.

When we examine who these prisoners are, we come out as in most investigations into criminal matters with facts that dispute the old wives' tales, the false beliefs we have held and based our judgments on.

We are willing to believe that there are a disproportionate number of blacks in prisons. That is indeed the case: Whites commit 64 percent of the crime, but the prison population is about half white, half black. There's inequity there. But instead of concentrating on that, my liberal friends raise Cain about all the blacks on Death Row. It turns out that there are a disproportionate number of *whites* on Death Row.

Fifty-one percent of those awaiting execution are white; only 42 percent black.[36] Yet it is blacks who committed a far greater number of felony-related murders than whites. My own suspicion is that all those on Death Row have earned their way there.

Only innocents fantasize about large numbers of guiltless men serving long terms, about hundreds of college youths doing lengthy time for being caught with a single joint. It happens rarely, and howls of publicity for reprieve are warranted when it does.

But the great majority of those in prison deserve to be there. Two out of three have been there before. A majority of those in state prisons are there for violent crimes, just the sort of thing they ought to be locked up for. A third of these violent prisoners are murderers.[37]

Now we seemed determined to find ways to get the guilty men *out* of prison. An embezzler, a counterfeiter, an inveterate shoplifter, a burglar, a corrupt politician or businessman—they all belong in jail. But it is a luxury we are unwilling to provide ourselves, as evidenced by New York and other states' refusal to vote for prison bond issues.

Certainly, we must find ways to get many of the nonviolent out, perhaps after only a brief, bitter taste of imprisonment. What makes it difficult is that probation and parole practices, particularly in the big cities, are pathetic, perhaps worse than nothing.[38] We need to concentrate more on halfway houses and similar alternatives. If run in a businesslike way (and some innovative prison reformers suggest they could be run fairly and efficiently as for-profit enterprises), they can perform a necessary function and save money at the same time.

Restitution projects, community-based "family houses" for those otherwise destined for prison or for those on the way out have shown some promise. Work camps—no; not chain gangs—open prison farms, weekend imprisonment, and community service all offer alternatives, and all need better management. The key is close control on both prisoner and facility, and the recognition that there are bound to be some failures.

The purpose of these alternatives to prison, it should be clearly recognized, is a practical one. It is humanitarian, but the principal justification is to free up cells for those violent ones whom even the American Civil Liberties Union acknowledges must be separated from society.[39]

Despite all the video series on police, all the police novels, and all the police magazines, how seldom we try to think about crime the way the police think about it! Yet what is going on inside the police-man's head affects us almost as much as what goes on inside the criminal's. And what is going on there right now is nothing very happy.

It's not so much the question of low pay. Police starting pay ranges well past teachers with M.A.'s in many jurisdictions. It's all the has-sle with courts, legal-rights procedures, and annual budgets. It's being better educated than the troglodytic sergeants and lieutenants who still oversee them in the anticrime fight. It's the insults the police take from suspects; the bad press; the horrendous, inefficient, bu-reaucratic, mind-dampening paperwork; the long hours, often with no overtime. And always, it's the danger.

For the danger is real. Death on the job is not frequent; but it still occurs often. Nearly 100 police are killed each year by hoodlums. Ninety percent of the dead police are victims of guns, often in the hands of men involved with drugs.[40] Meanwhile, new bullets are marketed—for no sane reason—that will pierce policemen's armored vests. And, appallingly in my view, too few steps are being taken to pass laws that would prohibit casual sale of these bullets.[41]

As if police didn't have enough worries, they are now at the center of the "deadly force" argument—when to shoot and when not to shoot. If a policeman fires, he risks calumny and pressures at the hands of citizens; if he doesn't, he risks his and his partner's life and perhaps the lives of those he is sworn to protect. If he seeks answers, they are often vague, whether they come from his chief, the city lawyers, or, as is increasingly the case, his union's lawyers.[42]

Statistically, police are in a tiny group of life-endangering trades whose only actuarial equivalent is the front-line soldier in wartime. In peacetime, there is only one largely followed craft which rivals the policeman's in danger: his opposite number, the practitioner of violent crime.

Although the amount of violent crime, as we have noted, has more than tripled since 1965, the same cannot be said for police. In cities, there were 1.7 police per 1,000 people in 1965. Now there are 2. Some forces have actually decreased.[43]

One good new trend, although it puts even more of a strain on police, is aggressive patrolling. This means more vigorous questioning of suspicious-looking people, more stakeouts, more vehicle stops for fugitives and stolen cars, more police posing as the elderly or as other potential victims, and more cops on the beat. It also means more care in making sure police do not abuse these recently reinaugurated tactics, and more attention to police officers' psychological needs.

Being a cop is about as stressful a job as a person can have. Faced with frustration from within, dangers on the street, a public that even when it approves does not really understand the daily scut work, the policeman is a modern Hamlet—torn between righting wrongs on his own, and waiting, perhaps, too long.

# Two

※

# The Business Approach

Sᴏᴍᴇ of the best readings in crime are in history. I found that everyone from Hammurabi through Homer and on into Aristotle and Plato was absorbed with crime. The Bible is full of great crime stories, the good Samaritan parable but one of many.

But nowhere was I so pleased during my plunge into the past as when I stumbled on the story of Patrick Colquhoun.[1] I felt a quick kinship with this energetic businessman turned crime reformer. Born in Dumbarton, Scotland, in 1745, son of a town official, he gave me an inspiring model for what I would like to do with my own life.

At fifteen, he ventured to Virginia, got into the bustling commercial life of the Colonies, and came back to Glasgow at twenty-one, off and running on a successful business career.

In 1783, by now a well-to-do businessman, he founded the Glasgow Chamber of Commerce, then ran for and was elected to the job of Lord Provost. He quickly began to devote himself to all manner of legal and social reforms.

In 1789, he and his family moved to London. There he was eager to try out the reforms he had developed in the smaller Scottish city. But Colquhoun was too cautious a merchant to sell a product he did not fully know. Before he promulgated his ideas in London, he studied the "market." He came up with statistics on the numbers of criminals (more than 100,000), the costs of crime, and the effects of alcohol and gambling on the workers of the city.

A strongly practical man of empathy and morality, Colquhoun was also longer on practice than theory. While other upper-middle-class Britons were applauding the French Revolution (while doing nothing to alter the poverty that had sparked it), Colquhoun was denouncing the revolution's excesses and organizing food kitchens for the poor.

Only after he understood London did he begin writing about it: its government corruption, its legal abuses, its prisons, which he found were turning men into monsters, and its disorganized and debased police.

In the police he saw his best chance to help his adopted city. Their function, he believed, should not be to dispense punishment, as they often did, but to prevent crime, and when they could not, to catch the criminals.

The Scotsman also drafted plans for licensing various trades to prevent sale of adulterated milk and food, to reduce fraud, and among other things to stop street singers from chanting dirty, seditious songs.

Because of his zeal in urging police powers, he was treated gingerly by the British bureaucracy. Many preferred things the way they were. But the merchants in the port of London were losing up to half their goods to river thieves, and they liked what they heard from Colquhoun. They asked him to investigate the mess at the port and to propose steps to set things right.

Colquhoun recommended a private "Marine Police," which was to be well-paid, professionally led, and politically backed by the merchants. In two years, the river police were so successful that the city of London began picking up the payroll. They became the Thames River Police, the forerunners of today's famed "Bobbies."

Indeed, the great British police reform bill of 1829, although it was passed nine years after Colquhoun's death, is considered as much a legacy of Colquhoun as of its more famous lobbyist, Sir Robert Peel.

I cite Colquhoun for two reasons: he was innovative, as the best of businessmen are; he did first things first, gathering the facts about London crime as carefully as he would if he were setting up a market in the Colonies for fine Scottish woolens or iron goods.

And I cite him from a third, more subjective, consideration. Patrick Colquhoun died before he saw his work done. I would like to realize my program against crime while I am still alive.

A man such as Colquhoun would be useful today in exploring the multibillion-dollar mess that the anticrime establishment has made of what was once, and can be again, its most promising weapon: the computer.

Computers, we tend to think, will take care of everything if we just program them the right way. Would that it were so. We in business dreamed when the Age of Computers began in the fifties that they were going to make free enterprise less work, more play, and more pay. They have, in fact, changed the way we solve problems, and in many ways they have decreased them. But it has been—and is—a road of ups and downs.

Initially, business rushed headlong into the computer market, bought equipment, put it into operation, and then realized we had become victims of our own predilection for novelty. Bankers found that they could not respond to depositors' complaints about monthly statements. Month after month the same errors appeared. Customers were furious (except when they came out ahead through some misplacement of a decimal point). Magazine computers sent out solicitation letters long after the subscribers had sent in payments.

Department stores—indeed, every kind of mercantile business—continued sending dunning letters to customers who had paid up. Consumers responded first with fury, then by taking their business some place where the computers worked.

Our solution to all of this was twofold—those of us who survived it. We called in the representatives of the computer industry to work with our own people. Just as important, we called in system consultants to take a costly but objective look at our set-ups, free of the biasing anger of our own people and the biasing apologetics of the computer manufacturers.

I explain this so it will be easy for the reader to believe me when I assert unequivocally that lives are being lost, hundreds of millions of dollars wasted, and horrors of delay, injustice, and inefficiency perpetuated because the criminal justice forces are not doing what we in business were driven to do.[2]

Houston is a stunning and illustrative example of what I mean. A few years ago, the city announced that its new police computer would solve crimes, increase efficiency, and do all the kinds of things business once dreamed its own computers would do.

Millions of tax dollars were poured into the computer. Because there was no need to show a profit, good money was thrown after bad. The system was weighted in favor of expensive equipment at the expense of expert workers.

As a result, tens of thousands of reports by officers and victims began to back up at the "mouth" of the computer. The machine could not even chew the data, much less digest it. Soon the data was a month behind the written reports, then three, then six.

There was no provision for bringing aboard a crisis crew of trained operators to feed the reports into the machine. Yet, as if in some criminological *Sorcerer's Apprentice*, the reports kept flooding in. Amid this wash of data were items on how specific criminals worked, their physical appearances, their nicknames, and their records—material of inestimable value in catching felons if it could but be summoned up.

In the last year, Houston has turned things around. True, the computer is not as sophisticated as some had hoped it would become. It cannot produce a dozen suspects' names on the basis of modus operandi, physical description, speech mannerisms, and so on.

But within twenty-four hours of a policeman submitting a report, it can retrieve data on national, state, and county fugitive warrants, on prison, jail, and arrest records, even on a suspect's transactions with pawn shops.

How was it done? Just as industry would have done it. Police executives were able to convince detectives and patrolmen that the computer was here to stay and could help them. Then the police management team redrafted forms to make it easier for the computer to handle arrest data, homicide reports, and so on. While in-service training was given to some uniformed men and women, outside experts were consulted on how to make the computer work, and outside civilian clerical personnel with computer experience were hired. The dinosaur, in a word, had been turned into a workhorse.

Denver is another case in point. Although over a million dollars in federal funds and a hundred thousand dollars in local money was spent, the city's computer, which had been expected to perform miracles, was doing the work of a few desks of adding machines, and less predictably.

The problem was "down time," the bugbear of all hastily set up computer systems. In somewhat the same way as Houston, Denver has drastically improved, although even now priority cases must sometimes wait while repairs are made or while less important programs are being run. To interrupt in the middle would build up both backlogs and costs.

A recent robbery case shows how improvements can lead to safer streets. A task force was set up on a particularly vicious robbery, with one detective manning the computer full time, contacting field detectives and offices, feeding in and extracting data from the computer.

When a car thought to have been used in the robbery was located, the computer came up with the names of five people with serious criminal records who frequented the area of the robbery. Based on physical description, the five suspects were reduced to two. Their mug shots were pulled, and the victims were able to identify them both so arrests could be made. At this writing Denver police are confident of convictions.

Before turning to more detailed recommendations for making computers work as electronic police, it is worth examining a most complicated institution, that in New York State. There, no single source can provide accurate information on criminal offenders. Instead, there is a patternless collection of independent and semi-independent agencies, each with its own expensive system.

The Department of Correctional Services has its system; the Division of Parole and the Division of Probation have their systems. The State Police has its, as does the Department of Motor Vehicles. Various municipal systems have their own. All work, more or less, but they do not work together.

This means, for example, that an upstate felon's conviction record may be unretrievable by New York City and vice versa. Or it may not be in *any* of the computer systems. One survey showed that as of 1982, court data on a third of the upstate arrests had not been fed in the statewide computer, and there were no computerized court dispositions on more than 70 percent of them. Criminal histories, parole and probation data—hundreds of thousands of criminal history items *simply were not available*. Blessedly, there has been improvement in the last three years, but the computer systems remain badly unintegrated.

In New York City, it was not so much Balkanization, but budgets that hampered CATCH, Computer-Assisted Terminal Criminal Hunt, one of the better operational criminal ideas in the computer field. Stored in CATCH is a gold mine of mug shots; fingerprint data; physical characteristics such as broken noses, scars, and missing teeth;

modus operandi, and other memorabilia about criminals.

At its best, CATCH operates beautifully. For example, a career criminal is arrested, his biography can be called up and sent immediately to the district attorney involved. This gives the DA a case file complete with previous victims, accomplices, and favorite haunts.

CATCH is also a criminal hunter. When an old lady could describe her attacker only as black with a gold tooth, the computer scanned 300,000 files, and found six such men. Three were in jail: one operated in the old lady's neighborhood. CATCH caught its man.

But CATCH was set up with IBM equipment years ago and since then has been much juggled with. For all IBM's diligent maintenance, new hardware is needed and more money is needed to pay for it.[3] By contrast, there are happier outcomes.

San Diego and the Federal Bureau of Investigation are examples where business principles have been successfully applied to law-enforcement computers.[4] In the California city, $2.4 million in federal funds, then another $2.6 million were spent wisely over a period of four years.

The system is used by a dozen jurisdictions around the big West Coast port city. Policemen on the beat vie with each other in feeding it information from their interviews. Recently the computer "made" a murder case in seconds based on a man's nickname and a description of his jacket.

At the FBI, the National Crime Information Center (NCIC) though plagued by minor kinks from its years of service, provides information in seconds anywhere in the United States on stolen cars, criminal records, and warrants outstanding. A state patrolman in New Mexico, in little more time than it takes for a radio call to his dispatcher, can find out if a car is stolen or its driver dangerous. A vagrant child molester in Oregon can be tied to a record of morals crimes in the East in under a minute.

The FBI will soon have a new National Center for the Analysis of Violent Crime tied into NCIC. It will use computers, behavioral profiles, hypnosis, and other techniques to help local police solve seemingly motiveless or "stranger" crimes.

The emphasis will be on serial murderers, rapists, violent child molesters, and arsonists. For the first time, not just criminal records, but the kind of information that San Diego and New York's CATCH have locally, will be available on a national clearinghouse basis. The

FBI's computers and analysts will be able to suggest the names of suspects on one coast for crimes committed on the other, based on how the criminal operates, his physical description, companions, and other clues.[5]

We expect the FBI to do a good job. We take it for granted. The local police tend to grouse about the FBI's vanity and egoism. But hardly any policeman in the nation would disagree that the NCIC has been one of the great boons to crime fighting in this century.

What do these two fine systems have in common?

Both were developed over a period of years, using a colleagueship of law-enforcement experts, manufacturers' experts, and highly skilled consultants from outside—that is, a business solution. Both were well funded. Both were set up methodically, as corporation computer systems are, to do specific things without unnecessary frills.

There is probably no one in either business or law enforcement who would not agree that both systems are "cost-effective." The results, *even in terms of money saved,* not to mention lives, have more than paid for the costs of the equipment and the skilled hands that man them.

There are many more Houstons and Denvers, unfortunately, than there are FBIs and San Diegos—or even New York City CATCHes. Out of 1,500 law enforcement computers, probably no more than 150 are working at the peak of their capabilities. Most of them are just automated criminal record files.

Such costly failures can happen again if federal or state funds once more become available. In the seventies, the Law Enforcement Assistance Administration awarded grants of hundreds of millions for space-age law enforcement hardware. Almost every city over 50,000 got its own computer.[6]

The computer companies were glad to sell them even though law enforcement is small potatoes compared with financial institutions, hotels and hospitals. For months computers sat in crates. When they were set up, the cities often refused to pay for qualified operators and technicians.

A former IBM official, M. Daniel Rosen, in *Police* magazine, cogently quoted a city police chief to the effect that "in the harsh world of profits, firing and hiring which is the private sector, competition forces you to innovate or fall behind. But a police department is an island apart from the rest of society."[7]

Amen to that. Yet even now it is not too late. In a well-run corporation as I outlined earlier, an aggressive vice-president would be named and invested with the authority of the chief executive officer and the blessing of the board of directors. He would be told to find a specialist and to look into the situation for a week. When he came back to the board, he would be asked, "How much will it cost? How much time will it take?"

If his answers were reasoned and firm, his resolve sure, he would be told to go out and get the job done. He would be backed on his recommendations to hire and to fire. It would be understood that for a certain time things were going to be worse, perhaps much worse, before they got better.

It also would be understood that heads might have to roll, that inefficient operations were going to disappear, that radical changes in jobs and even locations were possible. The computer "czar" would be expected to work on the project seven days a week, eighteen hours a day, for as long as it took.

If he did the job, he would be rewarded with whatever it took to keep him with the company. If he failed, he would be out of a job—and perhaps the company chief executive would go along with him. But nineteen times out of twenty, things would be vastly or at least greatly improved.

So it should be with a law-enforcement computer, whether it is a statewide system or a special system for corrections, the courts, or the police.[8] A "czar" has got to be named, vested with the support of the legislature, the governor and the courts, if they are involved. Computer wizards too often are lacking in administrative ability, but the "czar" preferably should have some background in computer work. He should be intelligent, ambitious, and aggressive—he should be the kind of man business tries to hire away from government. Or he should be the kind of man that government occasionally hires away from business for tasks of great moment.

In following this advice drawn from practical business experience, the governments can expect the same result we got: a lot of unhappy people who had been willing to go along so they could get along; a big bill from prestigious outside consultants; and a computer that finally works.

If that is all the "czar" did—apply business techniques to patch up an anticrime computer system that was foundering because government-type techniques had failed—he would save lives and dollars.

As in San Diego, responses to crimes would be quicker, killers and robbers and burglars would be more rapidly and surely removed from the streets, and loot would be more swiftly recovered from fences. The savings in medical costs of cities alone would pay for the reforms.

But it is not enough, of course, just to repair the bureaucratic wreckage of the past. Business is looking to computers to achieve breathtaking things in the future—helping produce better products, exploring new markets, testing novel products, and making financing and manufacturing more efficient.

Why in the world shouldn't anticrime forces do likewise?

For example, one aspect of crime that has fascinated me is called *incapacitation*. This is a fancy word for predicting who the most violent criminals are, getting them off the street, and thus substantially bringing down the crime rate. The idea is as old as the Greeks, but now it is on the point of breakthrough.

Studies by the Rand Corporation, by Yale University scientists, by the pioneer researcher Dr. Marvin Wolfgang of the University of Pennsylvania, and by many others are beginning to identify the kind of people most likely to be violent predators.[9] These are the tiny percentage of people who commit the vast percentages of crimes. The problem in these new diagnostic approaches is that some of those who fit every qualification are *not* violent predators.

Clearly, one cannot punish a person just because he *may* commit a crime. After all, he also may *not*. Computers hold the promise of a partial answer. I mentioned in the last chapter some of the common characteristics scientists find in the backgrounds of violent habitual criminals.

At this writing, no one has ever computerized all the most respected findings of the incapacitation researchers. The samples have all been gathered in different ways, and from different states. Some come from California; some from Pennsylvania; some from Connecticut. Some stem from interviews of prisoners; some exclusively from official records. Some involve thousands of criminals; some a handful of precriminal teenage boys.

I have talked with computer wizards in industry. They are intrigued with the possibility of setting up programs based on the various studies of incapacitation. They believe models can be predicated that would narrow still further the margin of error in predicting who will become a violent habitual criminal.

We already know that continuingly vicious criminal adults have long juvenile records of violence. They have at least one, probably more, adult arrests for violence. We are not talking here about an innocent. I believe that when the profile is drawn from a computer, when the sample is tested and examined by experts, such a profile can legitimately be used by the courts to help to determine who gets bail, the length of sentences—always within legal limits—and who gets parole.

The profile should be publicized far and wide. Those who fall within it must know that they are especially liable to long terms if they commit violent crimes. Finally, there must be some safeguard for those who can prove they are rehabilitating themselves. All that done, I am ready to support this radical means of keeping ferocious men from doing further harm to society.

If business-type computer work can identify this violent predator, down to negligible errors, then its importance can scarcely be exaggerated. One of the Rand studies shows that the most predatory 10 percent of high-rate robbers each commit 135 robberies a year. The worst of the burglars commit 516 housebreakings. The most active drug dealers cut 4,000 deals a year.

If these awesomely busy criminals are taken off the streets, it is hard to imagine that such a move will not decrease crime. A second Rand study shows that by jailing the high-rate robbers for longer terms, and shortening the terms of low-rate and medium-rate robbers, the robbery rate in California would drop 15 percent, the robber population in prison 5 percent. In terms of money, that is a lot less tax income lost on housing criminals. In terms of people, that would be an enormous easing of injury, fear, and medical cost.

There are other areas where computer usages that are standard in finance and industry could be applied to crime. Professor Alfred Blumstein, an engineer/urban scientist/author at Carnegie-Mellon University, has used such computer "models" in several areas.

He has shown that certain violent-prone age groups, as they move throughout populations, carry with them crime increases. As this "bubble" diminishes, so do crime rates. The benefits in projecting court, police, prison, and social welfare needs and costs are, obviously, gigantic.

Blumstein has limited his studies mainly to Pennsylvania. But applying his principles, exactly the kinds developed by industry in making sales projections, would be no great trick for every crime-ridden state and city in the United States. Industry does this sort of thing as a routine procedure—why not the criminal justice systems of our government?

Not even the best researchers, or the most magical computer geniuses, would say they could come up with perfect results. What they can guarantee us is something far better than the nothing that is being done in many jurisdictions now—something less costly, something far more likely to save lives.

In another data field, there are substantial information bases available on which juvenile delinquency measures seem to work and which ones don't. But any review of delinquency research shows that government and, to a lesser extent, private funding often goes to projects that are faddish and trendy, with approval influenced by how good a con man or how prominent a leader is putting forward the grant proposal. A computer cannot pick with precision what *will* work. But it can project pretty well what will *not* work. So, at worst, the investment of a few thousand dollars in a computer printout based on the potentials of a juvenile project will give the granters some assurance the grant is not going down a rathole. At best, the computer will produce a "reject" reading that will save hundreds of thousands and even millions of dollars.

As an analogy, the scans produced by business computers generally come up with two or three products that may sell equally well. The same programming will give us a flat "no" on a dozen. How much better to do a little wheel-spinning among the two or three than on twelve.

In the juvenile delinquency field, nine out of ten of the most promising programs set up prior to 1970 didn't do any better than if there had been no program at all. Things aren't much better now. One of the Justice Department's best arms, the Office of Juvenile Justice and Delinquency Prevention, candidly says that when good evaluations have been done, most programs prove "ambiguous, mixed or negative."[10] It dumfounds me that we do not listen to these professionals in such matters. If the data show a program will fail, and our computers can back that up, why do we pour in more tax dollars?

Ford, after all, did not try to revive the Edsel. And as mistake-haunted as industry is, we at least did not try a second time to sell the seatbelt "interconnect" to the public—as good an idea as it was in terms of safety—after they resisted and rejected it.

There are dozens of other areas where crime could be fought by commercial computer models. For years, the railroads, no prodigies of efficiency, have kept track of their freight so they know where they can ship what. It is not difficult to do such things well.

But most police forces, even when they have the computer capacity, do not keep track from minute to minute of their patrol cars, their detective cars, their motorcycle and scooter men, or their footmen, not to mention their police auxiliaries, civilian crime watchers, and the like. With a good system they can be located on an instantaneous basis.[11]

Computer experts tell me that such usage would simplify scheduling, especially if the crime rates of various city areas were used as a constant in the computer, would speed responses to "policeman in trouble calls," and would reveal goldbricks on the force (maybe that's a factor in unspoken police opposition to such systems).

Business also does this kind of computerization with its inventories. We know when we must send items express or when there is enough on the shelves to use ordinary surface or air transportation.

When fully in place, a parallel police system could alert the dispatcher if a violence call comes in from a city block with high murder and assault rates, and even announce if such a call came from a house where there had been serious domestic trouble in the past.

It makes no sense for a skilled policeman to be taking a report on a two-day old television theft if the computer shows he is needed on the double for a "man with a gun" call.

Sad to say, government, even when it recognizes a good industry procedure, does not always know what to do.[12] A costly study was done on setting priorities for these kinds of police responses. But its methodology has been questioned and now, at great cost, it should be done all over again. If a corporation's balance sheet had been in mind on that first study, it is my guess it would have been right the first time.

We are accustomed to calling an 800 number and finding in a minute or two whether there is room in our favorite motel or hotel, no matter how distant the city. Business developed this system and it works perfectly. Why is it not widely used in the prison system?

Corrections officials talk of overcrowding, but there are degrees of overcrowding and in some prisons there are temporary or long-term vacancies. While some states bar out-of-state housing of prisoners, legislatures are ready now to change such laws, particularly in states under court order to alleviate bad conditions.[13] The alternative is to free prisoners.

A nationwide "cell bank" for prisons could be set up on a desktop computer by a handful of people in a central office and a one-or-two-person operation in each state, probably doing the job part-time. When a cell is opened as a result of a prisoner going to a hospital, getting an early release, being transferred, or escaping, that cell would be available to a prison system with gross overcrowding. The finances of it would work out pretty much as a wash: the state giving up the prisoner would save money on his "keep," and the state taking him would be paid board.

Such an easily established system also could ensure that maximum-security prisons were not populated with bad-check writers who belong in minimum-security prisons, prison farms, and the like—some of which are now housing ferocious career criminals because of overcrowding.

If a modest computer system along these lines worked, it could be expanded to include juvenile facilities, halfway houses, other residential alternatives, hospitals for the criminally insane, and even jails.

Based on industry models originally programmed to determine the progress of cars on assembly lines, many courts are already conducting advanced data retrieval work. In several large cities, a prosecutor can punch up a case number and immediately see the date of arrest, the present status of the charges, and the continuances that could determine whether an unconstitutional "unnecessary delay" is imminent. He can budget time for the most serious criminals, decide where he has to plea bargain, and even see whether the defendant is in trouble in another case, all on the basis of a single "entry" to the computer system.

Industry uses computers in employment and personnel work, and here, too, anticrime workers can modify their procedures to achieve savings in time and money. For instance, we can feed the computer the qualifications for a job in terms of intelligence, education, experience, and language. We can scale each of these elements as to importance. The computer weighs the candidate against the scale, and we have a highly useful tool for our personnel manager and other officials in choosing the right person for the right job.

When I read a Brookings Institution study on the failures of the parole system, I saw clearly how a sophisticated, computerized use of present parole board scales could be used just the way I described.[14] The prisoner's disciplinary record, work reports, past history—his "profile"—could be measured against the success or failure nationally of hundreds of parolees. This scan would not be the *end-all* for the parole board's decision, but it would be a great aid in deciding who is ready to return to society and who is still a distinct danger.[15]

Another industry personnel tool, one about which I remain cautious, is the polygraph, the "lie detector." I am too skeptical of it to want to see it used in trials, but in a parole hearing, it is the *prisoner* who proposes he be freed.[16] Industry uses the polygraph for job interviews and, most often in the retail business world, to discover employee theft or other dishonesties. Parole boards could use it to test the sincerity, the *credibility*, of the parole seeker.

My recommendation would be that it not be administered either by the corrections agency, or by a private operator hired by the prisoner. Instead, a private operator, chosen mutually by the convict or his lawyer and the corrections people, would give both sides a feeling of fairness, justice, and objectivity. These three elements seem missing all too often in parole hearings today.

Not just law-enforcement officials, but academic researchers in the field, sometimes have difficulty communicating their thoughts. How else to explain the turgid writing of these experts? What, for example, is a "demographically disaggregated projection methodology"? What can we make of "offensivity" or a "punitative segregation unit"?

My point is not to mock this kind of writing. Actually, these phrases come from useful documents on crime. But why not simplify them? It would save time. It would prevent misunderstanding. It would reduce the aggravation of readers who must read these documents as part of their crime-fighting job.

When a company wants an annual report prepared for its stockholders, it either hires an able outside writer or uses an in-house professional. Government and government-sponsored researchers must follow industry in such matters. It costs only a few well-spent dollars to get a writer to make a report comprehensible so its value can be appreciated. As a veteran *Wall Street Journal* reporter once said, "You've got to dumb it down if you expect anybody to read it."

This same professional and businesslike way of doing things applies to publicity. Why shouldn't the best promotion person in an agency, or an outside firm, be given the job of getting widespread visibility for important studies? The two vital Rand studies on incapacitation and the Yale studies of Dr. Dorothy Otnow Lewis surely should appear at length in many popular media, not just *The New York Times* and a few other publications of record. This research is speaking about the heartbeat of the potential criminal; it is that important.

We should be able to discuss as readily and accurately this kind of gut issue research. I can assure you if a corporation had a product that significant, then either the promotion and advertising people would have word of it out to the buying public, or there would be a new promotion staff and ad agency.

There is another basic fault in law enforcement management that needs to be discussed in commercial terms. Businesses seldom do repetitious research. It cuts into profits. Government, with its profligate view of tax money, all too often repeats itself.

For example, the federal government recently decided to spend $1.8 million to study fear of crime in two inner cities.[17] But in both cities, fear-of-crime information is available on the tips of the tongues of police, social workers, and businessmen—everybody in town. The statistics on crime in these cities already fill file drawers.

This single unnecessary study is no exception. There are dozens more in the crime and justice area, hundreds throughout government. This prodigal waste of money could be redirected for police salaries; hard-nosed, business-type, management troubleshooters; and others who can deal with fear of crime by reducing both the crime and the consequent fear.

When industry develops a weak link, we cut it off, often with the greatest reluctance. I admire American companies who held out for so long for American-built components against the electronics industry. But I understand why others like General Electric and RCA realized that it had to come down to either "buying Japan" or not surviving. It hurt. Yet industry did what it had to do.

Unfortunately, this is not the way it works in government. The city of New York recently installed an intricate and sophisticated experimental television monitoring system in its Columbus Circle subway stop.[18] It cost $500,000. Crime went up 30 percent during the first year of the experiment. Obviously it did not work well enough to continue it. What did the transit bosses do about it? They allocated another $1.2 million, mostly in federal funds, for the same kind of system in the Times Square station. Again, why not spend the money, if it is available, on tough, young transit cops?

For purposes of this book, it is important to understand why that television monitoring system did not work. True, it was modeled on industry-tested systems we have used for years in plants and offices. But our systems are in what security people call "controlled environments." We can limit access to our buildings; we have a specific number of people in our workshops and in our hallways. We do not have rush-hour crushes, milling crowds around columns, mobs by turnstiles, and sudden jams.

With the best intentions in the world, law enforcement tried to turn an excellent and proven industry practice to its own uses. Its mistake was not doing what a company would have done: avoiding like the plague the use of this equipment in an atmosphere where it was doomed from the beginning to fail.

I am not opposed to innovation. Far from it. Some of the techniques that prisons, courts, and police have borrowed or adapted from business are working out excitingly.

The "robot cop" bought by New York, Denver, Phoenix, and other cities is a promising example. It is a wheeled robot that can approach a barricaded madman, barrels leaking deadly chemicals, or suspected bombs.[19] It can probe dangerous objects, pick them up, jiggle them a little, and study them with a mobile stethoscope, an X-ray, or a television camera. Meanwhile the human operator is safely 200 feet away.

The cost is high: from $25,000 to more than $60,000. But that cost is nothing compared to the serious injury to an officer. As without industrial robots, when its "glitches" are worked out, the "robot cop" will more than pay for itself.

The robot is only one of a long and varied list: industry provided the know-how for policemen's soft body armor; for arson "vapor sniffers" that can smell out kerosene, gasoline, paint thinners, or the fuels criminal "torch men" use; for tenacious police car tires that take speeds up to 125 miles an hour; for special dyes that blow up in bags of money handed over to bank robbers, turning them and the loot a brilliant and long-lasting red.[20]

There are also promising ideas from industry outside the equipment field that should be explored to see whether they have wide anticrime application. The Quaker Oats Company recently decided to give bonuses to workers who stay well and avoid health insurance costs.[21]

Such behavioristic ideas must be monitored carefully to make sure they do not keep sick people from going to doctors. But, with that qualification, might this bonus system also be adapted to prisons, to police forces, to the demoralized probation and parole workers?

Should we encourage cooperative prisoners with small bonuses? The idea is as old as the nineteenth century, when small gifts were given to prisoners for good behavior.

Quaker, an innovative firm, may also have some innovative ideas about how to use the bonus system. If I were a prison administrator, I would certainly be on the telephone to one of Quaker Oats' idea men to find out what might work in my institution.

It was out of just this kind of brainstorming that the prison Jaycees idea caught on. Many businessmen thought it was crazy to set up a Jaycee chapter in prison, a chapter made up of safecrackers and gunmen. But New York businessmen tried it at the Auburn maximum-security prison in 1969, and the Jaycee ideas of leadership, dignity, and responsibility "took."

At this writing there are more than 10,000 prisoner Jaycees in over 300 prisons in the United States, Australia, Canada, Kenya, New Zealand, the Philippines, Switzerland, and Sri Lanka. There have been failures, but in general the optimism and ideas of hard work and ingenuity seem to have paid off. In the last few years, some inertia has set in; but I hope it is reversible. Prison Jaycees is too good an idea to languish.[22]

A principal, if indirect, solution to crime is to learn about it as my "historical model," Patrick Colquhoun, did. It was my first step toward writing this book, even as your first step may be reading it.

No book, with its long publishing schedule, can be current with the state of the art in crime information. But there are simple, inexpensive ways to "keep up."

The best single information source is the almost totally unknown (and free) bulletins put out by the Justice Department's Bureau of Justice Statistics, Washington, D.C. 20531. Cleanly written and free of bias, these little fact sheets on victims, criminals, crime rates, the old, the young, the Death Row dweller, and so forth can be read in a tenth of the time it takes to work the simplest crossword puzzle.

It is sad that the Chamber of Commerce, the National Association of Manufacturers, and other business groups, at this writing, made no effort to put their members on the mailing list of the Justice Department's publication. Nor has the bureau done any missionary work in that regard. It is another example of government failing to "sell" its best products.

The National Institute of Justice (at the aforementioned address) puts out a biennial report that is almost as well-written and gives current information on the state of criminal research. It is also free, concise, and invaluable. For those who want to go even further, it lists a raft of other agencies fighting violent crime.

The House and Senate Judiciary Committees, Washington, D.C. (zip code 20515 for the House; 20510 for the Senate), produce free informative materials and provide an index of what's available. You can obtain these materials most quickly from your Congressman—if, as a voter, you put a little heat on him.

There are dozens of nonprofit or private publications; one of the most challenging is "IE" (Institutions, Etc.), put out by Jerome G. Miller, a knowledgeable (and controversial) corrections official turned philosopher. The address is 814 North St. Asaph Street, Alexandria, Virginia 22314. It is from Miller that I got encouragement for studying small, private, closely monitored treatment centers for violent youths whom everyone else has forsaken. In Chapter 6, I will deal more extensively with this concept.

The National Crime Prevention Council; the National Committee for Prevention of Child Abuse; and groups that audit lenient judges, drunken driver sentences, rape victims, elderly victims, and discharged prisoners also produce publications worth looking at.

Every library also has books on the subject of violent crime. And the National Criminal Justice Reference Service, Box 6000, Rockville, Maryland 20850, not only has a splendidly efficient library, with customized searches, but provides voluminous bibliographies on every imaginable crime subject.

Colquhoun, if he had had our vast information resources available, might never have gotten to the task of fighting crime. Nevertheless, I have listed many sources on the basis that, as in business, it is far better to do too much market research than too little.

With all that, I have still touched only on a fraction of the ways that crime fighters can use business techniques. The possibilities are myriad. In the world of business management techniques alone, there are countless applications, some of which I will focus on later.

The cop on the beat, or other members of the anticrime establishment, may well, and fairly, complain that I have told them what to do but not said much about why business doesn't do more. This omission is intentional. In Chapter 12 on "Volunteers," I will describe how business can pitch in.

I am not such a dreamer as to think that the commercial strategies I have touched on, no matter how cleverly and industriously they are applied, will put an *end* to violent crime. Nothing will do that. But they will help. And they will begin helping as soon as the anticrime bureaucracy adapts even the most obvious procedures that make a well-run corporation tick.

# *Three*

✳

# The Subteen Criminal

T HERE are some very young, very scary kids out there. A three-year-old was caught as she held a knife at her mother's throat. A six-year-old, blade in hand, threatened to cut off his brother's head. A seven-year-old boy got his pocket money by sudden, ferocious muggings of very old women.[1]

These are often the kind of kids who at two were repeatedly burned for the sport of it by their parents or otherwise abused.[2] Yet other times, the kiddie criminals come from seemingly stable, loving middle-class families.

In earlier chapters, I listed the characteristics that identify violent predators *after* they have begun their vicious years of criminality, at eighteen or older. At present, we cannot *predict* exactly who will become that malign. But valid research is getting closer. Already it tells us who is in the pool from which most career criminals develop.[3]

Sharpening our focus is vital. For almost anything would be better than letting kids grow up along ways that permit them to maim and murder. The financial costs are also horrific: $40,000 a year for us to keep an adult locked up, as much or more for a juvenile.[4]

To begin with, the sociologists are right when they tell us that the child most likely to become a violent teenager is a poor one, and not just poor, but one with problems even before he is born.

By before he is born, I mean back to the third generation. If the grandparents of a child are drunks, criminals, ne'er-do-wells, brutish, and cruel, then the parents pick up some of these qualities and pass them on to the grandchild.[5]

Twenty percent of the delinquents in one study had grandparents who harshly assaulted their children—the delinquents' parents. Fifty-four percent of the parents had marriages or liaisons in which physical beatings occurred, compared to the national average of 38 percent. In more than half of these violent incidents, one of the partners was drunk, the husband—or paramour—83 percent of the time.

Small wonder that when the child was born—unplanned 55 percent of the time—he came into a climate of violence.[6] There were often five or more siblings; the child was soon being violently, physically abused.

I do not mean a paddling or even a hairbrushing. These predelinquent children were beaten with sticks, boards, pipes, belt buckles. They were tortured with burning cigarettes, cut, thrown against the wall, hurled downstairs, or shackled to their beds. Three-quarters of the children who later became the most vicious, most dangerous, and least contrite teenage felons were badly beaten as kids. When it wasn't happening to them, it was happening to their brothers and sisters.

Most often it was the men in the house who beat them. These males also savaged the mothers, who sometimes armed themselves with knives or pistols and used them on their mates while the children stood by.[7] When children tried to help their mothers, as seems often to have been the case, they learned that no good deed goes unpunished: the furious men turned on them.

Among these children most surely on the road to murderous behavior, one study shows, 37 percent of their fathers were also murderous. Forty-three percent of their mothers had deep psychiatric problems. And in fact, more than half the homicidal children, as they grew older, tried to commit suicide, generally by jumping from roofs or out of windows.[8]

When the predelinquent wasn't experiencing the real thing at home, he saw a fantastic world of violence on television, where his mother sat him down as soon as he was out of the cradle so she wouldn't have to do any real mothering with him. By the time this kid was seven—the age, by the way, when English common law said criminal intent can be formed—violence was familiar and accepted. When he went onto the street, he was very ready for it.[9]

The Liberty City section of Miami has the kind of "street" I am writing about.[10] It has come under a lot of scrutiny since riots tore it apart in 1980. It was, and remains, a down-and-out, decaying, black ghetto.[11] The residents live in constant anxiety of being mugged, robbed, or murdered by their neighbors or visiting criminals who use it as a haven from police, much as French criminals did certain areas of Paris in the seventeenth century and as British felons used parts of London in the eighteenth.[12]

Slashings of prostitutes, drug-related shootings, assaults, penny-ante extortion, and domestic mayhem are endemic. When police answer calls, particularly if they are white, they are shouted at by hostile groups, who are sometimes stoned. So they prefer to ignore the calls, leaving Liberty City to fester, despite all the talk about reform after the riots.

For the subteen criminal it is an ideal culture. Many of its kids grow up into antisocial criminals because they are made to feel like junk, because they see their parents behaving like monsters, and because they are shunned, thrown out of the house, beaten, or otherwise rejected.

The Justice Department's Office of Juvenile Justice and Delinquency Prevention puts such dilemmas lucidly:

> Delinquent gangs and subcultures emerge in communities where the illegitimate opportunity structure is organized for involvement in and maintenance of criminal activities.
>
> The community may have a tradition of crime; intricate patterns of interaction among police, thieves, fences, lawyers, politicians, and citizens are typical; and youngsters in these communities are controlled by conventional adults but even more so by criminal adults.
>
> Older criminals select and recruit good prospects, bring them up through the ranks. . . . High delinquency rates persist in these types of communities because the tradition of crime is passed on to younger generations and new residents. The process, then, continues in a vicious cycle.[13]

Parents are trapped in these slums. When they do have jobs, they are employed at the lowest, unskilled levels. The average income often is below the federal poverty level. Indeed, the pressures often sunder husband and wife to the youngsters' eventual woe. A survey has shown half of all prison inmates come from broken homes.[14]

The children are also trapped. To be sure, there are suburban Eagle Scouts who become mass murderers. And there are the children of middle-class or of upwardly striving, lower-middle-class families who become just as violent as the children about whom I am writing.

But for the most part, violent twelve-and-under predators start out in ghettoes and as losers. Only 1 percent of them have IQs above 115, compared with 16 percent for nondelinquents. In school, when they do attend, they perform dismally. By the time they are twelve, they may be years behind expected performance levels.[15]

Also, by twelve, far more than half of them are suffering from some sort of diagnosable emotional problem. It will already have shown up in neurological, psychomotor, and related symptoms: pronounced tics, uncontrollable twitching of the fingers and limbs, inability to sit or concentrate, paranoid hallucinations, memory loss or warping about their violent (and nonviolent) deeds, inability to repeat backward as few as four numbers.[16]

An interesting, seemingly puritanical, but actually scientific test also shows what has been happening to their moral sense.[17] The test is based on the Swiss psychologist Jean Piaget's belief that at the ages of seven to nine a child begins to shift from thinking that things he does are wrong because they result in punishment to thinking about right and wrong in terms of what is good for society. The test uses pairs of easily understood stories.

The first story, for example, might tell of a child who bumps into the table on the way to supper and breaks fifteen of his mother's dishes. Its pair is a story about a child whose parents tell him to stay out of the cookie jar. The child disobeys and as a result breaks the cookie jar lid.

A youngster developing normally will see even at an early age that the first child is merely clumsy but that the second child is in the wrong because he disobeyed his parents.

But when 100 delinquents were tested, even though many of them were much older than nine, they still saw things in the premoral, infantile way: they thought the first child was guiltier. They believed that because the damage was worse, the punishment would surely be worse.

The tests show that whether a kid was rich or poor, white or black or Hispanic, smart or stupid, so long as he developed in normal ways, he was equally acute in distinguishing between right and wrong and equally firm in adhering to the right.

Some extremist social architects have suggested honing such tests, combining them with other examinations, and using them to weed out from the community children who "fail." Indeed, one of President Nixon's doctors once proposed testing all six- to eight-year-olds and setting up camps for those with criminal tendencies.[18] The whole train of thought smacks of totalitarianism and engineered humanity, and it should be rejected.

However, tests like the "moral scale" might be conducted and the results made available to parents. The government might offer intense family help to parents and children where a problem is evident. But I would favor having the government keep no record of the tests: it is too much, regardless of the theoretical value, to burden a child of seven, eight, or nine with a permanent record of "dubious morals."

The consequences of doing nothing about kiddie criminals are catastrophic. Recall, for a moment, the seven-year-old I mentioned in the first paragraph of this chapter who savagely mugged elderly women. He quickly began to amass a record of violence.

By the time he was fifteen, he had assaults, sodomy—a total of fifteen different crimes against him. But each time, the family court either gave him probation or dropped the charges. At school, his main academic interest was in drubbing his teachers and fellow students.

"We knew when he was here he was going to kill somebody and that there was nothing we could do to help him," the principal of his public school recalled. The truth was that the principal had only guessed at the extent of his student's viciousness. In the name of confidentiality, of protecting the rights of juveniles, the court did not tell the school of the boy's arrests.

"Every time I got caught," he said, "I would say: 'I swear I'll never do it no more. I promise. Just let me go.' Soon as they do, I'm out there doing it again."

Once he beat a girl into a coma because she called him a name; another time he shot and killed a man he thought had cheated him in a street game. The youth was open about his criminal career, perhaps because he knew it didn't really matter. When he was still fifteen, he murdered a grocer in what the police said was an armed robbery. The violent youth denied only the part about the robbery. The murder, he said, was "justified." The grocer, he explained, had insulted one of his girlfriends.

Subsequently, this underaged career criminal was sentenced to three years. The probation report that was filed on him said he needed "a strong structural environment . . . to obviate an aggressiveness that he cannot handle." Within a year, however, another probation report described his behavior as "excellent." It recommended that he be given more freedom.

So while still serving the sentence for murder, he was given a weekend pass to go home. Within hours, he and a friend found a gun, broke into an apartment, and forced a man to commit sodomy. They stole his leather coat. When our subject was caught, he was resentenced for robbery. At last report he was eligible for parole. Even as you read this, he may be back on the streets again.

The same kind of story could be told about many others: the ten-year-old who tries to murder his mother; the eleven-year-old who does murder his schoolmate; the fifth grader who traffics in hard drugs; the ten-year-old who commits forcible rape even before he reaches puberty.

Looking at subteen criminals statistically rather than individually, they are numerically not an insignificant group. Before they are ten, thousands of them are being arrested for serious crimes.

Almost 6 of every 100,000 twelve-year-olds and younger were arrested for robbery in 1983, 9 of every 100,000 for serious assault. In fact, 338 in this subteen group were arrested for forcible rape, 64 of them under ten years old. Altogether, subteens were arrested for nearly 100,000 serious crimes in 1983.[19]

These are only the *arrest* figures. There is evidence that at such young ages, a kid gets away with ten such crimes for every one arrest.[20] If that is true, then there were a million serious crimes, from larceny-theft to murder, committed in 1983 by twelve-and-unders, 82,000 of them vicious crimes if arson is counted.

That's a lot of subteen crime.[21] It is some solace that recently the rate has been approximately constant—even in areas like New York City, where certain violent crimes by the youngest criminals climbed for years.[22] A major recent problem there, as in other cities, remains the sophistication of youth crime gangs, and the violence used by them to obtain dope or the money to buy it.[23]

It is in the gangs that the underaged criminals are most useful. Only 1 percent of children ten or younger who are picked up go into institutions, compared to 20 percent in some cities for those who are seventeen.

So older criminals use teeny-boppers for making deliveries of "dime" packets of drugs, for shoplifting, minor burgling, schoolyard extortion, and petty robberies. The older members profit from the take but are insulated from the guilt. It is all very businesslike in the worst sense of the word.

It is horrendous to think of your wallet or your life being endangered by a ten-year-old child. Yet, here are these kids, still three years away from their teens, with no more feelings of decent restraint than a moray eel feels for a passing fish.

These are the children who grow up to be the violent adult predators: that 3 or 4 percent of criminals who commit 50 percent or more of the violent crimes in America. What can we do?

First, we must immobilize them. We are not talking about a twelve-year-old using his fists or even a stick. We are talking about a group of twelve-year-olds, one of whom has a small, functioning pistol. He is as willing to rob and kill as a criminal of eighteen or thirty or forty.

The logical start toward controlling them is to identify them. At present, fingerprinting and photographing juveniles and keeping records on them is in a state of anarchic and unnecessary confusion that, to a business, makes the Stock Market Crash of 1929 look like a well-orchestrated phenomenon.

Procedures vary in almost every jurisdiction, municipal, county, state, and national. In Washington, D.C., for instance, juvenile fingerprints and mug shots are exemplarily handled.[24] A police department general order lays it out clearly: "All juveniles 16 and 17 years of age, charged with a felony . . . shall be fingerprinted and photographed as quickly as possible after placement of charges." All others may be fingerprinted and photographed with "prior approval from the Youth Division Watch Commander." Written juvenile records shall be available to law-enforcement authorities and "teachers, principals and school security personnel" but denied to the public.

Simple, direct, rational. Would that it were so in other jurisdictions. But it is not. And the master file of criminals kept by the FBI at the National Crime Information Center does not accept juvenile fingerprints unless they have been "waived" to adult status.

The Attorney General's task force in 1981 urged the FBI to change its policy.[25] At this writing, for lack of funds and other reasons, the FBI has not done so. It would not make me happy to have a ten- or twelve-year-old's criminal record in a master federal file. Nevertheless, it seems to me the lesser of two bad choices.

Not to keep a file of violent young juveniles deprives inquiring police departments of records that might indicate whether the youth (or adult) in their custody has a history of similar crimes. If the police find such a record, they can proceed with their investigation with the knowledge that they may have the right culprit.

Right now, a kiddie criminal who crosses the river from Philadelhia to Camden, even though he has a horrible juvenile record in Pennsylvania, may well be unknown as a vicious child in New Jersey. With that kind of head start in his new home and by the time the courts get around to confining him, he may have graduated from assaults to murder.[26]

The same lack of communication often occurs between a city and its surrounding county, between neighboring counties, and among different authorities in the same city. Police are often forbidden to tell school officials; courts fail to keep police fully informed; there is a dangerous data breakdown; such concepts as juvenile record confidentiality become a travesty. Certainly it is important to protect juveniles' privacy, but not at the expense of dead shopkeepers and prison guards and apartment house arson.[27]

To give juvenile criminals privacy protection, we might, instead, handle their records as industry handles outdated records and even products. We hold records or items only so long as they are useful, then, to conserve costly space, we get rid of them.

By analogy, a juvenile's records, fingerprints, and mugshot could be kept in the computer and the files for, say, ten years. If, during that time, there were no further crimes, the computer entry would be erased, the records destroyed. That is only fair.

But if the record continued to build during the juvenile and adult years, it would remain for use by police, courts, schools, and correction authorities.

Merely knowing the subteen criminal, of course, is not enough. We must do something about him. Industry does not let people, even young ones, come into its plants and throw scrap iron into the machinery. It makes no more sense to let children continue to fire lead and steel into our homes and bodies.

Such children cannot be taken out of the community without the most careful regard for their civil and constitutional rights. We must be assured through the juvenile court system that every other alternative has been exhausted.

They must have been given probation in their home, psychological testing, and counseling. They must have been enrolled in special schools while they were staying at home. If the home is a disruptive one, then with all legal protections, they must be given a chance in a caring foster home.

But when, week after week, they persist in violence, society must step in to protect itself. There may be no option but hospitalization or a correctional school.

Correctional schools are, of course, the rub. Some of them are likely to return him to the streets bigger and meaner than when he entered. Generally the worst facilities are the largest, some with a population over a thousand, others with many hundreds.

From my reading, I believe that the most effective place to put these violent young children is in small, secure schools with no more than a few dozen inmates.[28] They are costly, but they are worth it. We are only talking about those few hundreds in the country who are so violent they must be restricted. The expense may be over $70,000 a year.[29]

But the cost of letting this rare brutal child loose will be far greater in terms of terror, medical expenses, court expenses, insurance payments, and defending damage suits than the cost of keeping him locked up with the kind of intense psychological, religious, and other help necessary to perhaps change him so he can reenter the community.

Even with this huge expense there are two caveats:

First, these kids must not simply be forgotten. It is not enough that they be represented by an *ad litem* social worker at the juvenile court proceeding where they are taken out of the community.

A lawyer must represent the child's interests at that time and even when the lawyer agrees with the initial finding, he must periodically—perhaps every three or four months—require the government to show that the child is being given proper treatment, and not just being warehoused.

At the earliest opportunity, at the lawyer's or the government's initiative, the child must be given a new chance, a new start in either his own home or a foster home. In some cases, a special halfway house may be useful. Most children will learn, or be helped if they are hospitalized in lieu of a correctional school, and will be free in a matter of months.

But for a few, even with the most dedicated care, even with the most exacting legal protections, it will be years before the fires of violence burn out. To think of a child spending his years from twelve to sixteen in a correctional school is painful, but I see no other way out of our tragedy.

And even when we do our best, there is this second point. We are going to make mistakes. Some of the kids we release even after our best efforts are going to commit more crimes of violence. I have come sadly to an important conclusion: There is no 100 percent crime cure. There is only better. Or worse. Or the same.

When the subteen criminal is not so obviously violent, there is less urgency, and time for more conventional remedies. Many, now costing us hundreds of millions, clearly do not work.

For example, it does not seem to do much good to conduct counseling with just the violent kid. Government programs—probation, social welfare, and others—keep on with this costly way of doing things as if the government were helpless to turn off the faucet. Studies show that unless you can also counsel the mother and the man in the house, and preferably the siblings involved, you might as well save talk and money.[30]

On a broader scale, anticrime fighters who are indigenous to the slum community laugh bitterly at how the city "parachutes in" social programmers and projects.[31] Bright and idealistic recent recipients of master's degrees in social work are transplanted to the slums expecting to convert their twelve-year-old clients from delivering small envelopes of "speed" or heroin to delivering the newspaper. It just doesn't happen.

Much worse are the almost unimaginable millions we have spent trying to graft on entire do-gooding bureaucracies. We staff them with imported administrators, assistant administrators, office managers, intake specialists, discharge specialists, "resource persons," clerks, typists, and janitors.

We renovate a tall building for this huge enterprise, which stirs sluggishly, generates a few clients, and then settles down to feed on its own funding. This behemoth ghetto is no more effective than a real giant would be if it tried to counsel humans on human-sized problems.

Why not, instead of wasting these millions, use the available data for projects with a chance of functioning, on enterprises based firmly in the slums themselves?

For instance, what seems to work, at least sometimes, is family counseling by preachers who grew up and stayed in the ghetto, ex-gang members and ex-cons who have gone straight, cops who were *born* just down the street, and social workers who *come from* the local community.

In some cities, lodges have been set up, almost spontaneously at times, by surrogate mothers and fathers, strong, often charismatic authority figures from within the slums themselves, who take on young violent boarders. The courts have moved kids from their own disorganized, crime-sloth-ignorance-and-brutality-permeated homes into the no-nonsense environment of these tough, zealous couples or singles.

The city or other governments pick up some of the tab; grants take care of other needs. The arrangements remain loose, even unpredictable, just as the results are. But if there is a 50 percent success rate, that is far better than the zero percent we are getting from most efforts.

To go into the sociological reasons why these small ad hoc centers work would require a sociological writer, which I am not.[32] Let me only say that in business, when we find something functions and is cost efficient, we embrace it. We don't sit around in endless encounter sessions trying to figure out the why's. We make money on it and try to replicate it.

Another thing that seems to work is religion. It may not be chic to say it, and most of the government-funded studies seem to ignore it, perhaps out of some misguided concept of what separation of church and state means. But in most of the few studies extant, it is clear that kids with strong, early religious ties have very low crime rates.

It shouldn't surprise anyone. In industry, if you believe wearing a safety hat will help save your life, or that washing your hands before you do a gelatin culture will improve your lab work, then you do not willfully break company rules that require these things.

By the same token, if you believe there is a God who will help save you as a person and improve your life, you do not willfully break what you believe to be His rules. Committing criminal acts—whether you are a Christian, a Jew, a Moslem, or of any other major faith—is a breach of religious rules.

The efficacy of religion as a dam against crime proves out.[33] A study of 10,779 youths, many as young as eleven, showed that children with no religious affiliations committed twice as many crimes as those who professed a faith. Kids who went to some religious activity twice a week or more committed fewer crimes. The same findings applied generally to truancy.

Youngsters whose parents were religious—whether they themselves were or not—also had low crime rates, particularly if both parents were of the same faith. Significantly, the survey was *not* of rural low-crime kids, but urban kids, from Nashville and its immediate suburbs.

For those who are still squeamish about the church-state problem, consider that the government already gives grants to church-related schools and legions of church research and charitable organizations.

Why not take some of that federal, state, and city money we spend on urban "parachutists" and subsidize a minister of youth education in a bustling ghetto church or some young divinity graduate eager to get back to his home community? Why not fund an athletic director in a slum parish, a musical director, or an employment specialist?

Let the work be done through the ghetto church, and be careful not to shun the Christian fundamentalists, the Black Muslims, and others who may not be in tune with mainline churches and synagogues. Some less "fashionable" religious groups show the best results in reducing crime rates.

My advice, a little less businesslike than I have been up to now, is that we should not worry too much about detailed evaluation units or about cumbersome administrative controls. We must only try to pick an honest, able minister and then pay the freight for a few years. It won't be much. There will surely be some goof-offs, even some thieves. But we are not talking about the wildly expensive poverty programs of the sixties. We are talking about a few tens of thousands here, a few there.

Of course, the twelve-and-unders in these slum churches are not likely to be your usual Westchester County Sunday schoolers. But if the example of a few good men and women turn even a small number of these youngsters—however waveringly—toward the God of Jesus or Abraham or Mohammed, then that money will have been expended not only morally but cost efficiently.

If you doubt it, think of the $35,000 and up a year it costs for custody, psychologists, remedial education specialists, and guards, to confine a kid who is advanced so far into senseless violence that he is almost, or entirely, beyond help. And if that still does not move you, imagine how a small calibre pistol looks at close range in the hands of a scared and ruthless twelve-year-old outside your garage door at 10 P.M.

In one area, industry is in no position to point fingers at anyone when it comes to kiddie crime. I am talking about television violence. With publication of the National Institute of Mental Health (NIMH) report, there is no longer doubt in my mind that violent acts on television contribute to violent acts in real life.[34]

The NIMH looked into about 2,500 large and small research projects done in the last decade. It found a causal relationship between television and aggressive behavior and a consistently high level of violence on television. *Reader's Digest* and other reputable publications and private groups have joined the cry for a radical diminishment of television violence.

The man many consider the preeminent American philosopher on juvenile crime, Professor Marvin Wolfgang of the University of Pennsylvania, believes that if social class is constant, "the longer one is exposed as a young child to violent displays in the television world and other kinds of media, the higher the probabilities are that one will have an augmented aggressivity in his personality."[35]

Increasingly, the rebuttals of the television industry ring false— like those of the tobacco industry in the sixties as they insisted that there was no proven relationship between cigarettes and cancer.[36]

I, at least, am prepared to believe, as the experts do, that children from around the age of two are affected by television violence and that the effect is a bad one.[37] I believe police when they say that a kiddie criminal's quick, lethal draw with his Saturday night special during a robbery or a ten-year-old's tragic reenactment of a television hanging is related to what those kids see on the "tube."

Psychologist Leonard Eron of the University of Illinois feels that children from six to eight begin to confuse real life and television, a dangerous illusion. Cartoons, he points out, are particularly violent. One monitoring organization measured forty-eight violent acts an hour in a Bugs Bunny show. Adult programs such as "Fall Guy" averaged thirty-eight.

The kind of children I have been writing about here—the potentially violent—are those most susceptible to television violence, to its forceful illusions. For one thing, in a world deprived of positive cultural influences, the television is something these children can identify with. For another, from infancy, it is in these homes that children are most often left to spend mindless hours before the screen, uninterrupted by even the most ordinary enrichments from their parents.

It is childish for industry to claim it is not aware of what it is doing when it sponsors television shows full of violence. Businessmen, after all, were canny enough to cut back on using models smoking cigarettes in their ads. We know it offends nonsmokers who we want to buy our products. Yet, because we know people like to watch violence, we encourage it by sponsoring violent shows. In our hearts we know we are doing wrong, but none of us wants to stop unless everyone does.

The networks would back away from violence if industry took a united stand against it. As one businessman willing to take that stand, I invite others to join me. If our efforts prevent a single street murder, a single ill-advised attempt by a kid to imitate a television hanging, it will be worth our while.

If we can make the sponsoring of violence as much a renegade business practice as we now regard the poisoning of drinking water with industrial waste, we will have done something our children will be able to praise.

There is no single business-style remedy for subteen crime. I have pointed to a few commonsense avenues open to us. Many of them have been put forward by others, but always in fragmented ways.

Here are some possibilities:

• We can push for federal funding of an office on spouse abuse and increase the funding for the tiny bureau now handling child abuse.[38] It can be done with a fraction of what we would save by ending projects that have been proved dubious or ineffective time and time again.

• We can try to educate judges to understand that physical abuse by a man of a tiny child is just as serious as holding up a store. Indeed, the man who sticks up the store in all probability was abused by another man when he was a child.

• We can seek government sponsorship of programs to get kids out of the slums, if only for a few days a year, and into a world of lakes, trees, and field sports. Sure, it's an old-fashioned idea. But it may permanently shock a youngster into recognizing that there is a different world beyond the street world, to everyone's benefit.

• We can end most probation as we now know it for the juvenile criminal. We can replace it with what probation has become anyway: a means of keeping track of where the kid is. The manpower and money should go into family counseling. Right now, probation for this age group is a sad ritual, as meaningless to the probation officer as it is to the kid.

• We can use some of the computer suggestions I made in the last chapter to speed up the juvenile court process. Those with early violent offenses should be securely confined, if only for a weekend, as soon after the last offense as possible. Punishment should come while the recall of the crime is still fresh. Now, when kids are put away, it is so long after their crime that they feel no relationship between their criminal action and society's reaction.

• Some institutions mix twelve-year-olds with seventeen-year-old criminals. This can be ended without much cost. The return is substantial. The less exposure a youngster has to older criminals, the less likely he is to adopt the older youth's criminal techniques and ways of thought. Looking at it cynically, at worst, he may embrace serious adult crime a little later if he is kept with subteen criminals his own age.

If the means of decreasing the numbers of kids who turn early to crime seem costly, consider the savings I have recommended to balance off the costs. If they still seem high, remember that anything we do to put off the beginning of a criminal career by a few years, or perhaps cut it off before it starts, is worth the money. Our families will be safer, our taxes lower in the long run, and our hope for a less distressed America more realistic. At ten and twelve, a few things can be done and the investment is worth it while the social "interest rates" are low.

# *Four*

## ※

# Juvenile Predators: Thirteen to Seventeen Years Old

ANDREW Vachss is talking to a group of youth crime experts. He is a *magna cum laude* lawyer, a juvenile-maximum-security unit director, a professor, a ghetto caseworker. Nobody talks about thirteen- to seventeen-year-old violent delinquents better than Vachss.[1]

Now who *is* this kid? [Vachss is saying]. This kid is characterized by a complete lack of apparent empathy for other human beings. He feels no pain but his own. This is the type of kid who will kill three people on separate occasions for no apparent reason—a subway robbery, a push-in mugging, blowing somebody away because they looked at him wrong—show no remorse, and then come in to the office of an institution just *enraged*, veins bulging out of his neck, sweat pouring off his forehead, eyes wild, incoherent almost to the point of tears . . . all because someone broke his portable radio. And he'll see no contradiction whatever. He simply does not feel anyone's pain but his own. This is a *learned* response. People are not born like this.

The second characteristic is that he has no perception of the future. None. If you ask a kid like this, "What are you going to be doing next year?" you will get an absolutely blank stare. Not because he's stupid, but because he simply cannot conceptualize such a distance from *right now*. If you want to speak with this kid, you have to speak within his time frame, and that time frame isn't ever more than a few hours from the present. . . .

In his world, everyone commits crimes. *Everybody*. Some small percentage are arrested. A still smaller percentage go to court; an even smaller percentage go to trial. A smaller percentage still are actually found guilty (or adjudicated delinquent if you prefer). Lastly, an even smaller percentage are actually incarcerated.

He sees no connection between his acts and the consequences. He is marked by a chronicity of violence, usually an escalating pattern. Violence permeates his existence until it *is* his existence. It is not the *extent* of his criminality that frightens us, but its *regularity*. Crime is not so much an "occupation" in the sense of a professional criminal, but a way of life.

He has translator mechanisms in his head. You think of *earning* money; he thinks of *taking* money. You think of romance; he thinks of rape. Criminal sophistication is almost totally lacking.

He doesn't plan in any real sense; he's not organized in his criminality. Even what to do with the money is not pre-planned. He gets up in the morning about 11:00 A.M., puts on his sneakers, listens to the radio, looks in the refrigerator, sees nothing there . . . maybe some old cornflakes. He hits the street with his friends, hangs out.

He waits for an elderly woman to come home from the supermarket; follows her to her house. He gets on the elevator with her; she presses the button for the fourth floor; he presses it for the second floor. He jumps off at the second floor and runs up the stairs, watches her open her apartment door, slams foward, shoves the door open and the woman inside, kicks the door shut behind him, smashes the woman in the face until she hits the ground, snatches whatever little money she has.

He goes back downstairs to the same corner. If there was enough money, he may buy some soda, some pizza, some marijuana; he may go to a movie downtown.

Sooner or later one of the elderly women dies. And *then* the crime is in the media not as an organic continuation of a lifestyle but as some kind of nova-blast of episodic crime. But that's not the way it really is, and we know better.

We're not talking about some human being that just snaps out and hurts other people. We're talking about a person who has violence so inexorably woven into his life that a fatality is, in fact, *predictable* at some point in his career.

Who are his role models? Those who are, in his mind, successful criminals. He doesn't know any *real* successful criminals. He knows no embezzlers. He knows no computer criminals. He knows no politicians. He knows only what he perceives as success. And what *tells* him someone is a success? A diamond ring, fine clothes, a car. Not a home, because his perception doesn't extend that far.

He focuses on the *things* you can carry around with you. And when he goes to jail, that perception doesn't change. So when you read about one kid stabbing another to death over a pair of sneakers in a juvenile institution, don't dismiss it as insanity. It may be insane, but it's *consistently* so.

So who are the role models? Pimps, dope dealers, armed robbers. And when this kid thinks armed robbery, he's thinking like a cowboy. He's thinking about the guys who kick in the door of a social club, blow away three or four people, and end up with five hundred dollars. He doesn't even *conceptualize* a large-scale robbery, such as an armored car job.

Do any of you know what so-called "wolf children" are? They were the children found in Europe years age who had, apparently, been raised by wild animals. They were completely amoral, unsocial. They were feral things. They lacked any semblance of social control; just responded, as animals, to stimuli.

We've got our own "wolf children." We've got them for sure, and if you don't believe this, I don't know where you've been. We've got them and they scare the hell out of us.

The public has a right to ask us: "What are you going to do with them? More experiments? More research and development? No thanks. The risks are too high. Go ahead and conduct your experiments. Take a chance and see if maybe you can help this kid. But do it in some place where the kid can't come around and visit me at night."

I have quoted Vachss at such length because among the millions of words I have read, no one has ever put better the nature of the violent juvenile delinquent, unless it is, unwittingly, the delinquents themselves.

In a *CBS Reports* broadcast, young murderers were probed on their feelings about killing innocent people. One explained:

I shot this dude in the head for no reason, you know, I just knocked on his door, and I—I didn't want to, you know, go inside and, like, just, you know, be physical with him, you know. So . . . I just let off on him. . . .

How did I pick him? It was just the average little house, you know. It wasn't no picking to it. I was just smoking like, new chemicals, you know, and really, you know, I—I wasn't scared, you know. I ain't, you know, never been scared, you know . . . if I get caught, hey, I just get caught."

A sixteen-year-old in an institution for both murder and attempted murder, told of how he randomly killed a truck driver:

We were just driving down the street, and we saw some guy in a blue pick-up truck . . . and I looked over at him, and he said—said "Go ahead." So I just pointed the gun out of the car, just shot him right underneath the ear. . . . The reasons are just—well, we were just kind of high right then, but—I don't know if it was just for the fun or what, but we just decided to do it. . . .

The attempted murder, well, that was done on a—a security guard. . . . He started running up a hill and started saying something, so we—I shot him in the stomach. And then he was still yelling and everything, so we just kept on shooting him until, like, he passed out.

A teenager, this one from a family of some means, told why he became an armed robber and murderer:

When you rob people, sometime some of them will try—they try to fight you and don't want to give up the stuff. Then you have to shoot them. . . . It was in the summertime. I didn't have nothing to do then. . . . I wanted to buy a motorcycle, and I didn't have no money. I didn't feel like asking my mother to buy it for me, so I said I was going to get my own money. I went out, we started robbing people, taking their money. . . . It happens every day. People get shot every day. People get robbed every day. People [*sic*] house get broke in every day.

Another adolescent gunman touched on a theme we have explored before:

It's not hard to kill somebody. . . . It takes a little kid to pull the trigger of a gun. . . . It don't affect my head. You know, I don't get paranoid, you know. That's how I grew up, you know. . . . I like the feel of a gun, you know. . . . And just the idea of pushing the shells in, you know. I guess, you know, a lot of it comes from TV too, you know—just watch them dudes pack their guns, and I'm ready to—you know . . . just like on TV.

Those are the voices of the subteen criminals we examined in the last chapter, but which now have come to full and poisonous bloom.[2] How rampantly they have blossomed is shown by FBI and other Justice Department data. It says 30.9 percent of those arrested for serious crimes in America are under eighteen, although they make up only 27 percent of the population.

Twelve-year-olds and younger, as we noted earlier, are being arrested for robbery at a rate of about 6 per 100,000. At thirteen and fourteen, the rate skyrockets to 110; at fifteen it is 222; at sixteen it is 289; and at seventeen, the rate is 314, the highest for any age group—juvenile or adult.

The overall violent crime rate for seventeen-year-olds is 667 arrests per 100,000, second only to the 685 for eighteen-year-olds. While the seventeen-year-olds are the most active robbers, they have not yet hit their full fury as murderers, rapists, and serious committers of mayhem. That comes later.

In the nonviolent crime area, the sixteen-year-olds, according to a recent FBI survey, were slightly ahead of fifteen- and seventeen-year-olds in burglaries, theft, and other property crimes, with almost 3,700 arrests per 100,000. That was the highest rate for any age group.

All these figures, it must be remembered, are only *arrest* rates. While these are the best available data, they are still iffy. The data include multiple arrests of the same juveniles. Local police, before sending their reports to the FBI, may fudge them for political or administrative reasons, miscalculate, or include juveniles waived into adult jurisdiction. Or they may simply not send in their figures at all.[3]

The actual number of crimes may be ten or more times the FBI arrest totals because so many criminals get away with, literally, murder, before they are caught. At that level there are 800,000 violent juvenile crimes a year—rape, robbery, murder, and serious assaults.[4]

It may be small consolation but better than none that juvenile crime is less likely to cause serious injury than crimes by adults. In 72 percent of the juvenile violence—not including murder—there is no permanent injury. The rest cause some injury, but only 7 percent of the victims require medical attention.

There are other ways of assessing juvenile crime. One way is to ask the victims; the other to ask the criminals once they have been caught. These techniques support the FBI data in some cases, contradict it in others.

The 20-percent figure for violent juvenile crime is basically backed up by the victims—actually a sampling of 60,000 households and 50,000 businesses whose answers are then projected on total population figures.[5]

However, the victim surveys indicate the rate of violent juvenile crime is decreasing substantially, except in a number of major cities, while the arrest figures show it as more or less constant. The victim surveys show that juveniles commit 8 percent of the rapes, fewer than half of the 15 percent indicated by the arrest data. And victims say they were robbed by juveniles only 24 percent of the time, not 27.

The victim surveys show that in committing such crimes as robberies, juveniles use guns or other weapons 27 percent of the time, compared to 36 percent for those eighteen through twenty, 41 percent for twenty-one-and-overs.[6]

The third way of finding out more about criminals, and one growing in popularity, is through "self-reports," that is, interviews or questionnaires given to young criminals and often compared with data from nondelinquent "control" groups.[7]

When the controls and the criminals are lumped together, the self-report studies show that from 80 to 90 percent of all persons under eighteen at one time or another did something for which they could have been arrested. This could include minor pilfering, sampling a "joint," or hitting another kid hard enough for it to be simple assault.[8]

But more serious, the self-reports show that even before the age of fifteen, those who go on to become violent habitual criminals have gotten themselves heavily into crime. In their talks with interviewers, "self-reporters" say their crimes were unspecialized—a robbery one day, a burglary the next, a rape or fight the third, a car theft the fourth. Many of them were using hard drugs—powder or pills—but also some heroin. They were, as the criminologists say, already "seriously deviant" in their mid-teens. We encounter them in the media all the time.

From just a few days' newspaper clippings, we learn of the sixteen-year-old who put a gun on three social workers and held them hostage for two-and-a-half hours. He was angry because no one would adopt him.[9] There was another teenager who shot his parents and his two younger brothers because his parents were "too strict." There were three boys, fifteen, sixteen, and seventeen, who tried to rob a plainclothes policeman in the subway, stabbing him in the process. The officer shot two of them.[10]

These teenagers are now the ultimate American nightmare.

West Los Angeles is not a violent area. But, on Sunday night not long ago, two teenagers started walking at dusk. First they stopped a man who was pushing a baby carriage. They asked for money. He had none. They let him go.

Then at a nearby street corner, they stole $8 and two wristwatches from a married couple.

Then the two teenagers stopped two elderly Chinese women. One of the boys waved a pistol, and when one of the women tried to push it away from her face, he opened fire and killed both women.

Unhurriedly, the boys started walking again. Soon they came on three people who were out strolling together. They took a watch from one of them, and then, as casually as they had let the man with the baby go free, they shot and killed one of the three people they were holding up. He was a French tourist who had offered no resistance. The boys never said a word.

Finally, they reached a drive-in restaurant. An elderly man was standing outside. It is believed they argued with him. Moments later, they shot him, left him dying, and disappeared.

Young murderers like these have become as much the terror of the schoolrooms as they are of the streets. Not too long ago, a fourteen-year-old armed with two pistols resolved an argument over a pen by killing a fifteen-year-old classmate during study hall. He then shot another youngster before killing himself.[11]

Some 68 percent of the robberies and 50 percent of the assaults of children aged twelve to fifteen take place at school.

The National Institute of Education has estimated that 112,000 students were robbed and 282,000 attacked (42 percent with injuries) every month. Some 5,200 teachers were struck each month, and almost 20 percent required medical treatment. Other studies, while questioning the student figures, confirm the overall seriousness of school crime.

The Department of Justice, in an analysis of information gathered by the National Crime Survey, said:

> Nine out of ten in-school victimizations suffered by students and three out of four of those suffered by teachers and others were not reported to the police. Victims who failed to inform police most often said either that they reported it to someone else, or that it was not important enough, or that they thought nothing could be done.[12]

As a result, only a tiny number ever wind up as formal assault charges or are even reported to school system officials.

Much has been made of youth gangs, and with good reason.[13] They are a constant threat to citizen safety in New York, Chicago, Los Angeles, Philadelphia, Detroit, San Diego, San Antonio, Phoenix, San

Francisco, and Boston. Those ten cities, although they have only 18 percent of the population of cities over 10,000, have two-thirds of the nation's gang members.

In New York City alone, in a recent year one-eighth of the country's juvenile arrests for serious crime occurred. The arrests there for serious crimes by fifteen-and-unders are four times the national average. In 1984, the city's violent juvenile rate was going down in line with a national trend.[14]

Gang violence in New York, bad as it is, does not match the situation in Chicago or Los Angeles. In fact, dangerous gangs operate in towns all the way down to the 10,000 level. In 1981, the Attorney General's task force on violent crimes estimated there were 2,200 gangs with 96,000 members in 300 cities and towns.[15] In sixty of these cities, there were 3,400 gang-related murders between 1967 and 1980.

Lately, the gangs have begun moving drugs across interstate lines much like organized crime, according to the task force study. The return is enormous. A fourteen- or fifteen-year-old delivering drugs for older gang members and armed with a pistol can make up to $600 a day if he hustles.[16]

Other gangs may be less involved with drugs and more involved with preserving a "macho" image for members, filling their needs for a family in a world where blood families have disintegrated. Significantly, when one gang member challenges another, it is generally with the ultimate masculine weapon, a firearm.

Still other groups are organized for gambling operations, prostitution, theft, burglary and fencing, robbery, extortion, arson, and even murder.

Chicago Police Chief Richard Brzeczek put it this way: "The street gang has a better hierarchy of membership than one would find in legitimate business, the military or even the farm system of organized baseball before expansion."[17]

These gangs range from small predatory groups of five up to organizations of fifty or more with stratified duties specified for kids of ten as well as prison-hardened criminals of twenty-one or older.

Professor Walter Miller of Harvard, the most renowned researcher of law-violating groups, estimates that they commit 71 percent of serious juvenile crimes.[18] Other studies put the figure lower.

Whatever the numbers, I can assure you that the meaning of youth gangs comes home not as a statistic, but as cold, stark panic when, while your car is stopped at a light in the ghetto, you see four fifteen-year-olds, the first with a gun, walking toward your left front door.

It is a time when you bless the efficiency of rapid acceleration, and later ponder a long time the fragility of life, particularly life in the city.

We heard from the teenage murderers, the "cool" argot of the drug user: words like "chemicals" and "kind of high." But drugs are not merely talk, not merely the fads of the young. They are components of the violent crime in America.

The Justice Department reports alcohol or drugs or both were factors in 60 percent of the violent crimes by juveniles.[19] Another study shows 41 percent of vicious crimes by adolescents were immediately preceded by alcohol use, 23 percent by drug use. Looking at it slightly differently, a third survey reported only 29 percent of young criminals had not used either drugs or alcohol or both just prior to their violent acts.[20]

A California research project showed that a quarter of the juveniles were drunk at the time they killed or tried to kill. In another study, the rate of violent crimes leaped from 10 percent before the adolescents began narcotics use to 35 percent afterwards.

Narcotics-related crimes are, in a sense, double-barreled. Sometimes the young criminals are under the influence of "speed" or other amphetamines or barbiturates or heroin when they commit violent acts. Other times they rob for cash to buy the drugs, or break into drug stores or doctors' offices to steal them directly.

While statistics vary on precisely how great a role drugs play in crime, few deny that they can encourage violence. Indeed, tests show that alcohol can turn even respectable college kids into seething cauldrons of antisocial hostility.[21]

Three groups of students were given bourbon, a placebo that tasted like bourbon, and nothing. Then they were given competitive tasks designed to heighten their frustration. If they accomplished the task, they could administer an electric shock to their opponent.

The bourbon-drinkers viciously electrified their opponents. When the students were given vodka instead of bourbon, they shocked their adversaries even more severely, presumably because vodka contains fewer congeners and so builds up faster in the blood. The "control" groups reacted much more mildly.

In summing up drug research as it relates to crime, the Justice Department said: "The onset of substance abuse during adolescence is a direct spur to subsequent delinquency and serious criminal behavior." On alcohol and crime, the Justice report continued: "The criminal alcoholic typically has a history of violent behavior . . . from adolescence, or even earlier . . . usually murder, assault and rape."

The reports are not judgmental about alcohol *use*, only about alcohol abuse. They say unequivocally that for those who already are afflicted with what Andrew Vachss calls the "criminal carcinogens," drinking and drug abuse can be fatal—for other people.

# *Five*

※

# Juveniles and the Courts

SOME criminologists believe only 3 out of every 100 juvenile crimes are cleared up with an arrest. Others say 10 in 100, or 1 in 5. Actually, it may not be too important to close that formidable gap in our knowledge.[1]

What is important, however, is to remove from the streets that minuscule number of young predator criminals from thirteen to seventeen who commit much of our violent crime.

The juvenile court systems are the means by which this must be done, but right now in many jurisdictions they are in shambles.[2] Unless we can bring some order to the courts, we cannot stem juvenile crime even when arrests are made.

To understand what can be done—and much is possible—it is necessary to go back to where it all began and to define why it went so terribly wrong. For millennia, young criminals were treated no differently from older ones. Even in the nineteenth century, England did not scruple about hanging ten-, eleven-, and twelve-year-olds for offenses no worse than the theft of a piece of silverware.[3] Less than a hundred years ago in our own country, youngsters were always tried as adults and were often locked in fortresslike prisons with criminals in their twenties and thirties.[4]

Toward the end of the nineteenth century, however, reformers began preaching segregation of kids from adults not just in jails, but in the courts. Finally, in 1899, Chicago set up a juvenile court so that young criminals could "be taken in hand by the State, not as an enemy, but as a protector."

Ten years later, New York passed a similar law saying that children henceforth would not be considered guilty of crimes "but of juvenile delinquency only." The courts would not punish, but rather would help, troubled youngsters.

As the system spread throughout America, a natural trade-off emerged. In return for being treated differently, juveniles would surrender certain rights of due process. Most important, they would not have the right to counsel, but would rely instead on the fairness, discretion, and good intention of the juvenile court.

In the early 1960s, the more liberal states began to pass laws giving juveniles more and more legal protections, including the right to counsel.[5] In effect, the new laws turned the proceeding into a quasi-adult trial.

Liberals across the country applauded the statutes. The Supreme Court and the President's Commission on Law Enforcement commended them. The state laws were ahead of the times, but not for long. In 1967 the Supreme Court handed down the epochal Gault decision. Based on the case of a fifteen-year-old boy who got six years for making obscene phone calls, the ruling gave juveniles in *all* states the right to counsel and most other rights of adults.

But while the legislature and the courts were increasing juvenile criminals' rights, on the streets the violent young criminals were increasing in numbers.[6]

Policemen on the beat, prosecutors, and some judges began talking about these more violent teenagers.[7] Newspapers started carrying prominent stories of teenaged gunmen murdering homeowners, torching derelicts, and raping old women.

The requirements of due process in juvenile cases meant increased funding not just of prosecutors, but of the legal defenders who in many states would now counsel these young criminals. The fiscal problems at city, county, and state levels often made already overloaded systems unmanageable.

To be sure, some juvenile courts made the transition without problems and have continued to function without serious hitches. But in most cities overcrowding and confusion have become nightmares.

The horrors begin the moment a youth is turned over to the court and are amplified at every stage of prosecution. The legal defenders who are paid by the government to take on the defense of the juveniles, overworked as they are, at least deal with individual clients. Prosecutors, many of whom are only serving until they can get out and make better money elsewhere, often must represent whole "sections" of cases. They literally may only have time to snatch up a trial folder before they are required to put their case before the judge.

With neither preparation nor clerical staff, they may have no time to persuade witnesses to come to court. They lack manpower to enforce subpoenas. Sometimes they meet witnesses only minutes before a crucial court session. When cases are put over, it is always tough for them to marshal witnesses again for a new hearing.

Then when witnesses do show up, legal aid workers can chat with them informally, asking them to drop their charges.[8] Congested waiting rooms for witnesses make court appearances even less appetizing, particularly since the defendant, his family, and his friends may be sitting in the same room. Beatings and other intimidation are not unheard of while victims and their witnesses wait for a hearing.

To make matters worse for the victims and their witnesses, cases are often scheduled in the morning, even though they may not be called until midafternoon.

The judges, traditionally the movers and shakers of the court world, have lost much of their power and influence in juvenile courts. Like all judges, they dislike appeals and particularly reversals. With the more skilled appellants in the ranks of the legal defender staffs, the judges stand good chances of reversals, and they have pulled in their horns accordingly. It is, after all, much easier to appeal a finding against a defendant than vice versa.

Probation officers were once answerable to judges and worked under their supervision to come up with placement alternatives for offenders. Now in many cities, the probation department is a separate unit, no longer under the judges' direct authority.

Social workers tend to push for soft handling of juvenile criminals and regularly challenge the probation officers' placements if they seem overly harsh.

The cumulative effect is a severe warping of the system in the name of protecting young criminals' rights. Of course, they *should* be protected, but there has to be some compromise so the rights of the citizens are not menaced on the streets.

★  ★  ★

While the *theory* of the courts operates against the citizenry in one way, the *practice* is achieving those same morbid results in another. For the courts have a management problem of staggering proportions.[9]

Records are regularly lost. The telephone system doesn't work—it sometimes takes a half-dozen calls even to find the right office. One department has no idea what the other is doing, even on the same case.[10]

Incredible as it may seem, there is no central pool of information on juvenile offenders anywhere in the country. Let us say that a fifteen-year-old with multiple arrests for violence in Brooklyn gets aboard the subway, travels to Newark or even to the Bronx, and commits an armed robbery. He is then arrested and taken to court. He could be treated as a first offender. No one may know of his previous record.

Furthermore, even if a juvenile pursues his entire criminal career in the same city, it is possible there will be no single record of all his offenses. Streetwise offenders can give the court and the probation clerk several aliases rather than their right names.

Since a new petition is filed each time a juvenile comes in on a new charge, the various cases are at different stages of prosecution. Lack of coordination means that the prosecutor may not even know when there is more than one charge pending. The probation and court record filings may not even use the same numbering system.

Morale in the juvenile systems often is almost nonexistent. Probation departments complain of overwork, but when one citizens' group inspected a big city department "only a few officers were busy."[11] And they often did little to locate offenders who failed to keep appointments ordered by the court. Budget cuts have been near-lethal for the department, and salaries remain low. The handful of dedicated officers are often on the brink of stress fracture.

A few episodes may illustrate many:

A "child" rooftop sniper was charged with attempted murder and sent to prison, but his sentence was reduced on appeal. While the probation officers were pushing to put him away again, the legal defenders were trying to assign him to a community-based facility. The murderous adolescent, meanwhile, was cut loose to roam at large while the two antagonists decided what to do with him.

In another case, two teenage gunmen shot a youngster in the head, killing him. The charge was reduced to "reckless endangerment." In still a third proceeding, five fifteen-year-olds kidnapped two girls and raped them repeatedly. The allegations began as rape and possession of a deadly weapon. The finding was sexual misconduct, a misdemeanor.

New York's then-deputy police commissioner, Kenneth Conboy, in urging more aggressive prosecution, described two of the types of juveniles being dealt with by the city's Family Court. He describes one young criminal:

> . . . from the time he was fifteen years old, [he] made hundreds of dollars a night prowling the city streets from Times Square to the upper reaches of Park Avenue, robbing everyone from . . . men with attaché cases . . . to clerks in small shops.
>
> The young man had little to fear even though he was arrested eleven times and convicted five. He was allowed to walk out of the courtroom again and again. He made it clear that while the city feared him, he had very little fear of the city or the massive system it had set up to deter, try and punish him.
>
> "They got me now," he'd think—and then they wouldn't. "I'd go to court and they'd say, 'Well, the lawyer's not here and such and such is not here.' So they'd let me go, give me a date to come back to court and I never come back—till I got busted again."

A second youth was one of a group of 500 offenders who New York City transit police felt were responsible for 40 percent of all subway crime. He had a record of sixty prior arrests. Eighteen months later, he had been arrested nine more times. The stiffest sentence given to him within that year-and-a-half was ninety days.

Legal defenders are doing their job under guidelines set down by their official manuals. Their duty is to defend their clients with zeal and get for them the best possible disposition from the client's own point of view. This means using their cunning to get even the most venomous young killer out on the street again and again if it is legally possible.

Some public defenders have found their predictable daily victories on behalf of juvenile predators so repugnant they have quit. The kid they free in the morning, they know all too well, could be committing another crime that same afternoon. Other legal defenders look on their work as a sort of grisly competitive sport, complete with tally sheet. Still others are idealistic, "turned on" to defendants' rights to the exclusion of everything and everyone else. Finally, there are the bureaucrats, those who function anywhere, under almost any kind of regime, and who salve their misgivings by telling themselves every morning, "I am just doing my job."

Meanwhile, adult-style protection of juvenile rights has spread into the appellate process. During the sixties, it was almost unheard of for a juvenile case to be appealed. Today, kiddie cases flood into the appellate process, slowing down dockets, and backing up trials and hearings even further.

About two million juveniles are arrested each year. For most of them, it is their introduction to the criminal justice system. Immediately following their arrest, about half are released or else handled within the arresting agency, that is, talked to by the police.[12] The rest are referred to the court officers or to prosecutors.

About half of these cases are then dropped, usually because of insufficient evidence. The result is that almost 80 percent of all alleged juvenile offenders have the charges against them dismissed or otherwise dropped.

Of the juveniles who do find their way into court, more than 70 percent are first-time offenders. Most of them are given suspended sentences, placed on probation, or lightly admonished.

Detention and adjudication in a formal court hearing are likely to occur only for repeat offenders; stiff sentences given only to the most recalcitrant or vicious.

By one estimate, more than 60 percent of youths arrested for robbery get the charges dismissed. Only 4 percent of those arrested for violent crimes ever serve time. In fact, only 13 percent of all formal juvenile delinquency cases end up with defendants being placed in *any* kind of institution—jail, halfway house, camp, hospital, or foster home—even for a day.

Some of the inmates in juvenile facilities are not there for crimes, but are "status" offenders, children who are runaways or truants, or were judged beyond their parents' control.[13]

Although they may not come into a juvenile facility as criminals, the odds are that they will come out that way. Some 86 percent of youths who go into an institution get into trouble again and are back before juvenile court. This time, when they go back to a "reformatory," they are far more likely to be there for something serious.

When a vicious juvenile is put into an institution with youths less accustomed to violence than he is, he often runs amok.[14] The staff of the institution generally responds to him as a special case. Consequently, he is assigned a role. He helps the staff to keep order, and he uses violence to do it. When he does, he turns the institution into a living hell for those juveniles who shouldn't have been there in the first place.

In the last few years, the mood of the public on violent juveniles has been changing. As a result, in the late seventies, state legislatures began passing laws intended to make things tough for young predators.

Assistant district attorneys, specialists on criminal law, now handle some of the most serious juvenile crime cases. In proceedings where these prosecutors oppose Legal Aid counsel, the battle is far more evenly matched.

When assistant district attorneys prosecuted a group of first offenders in one jurisdiction, all of them charged with serious offenses, 81 percent were found to be delinquent. Meanwhile, a similar group of first offenders, all of them charged with crimes of approximately equal severity, were opposed by ordinary juvenile prosecutors; only 24 percent were judged delinquent.

An anticrime measure that carried it a step further has had far less certain results. For years, in many jurisdictions, sixteen-year-olds and up could be waived to adult courts for trial as adult criminals. But recently some states have passed laws also permitting adult trials for fourteen- and fifteen-year-olds who commit certain felonies, and thirteen-year-olds who commit murder.[15]

In a recent six-month period, 622 youths in one state were convicted under the adult laws and 515 were "sentenced." Of those sentenced, 205, or 40 percent, drew probation. As a practical matter, all 205 of these convicted criminals were put back on the streets.

This is consonant with statistics from around the nation on all youths waived to adult courts.[16] When sentences are given, they are a year or less in 40 percent of the cases. Judges simply cannot bring themselves to put youngsters, even violent ones, in prisons with adult offenders. Nor am I disposed to. But there are ample means of achieving the necessary segregation of young convicts without reducing prison security.

★   ★   ★

If ever a quagmire called out for efficient draining, the juvenile courts are candidates. The hundreds of millions that could be saved, the numerous lives, and the vast amount of property that could be made more safe boggle the imagination.

Studies of the mess proliferate. The data is already there. What is needed is the kind of professional multidiscipline approach that industry would take to revamp a badly ailing subsidiary. Efforts by some cities in this direction have been made. But often they have failed because they have lacked authority. They have not had the backing.

The kind of team a big corporation or a top management-analyzing company uses is what I have in mind. It is made up of seasoned professionals from many areas, people who have nothing to lose by being both honest and tough. There is always an accountant; someone from one of the "social" disciplines such as psychiatry or psychology, whose specialty is management problems; a veteran first- or second-level executive who has gone into consulting, not because he was fired but because he can make more money and have more independence as a consultant; a legal specialist to see what the laws permit or *will* permit when amended; and a public relations or information type to estimate the effect on the public.

The team is always headed by an open- but stern-minded individual of high repute and ability, the kind of person who is used to talking with candor and confidence to presidents, governors, mayors, heads of legislative bodies, and the like.

Before such a team even goes into the situation, it must have— painful as this may be for politicians to accept—an *a priori*, preferably public, commitment that action will be taken.

What so often happens with these team efforts in government, either local or national, is that everybody applauds the recommendations, then the weevils get into them and they are spoiled. Juvenile court problems are so glaring and so well-documented that beforehand approval of radical changes is both possible and necessary.

The legislature and government must agree generally on what kinds of new bills will have to be passed, and what kinds of state funds made available, and the mayors, even more importantly, must be ready to act.

The courts' management problem is the first one to resolve. Strength cannot be guaranteed if most of a structure's beams and supporting timbers are rotten.

To start with, the filing systems must be rationalized, even if it means inefficient clerks must be fired and lax or incompetent supervisors replaced. Cities should be able to expect a full week's work for a full week's pay. It is essential to have reliable data to operate either a business or a government.

Court personnel must be able to punch up a name and a date of birth and find out from a properly programmed computer not just how many cases are outstanding against a juvenile, but what the status of each one is. Aliases and, where possible, juvenile records from other jurisdictions must be cross-programmed.

As another early step, if the present juvenile prosecutors are to continue to handle criminal cases, they must take them at the beginning and follow them through. These prosecutors must be as well-trained as their "big brothers" in the district attorney's office.

Juvenile courts must be made more monolithic, as the federal courts system is. The judicial branch of the government is not the preserve of the lawyers, either defendant's or city's, but of the judges. The guidance and authority of the courts must be returned to the judges, and their selection removed once and for all from politics to ensure guts and competency.

This means return of probation offices to the judges. Probation officers should be divided clearly into those handling adult and those handling juvenile cases. In my view, a better means of keeping track of unsentenced juveniles is possible. That is the main function of probation officers now. As I said earlier, they might better work with families than with individual young criminals, perhaps in cooperation rather than opposition to the social workers.

The waiting rooms for victims and witnesses are often a disgrace. If they cannot be kept orderly by policing, then victims and their witnesses should be given the dignity of separation from the defendants and their allies.

Scheduling of cases is sometimes shameful. Delay almost always works for the defendant. When cases are set, they should be heard. And they should be set at specific times, at least closer to their real hearing time than five or six hours later. When delays are necessary, those who have most often had their hearings postponed should have first priority.

If business violated simple commonsense rules with its employees, they would be out on strike and justified to do so. Yet we subject innocent victims of crime and witnesses to indignities that even the juvenile criminals do not suffer.

While they must be given back their "judgehood," our judges must also be urged in the strongest terms to adopt and follow consistent sentencing practices. At present, legal defenders, and in some cases prosecutors too, "judge shop" in the most blatant way. There should be no judge whose reputation for leniency earns him a nickname like "Back on the Street O'Fleet" or whose harshness warrants the sobriquet "Life and Thirty Gerty."

Plea bargaining, while sometimes necessary to keep down the number of cases going to trial, can at least be regulated. Some of the computer techniques I have suggested for incapacitation, based on past records, number of offenses outstanding, the national average for such crimes, and so on would make ideal guidelines for plea bargaining. When there are wide variations on plea-bargaining "deals," a memo on the reasons why should be entered into the files. The same would apply to judges' sentences.

As I offer these suggestions, a few of the changes I have recommended are on the way. But they are far too limited, and the process is taking far too long.

Even if all this were accomplished tomorrow, even *because* it was accomplished tomorrow, there still would be a major problem: There are going to be more young offenders in institutions. The reforms will mean more of these predators will be off the streets and in secure settings. At present, there is no appropriate place to send them. Redistributions can go a long way toward solving the problem. But at a cost. There are other avenues that are only now beginning to be explored.

# Six

✳

# Locking Up Juveniles:
# The Search for Alternatives

L ED by New York and Massa-
chusetts, reformers in the early 1800s began looking for ways to keep
children out of adult prisons. A "House of Refuge" was set up in
New York in the 1820s.[1] In Boston, a similar "House of Reforma-
tion" came under the management of a radical young Episcopalian
preacher named E. M. P. Wells in 1828.[2]

This novel facility concentrated on delinquent youths under fifteen and used organized play and gymnastics to teach them to get on
in society rather than traditional classroom lessons in grammar, pen-
manship, and math. The purpose was pragmatic: to get the adolescents home and to work.

Thirteen years later, in line with this goal, Boston set up a probation program where selected juveniles were released from institutions and consigned by the court to agencies, foster homes, or even
single foster parents.

By 1900, there were thirty-six states with special institutions for
children, most of them based on industrial school concepts. The
housing was generally in "cottages" rather than in cells—but with
high walls to deter escapes.

The worst of them were ghastly. As late as the 1920s a "disciplinary officer" went from cottage to cottage in one reform school with
a whip to lash fractious children. They were called out and delivered
up to him by the house father. More serious offenders were thrown
in solitary confinement for more than a month without mattress or

shoes. There, they slept on wooden boards nailed to concrete floors, in some cases handcuffed to pipes twenty-four hours a day.

But the best of these early reform schools were genuinely trying to rehabilitate. That remains the motive in today's institutions. Sheer numbers, however, often make them the same kind of human warehouses that adult prisons have always been.

What do we do with so many criminal kids?

Of the two million arrests each year of suspects under eighteen, perhaps a half million are repeaters, leaving a million to a million-and-a-half individual kids.[3] As I wrote earlier, most of these cases are dropped or the young criminals are put on probation—given a second (or third or fourth) chance.

Of those cases that aren't thrown out, only about 60,000 result in confinement in a juvenile facility. About 5,000 more are juveniles so vicious they are sent to young adult prisons.

Some of the arrested juveniles are held in jails pending their trip to court. In fact, sometimes adult jails are used interchangeably with juvenile lock-ups. The upshot is that a half-million juveniles are held in adult jails every year in spite of federal laws banning the practice.[4]

These jails have become rape factories for the juveniles who are locked in them. The suicides, although less numerous than believed, are nevertheless shocking. Beatings, torture, and theft are common offenses against these young prisoners.

In the juvenile facilities, the situation is often not much better. Instead of men abusing fourteen- to seventeen-year-olds, it is seventeen-year-olds abusing fifteen-year-olds or younger boys.

Nobody pretends that the average juvenile prisons do anything much to rehabilitate their inmates. As proof, 50 to 80 percent are reimprisoned after they are released. Often the young criminal, who is locked up for a string of muggings the first time, returns the second time with several armed robberies or a murder on his record.

By then, almost everyone now seems to agree, the only benefit of incarceration is that it confines the juvenile's criminal attentions to his fellow criminals instead of to the rest of us. That's something, but it's not much.

Recognizing that this cycle is a primitive and basically inhumane way to treat juvenile offenders—even the worst of them—juvenile crime authorities have come up with one alternative after another.[5] So far the pickings are lean, as evaluators make clear.

"A hard look at the programs reveals that there are a limited number of things which can be done to or for serious delinquents, although the ways of doing them can and do vary considerably," says an exhaustive Justice Department study.[6]

One social scientist studied 235 government-backed antidelinquency projects and found that in 233 cases, there was no significant effect one way or the other.[7] In the other two cases, the youths in the program did worse than a "control" group.

Another study found that over a twelve-year period, at least 6,500 projects had been launched to control delinquency. It examined the 127 most carefully evaluated ones and found that even where results were available, the projects "had not successfully prevented delinquency . . . we found little reason to believe that a major breakthrough in delinquency is forthcoming."[8]

One particular field of endeavor in the antidelinquency fight is diversion: taking offenders out of the system at the time of their arrest, or just before they are sentenced, in any case before they are sent to an institution or put on probation. A national study was done on eleven once-promising projects.[9] The diverted youths got into just as much trouble as those who were either simply lectured and cut loose, or those who continued in the court system. In some cases, the diversions didn't even save any money. In one recent project, one of the project administrators carefully selected by the government ran off with all the money.

In another experiment it was decided that 223 first-grade boys, selected on the basis of how disrupted their family life was, were likely to become delinquent. Teams of psychiatrists, teachers, and social workers worked with the youngsters. Ten years later, their records were checked. They had turned out to be every bit as delinquent as those kids whose families were similarly disturbed, but who had not been counseled.

In a similar program, teachers, police, clinical testers, and psychologists visited the homes of children from six to eleven. Their assessments were used to pick the ones who would probably become criminals. For five years, these children underwent intensive personal counseling and observation. The effects were no more useful than if the children had been left alone.[10]

Summing up two decades of frustration, the Office of Juvenile Justice and Delinquency Prevention, surely one of the most worthwhile and straight-talking little bureaus in government, said: "The empirical evidence suggests that past efforts at delinquency prevention can be characterized as largely ineffective."[11]

In approaching the subject as a businessman, I have read enough to know that here the road sign says, "Caution, road under construction."

The first problem is what to do with the habitually violent juvenile, whom I have earlier focused on because he commits a wildly disproportionate amount of violent crime. His breed is not numerous. Some experts estimate that no more than a few hundred juveniles in even the most populous states are truly dangerous, nonstop predators.[12]

But these constitute the seemingly insoluble problems. No halfway house can be expected to hold them. They disrupt even large, well-organized facilities. When they explode in confinement, they get the "works," but that, too, has its anguish.

"For violent, assaultive delinquents," says one Justice Department report, "there must be added the medical remedies of psychotropic drugs, plus restraining and stimulating techniques traditionally used in mental hospitals."[13]

Translating that jargon into English, they are drugged with Thorazine or some other powerful tranquilizer, buckled into a straitjacket, and chucked in what a veteran adult convict would call the "hole"—solitary confinement.

But eventually, unless he can be proved psychotic enough for confinement to a mental hospital, he is going to be cut loose on society. And so you have this, by now, well-muscled eighteen-year-old, unpenitent and homicidal, with the emotions of a disturbed ten-year-old, out on the street. He won't stay there long, but while he does, he is as unpredictable and as dangerous as an unexploded pipe bomb.

In Chapter 4, I mentioned a figure of $40,000 to $70,000 a year for a try at converting this criminal into someone at least less dangerous. Right now, on the street, he is good for $50,000 or more in costs, depending on whether he kills or merely robs, torches, or maims—and on how high a price a person puts on a jewelry case or a house or warehouse or a blinded eye or a life.

Here is why it costs so much to keep this young criminal in a therapeutic but secure facility:

The few "alternative residences" showing any promise are small and custom-built; the ratio of staff to inmate is one-to-one or better; and the staff are bright professionals who expect and can demand good money; the outside experts called in for special teaching, psychiatry, and the like also are costly.

To make matters worse, the life expectancy of such facilities is not great, in part because of funding problems, in part because the stress of running them sometimes causes staff problems of rending and insoluble proportions. Indeed, one of the facilities recommended to me by a Justice Department source as an example of a success had folded before I could even begin my interviews.

One project that seems to have all the elements of success is Pennsylvania's South East Secure Treatment Unit (SESTU) at West Chester.[14] Set up for only twenty-five youths, it takes males from fourteen to eighteen with an average of nine previous arrests, all of them serious and at least some of them violent. The residents generally have IQs of about 70 and they have failed already in from one to six less secure settings.

The program is not yet six years old, and one of my questions put to the staff was whether they thought it would last long enough for this book to be published. In this case, it probably will.[15]

One of the crucial elements, unfortunately, in all of the successful programs is their uniqueness, which is a function of their "management team." We tend to think of certain companies as the creatures of their founding geniuses: Henry Ford, Andrew Carnegie, Alexander Graham Bell, the Wright Brothers. Sometimes the companies they set up thrive under new management; sometimes they fail; sometimes they change radically.

At SESTU, it is no different. Fred McNeal is founder, director, and guiding genius. When he and his able associate, Alton Wedde, first set up the facility, there were fights, broken windows, even an escape. Since then, as of this writing, there has been only one additional escape, and no severe injuries from fights.

SESTU also exemplifies a second element in all the successful alternative approaches: it takes a pragmatic and eclectic view toward its wards. What works, within acceptable limits, SESTU tries.

McNeal has drawn his staff from a range of professional disciplines. He has, besides Wedde, a staff psychologist, twelve counselors, twelve houseparents, and two general supervisors, and he uses four county teachers and aides. All this for twenty-five kids.

Although McNeal was issued three pairs of handcuffs by the state when he opened SESTU, he has so far had to use them only one time. Nor has he administered psychotropic drugs to control his kids, or used straitjackets, or a "hole."

The emphasis is on a practical mix of academics—most of the inmates came to SESTU as near illiterates—prevocational achievement, and the simple skills for surviving in society. Most new arrivals do not know how to shop, how to look for a job, or even how to live properly in an apartment. The goal is to build self-esteem.

This has meant tough, endless hours of individual and group therapy, trial-and-error training in the use of the most simple carpentry, construction, and machine tools. It has meant one-on-one tutoring in speech and writing for kids whose basic vocabulary was made up of four-letter words. It has also meant, for McNeal, firing employees who got in unresolvable conflicts with kids because he was unwilling to evict even the most recalcitrant inmates. Only the psychopathic kid is turned away.

The core of the work is a point system. Each week a "student" can earn 400 points for schoolwork plus 600 points for his living area upkeep. For his lodging, he pays 800 points a month. If he passes muster, he can pay out 1,800 points a month for a private apartment. He also can spend points for supervised trips to a rollerskating rink, to the movies, or to an outside gym. He can use others for games, decorated shirts, models, or cheap watches. Or he can goof off, do nothing, and as McNeal says, "get the three hots and a cot that the state says we have to give him."

The youths, abandoned by most as lost when they come to SESTU, stay there twelve months. They are then placed, in most cases, back in their homes, or if that is too disruptive for all concerned, with close relatives or a foster residence. In each case, a good deal of family counseling—the third element in all successful programs—is first undertaken as a vital complement to the one-on-one counseling at SESTU.

When possible, a job is obtained for the SESTU "graduate" before he leaves the program. Although McNeal's efforts are still too young for an accurate evaluation, the results so far show 35 of his 62 graduates have not been arrested after they left SESTU. That's a 44 percent recidivism rate compared to the 70 to 80 that kids like the ones he takes could be expected to show. Neither he, nor the state which funds the project at a current cost of $45,000 per youngster, expects it to achieve 100 percent success. After all, the children who came to it were 100 percent failures.

A dissimilar but also successful alternative to youth penal warehousing is the House of Umoja in the Philadelphia ghetto. In an earlier chapter, I suggested financial aid for indigenous community anticrime efforts, and it is organizations like the House of Umoja that I had in mind.

Its founder is Sister Falaka Fattah, nee Frankee Davenport, a Black Nationalist, a mother of six, who, unfortunately, cannot be replicated. Like McNeal, she is unique. But America and crime victims are fortunate that society, somehow, keeps giving birth to these remarkable people.

The name *Fattah*, which she and her husband took when they gave up their "slave" names, means "revealer" in Arabic. *Umoja* means "unity" in Swahili. Her own words about the House of Umoja give the authentic flavor of her powerful and persuasive personality:

[The house] had its beginnings in 1968, at the Black Power Conference which was held in Philadelphia, and attended by over 5,000 delegates from all over the country, parts of Africa, and the Caribbean Islands. It was the concern of these conferees that because of the riots that had occurred in the 1960s that if long-range plans were not developed, that black people, people of African descent, could become as extinct as some of the Indian tribes.

So, the concern there was for long-range planning and for the liberation of black people. Out of that workshop came the House of Umoja as a publishing house, and a magazine was produced of which I was the editor, *Umoja* magazine.

We developed an editorial policy that we would not submit in our pages any problems for which we did not have any solutions. So, when hundreds of letters came across my desk about the gang problem—at that time Philadelphia, in 1969, was known as the Gang Capital of the country—this was a problem for which we had no solution.

So, I asked my husband—he was the only person on the staff that had any "street smarts"—to please go out and at least check into this situation and at least tell us why it was in Philadelphia that children killed each other.

He spent a lot of time in the streets, he had been a former gang member himself. He went to funerals and hospitals. He hung out in the bars—he had a perfect excuse for staying out late at night. He went to the pool rooms, etc., and after a while he began to develop an idea of what was going on.

We found that when black people moved into Philadelphia from the South, they did not move as a family group. That they did as many immigrants did, first one family member would come and they would get themselves settled. Then another one would come, then another one would come. So that that was the beginning of a breakdown within the family structure.

You would see young children walking the streets, and they would have keys around their necks. That key basically meant that there was nobody home, and this key simply gave them entrance into their home if they wanted something to eat. Among the gangs we found that for a lot of them the tradition of sitting down to a dinner meal together and having social interchange did not exist.

What Black Dave, to use her husband's street name, and Sister Fattah also found was that the young people were transferring their loyalties from family to the members of youth gangs. And one of these gang members was their own son.

Their response was to take in fifteen members of their son's gang— a total of twenty-three people in their small, five-room house. That was the beginning of the House of Umoja as an alternative to prison for violent youths. Sister Fattah continues:

What we did was, sold and gave away all of our furniture and then we bought camping supplies and simply camped inside of our house. We were not aware that there are other ways that you start programs. In fact, we did not know that we were starting a program. We just wanted to see if having a strong family unit would make a difference in the violent behavior of gangs.

What we found after having 200 youths live with us—and there usually were from fifteen members to perhaps 30 at a time—we found that those that lived with us did not return to gang warfare. However, it had no effect, whatsoever, in terms of the slaughter that was going on out in the streets.

So that in 1972, when Mayor Rizzo asked for all the gang members to turn in their guns, what we did was, we had the gang conference. We simply asked the 200 youths that had lived with us to contact the leaders of their gangs and ask them if we could sit down and discuss a way that we could live in peace. Over 500 came to the conference.

Since that time it has been pretty well documented that it was a successful conference because of the first 32 gangs that made peace,

22 were able to keep their peace pledges. Later on in 1975, those gangs that had made peace pledges rose to 80. At that time there were about 85 active gangs.

I think that is not the only factor, though. I think the reason why the conference was a success was not that we called them to the meeting, but because we had the cooperation from within the prisons. Because the entire year 1973 we visited every prison in Pennsylvania where gang members were held.

As far as gang traditions are concerned, it is the person in jail who is doing the time for whom the corner has the most respect. So, we went to them and asked them to give us their support in having the conference. I think it is incorrect to think that people in prison or people on the street have no redeeming features.

As of this writing, those who have lived in the House of Umoja, now greatly expanded, is approaching 600. They range in age from fifteen to eighteen, many there voluntarily, the majority sent to the House by the city courts.

Wake-up time is 6 A.M. and there is emphasis on good meals, school, field trips to museums, and vigorous exercise. For those who break the rules—violence and profanity are banned, television limited—there are fines, read off at a weekly "adella," or House council meeting. Each member gets a $10-a-week allowance that is docked when fines are ordered. Those doing particularly good work in ending gang violence become a *Fattah*, an honorary title.

"The only youths that we do not accept," says Sister Fattah, "are those who are psychotic, and they need to be treated at a mental institution, or those who are on drugs, and I think that there are plenty of programs that deal with that."

Of late, the House has branched out into a miniconglomerate of programs: a training school for security officers, an escort service for the elderly, a home renovation unit, a lunch and day-care program for neighborhood children, a work crew service, a team that installs dead-bolts in residences, a community musical group, and a guard service for businesses.[17]

Its money comes from both government and private foundations and corporations, its critics generally from within the juvenile delinquency structure. They complain that it is unstructured, and in a sense it is. I too am skeptical of some of the more extravagant claims put forward by boosters of the House.

Sister Fattah is an indefatigable testifier, speaker, and writer—she could easily earn in the six figures as a corporate vice-president for public relations, advertising, or promotion. She does not hide the House of Umoja's light under a bushel.

Be that as it may, the evaluations that have been made show that she and her husband have fashioned an organization that works and have infused it with something both African and American that has done much to reduce violence in a violent city.

Given its emphasis on self-help, family, church, and school, it is not surprising that one of the major backers of the House of Umoja is a conservative think-tank, the American Enterprise Institute. There, some of the most imaginative analyses in America of indigenous ghetto anticrime groups are being carried out by Robert Woodson, a black man, a Congressional consultant, and formerly an official of the Urban League.[18]

He calls the ghetto groups "mediating structures," and he has detailed how programs have worked in Los Angeles, Puerto Rico, St. Louis, Detroit, and other cities. It is interesting that Woodson and I, starting from different perspectives and different premises, should both frequently come back to the important role that religion can play in steering juveniles away from delinquency.

Woodson's speeches, articles, seminars, books, and testimony are among the most mordant, in some respects, and most exhilarating in others, that I came across in my businessman's look at crime. For anyone reading seriously about crime, they are "musts."

If Sister Falaka Fattah's efforts sometimes have seemed to run counter to the juvenile crime establishment's likings, New Pride, of Denver, is the darling of youth crime "mainliners." It also seems to be working, and not really surprisingly, for some of the same reasons as the House of Umoja and SESTU.[19]

For one thing, it is based on the drive of a single dramatic personality, Thomas James. He and two colleagues, Jeanne Granville and Peggy Lore, had worked with inner-city programs for years before they and the Red Cross got together in 1971.

All knew very well that what was lacking among Colorado youths getting out of juvenile institutions were skills and jobs. Without skills, there weren't going to be any jobs. Most of the young men could not even read or write. Many had learning disabilities, that frequent and stubborn companion of the juvenile criminal.

In 1973, New Pride was formally launched. Today it has the blessing of not just the courts, but the Chamber of Commerce, the city and state leaders, and the federal Justice Department.

Youths from fourteen to seventeen are referred from juvenile court as a last resort before they are institutionalized. The typical New Pride arrival is a dropout functioning at a fifth-grade level. He has a history of school failures and expulsions. A black or Hispanic, he has been a serious, often violent, offender. He comes from a chaotic one-parent home.

New Pride declines to take "incorrigibles" and those too dangerous to be left in the community, since the New Pride clients all live at home. In fact, one of the conditions for acceptance at New Pride is that the juvenile criminal's parent or parents, and preferably the siblings, must agree to counseling.

For the juveniles themselves, the counseling is almost daily for the first six months. Also during that period, the teachers, both professionals and volunteers, meet regularly with the clients in specially prepared courses.

In the second half-year of the program, the clients are trained intensively on how to get and hold jobs, generally janitorial, in the other service industries or in construction. For instance, the federal Department of Housing and Urban Development recently awarded New Pride a $190,000 contract to renovate forty houses. New Pride frequently pays the salary of its clients for two months, whether the job is full-time or part-time.

Throughout the program the kids are required to attend schools, and there is a great deal of emphasis on returning to public schools after the program is over—for degrees where it is practical or possible. So far some 600 juveniles have been in New Pride, and the results are impressive.

Surveys show that 25 percent of the New Pride youths are rearrested within twelve months of their "graduation" compared with 30 percent for a comparable group who had not participated in the program.

James himself estimates half his kids somewhere down the line are rearrested compared with 78 percent of the serious offenders who are not in the New Pride program. Only one in five of the New Pride participants is picked up for felonies, he says.

A few years ago, New Pride "replications" were set up in ten cities. Three foundered rapidly. Three more were dropped because of federal budget cuts. The other four, at this writing, are still perking along. The graduates of the new New Prides have shown substantial gains in math and reading, important elements in the self-esteem James tries to build into New Pride graduates. Truancy has dropped, and employment has increased. There is also a promising, although not dazzling, decrease in postprogram arrests in the replicas.

In Camden, New Jersey, for example, the New Pride spin-off seems to be prospering.[20] Like New Pride in Denver, it concentrates on jobs. It teaches clients how to fill out job forms and meet and talk to personnel people. It videotapes each young criminal's job interviews so he can see what he is doing wrong—and right.

The program also teaches such basic skills as check writing, map reading, drawing up a weekly budget, and applying for a driver's license—skills taken for granted by most middle-class youths.

The juveniles operate a downtown delicatessen and a farm. Other food services are planned. In other states, New Pride juveniles run a lawn maintenance service and are building soccer fields.

From a businessman's perspective, New Pride and its offshoots look promising. Forgetting for the moment the huge outlay in taxpayers' money for the failed duplications, it is far cheaper than operating institutions. In Denver, locking up a juvenile criminal costs $18,000 a year. For New Pride, the cost is less than $5,000.

It is also a benefit to the clients. Most institutions no longer pretend that they can rehabilitate inmates, even young ones. New Pride, as the business-produced Figgie report notes, stands out "significantly from the majority of corrections efforts at crime control." Its focus remains emphatically on job skills. It is putting juvenile criminals—not all, but many of them—back into society as productive members.

Not all the promising programs succeed as New Pride has. One such enterprise, which expects to be out of business by the summer of 1985, is the Shelby County Violent Offender Project in Memphis, Tennessee.[21]

Its innovative ideas make it worth describing. It was set up in a former tuberculosis sanitarium and designed specifically as a small facility. Its theory was that offenders should gradually be moved from the most secure confinement to less restricted supervision until finally they were ready to try their wings in the community.

The first phase required the residents to live under 24-hour supervision; their single rooms were secured from 10 P.M. to 7 A.M. Each young offender was handled individually, but typically he remained at this so-called "Structured Level" from four to six weeks. During this time he was tested, a program was worked out for him, with his assistance, and project officers gauged his potential for violence and escape.

In the second phase, or "Supervised Stage," the young inmate moved to a double room which he could decorate and personalize. He could have his own radio or television and he no longer was locked in at night. As his behavior improved—under close monitoring—he received additional privileges. He made trips, generally back home, but always under the supervision of a staffer. Family counseling was part of the program. This stage generally lasted from four to six months.

At this point, the staff pushed the youngster to bring his educational level closer to where it ought to be. It was also at this stage that the offenders became most rambunctious, precisely because they could sense freedom. How they came to handle this increased freedom determined how soon they moved into the next phase, called "The House."

"The House" put residents in former sanitarium staff housing on the grounds, three to five kids at a time. They prepared their own meals, did their own laundry, cleaned up the house, and either worked off the grounds or went back to school.

During the course of his stay, the young criminal was in touch with one or more conventional social agencies in the community. When the center cut him loose, these agencies stepped in for individual and family counseling and help with jobs and school.

With a staff of eighteen, annual costs of $360,000, and an expensive evaluation system built into the project, it was always in danger of collapse. The funding was federal, and there was no county or state money to support it once the federal government pulled out. My personal opinion is that if the management of the project could have convinced a meeting of hard-headed corporate auditors that the idea made sense, some mix of corporate and state or county funds might have been found to keep it going another year. Surely, its record of only two recidivists in its thirty-two graduates made it worth saving.

A far simpler program that should be established in every county is exemplified by the Taylor County (Texas) Juvenile Justice Association.[22] A policeman, a probation officer, and a YMCA worker got together in 1979 to form a communications network of all the child-care agencies, delinquency researchers, and academics interested in youth crime. Up to then, there had been no single body to discuss problems and solutions.

One outgrowth has been a Reassignment School, which accepts students suspended from the public schools system. It serves to get them off the street, further their education and, when and if they shape up, get them back into the system. Police believe its effect has been, among other things, to cut daytime crime.

In Washington, D.C., and now in five other cities on a trial basis, a different kind of school has been created for young offenders. It is called the Street Law Diversion Program and is a twelve-week course for juveniles from ages thirteen to sixteen.[23]

These are first-time offenders, perhaps well on the way to a career in violent crime, who meet once a week for two hours and vigorously argue their rights as well as their responsibilities under the law. Mock trials are held; crimes and arrests are acted out; trips to court are made; and attorneys, police, and judges are invited in to talk about their own roles in law—all as volunteers.

Because of the volunteer help, the instructional cost is limited to a director and a teacher. The few dollars needed to subsidize the kids' trips to and from the course are the main added expense, so costs are low. Initial reports indicate that juveniles who take the course are more likely to avoid further crime than those who have not participated.

In Florida, a program called Clinical Regional Support Team (CREST) used student volunteers from the University of Florida as probation officers for juveniles.[24] The Justice Department has found that these "youth advocacy" setups, using young people, are often a successful and inexpensive alternative to conventional probation or other counseling services. The Florida experiment cost only a quarter of the regular probation officers' per-hour expense.

This type of program, it seems to me, would be the perfect partner for ideas already put forward by the American Bar Association and the National Legal Aid and Defender Association. These two groups are trying to find ways to get nonviolent offenders out of institutions.

These nonviolent offender plans often combine community service—under tight supervision so there is no shirking—with some form of restitution. Sometimes judges give the offenders a taste of imprisonment at night or on weekends.

The problem is that operating these restitution agencies often costs many times more than the restitution produced. The use, in Florida, of student volunteers, particularly those in the social studies, could cut costs and perhaps make the traditional tension between young offenders and their overseers less embittering.

Another innovative program, this one under the aegis of the National Institute of Mental Health, uses a "teaching family" model. In a specially selected family setting, delinquents are instructed on how to manage their lives, make responsible decisions, and function in the community. Three or four offenders, although sometimes only one, are placed in each "group home."

The National Institute of Mental Health is trying these techniques in some fifteen homes around the country, so far with encouraging results.[25] The residents, of course, have to be picked carefully and paired with their new "family" precisely.

A state-funded enterprise along these lines, the Environments for Human Services (EHS) seems to be working in Virginia.[26]

For example, in 1983, a black seventeen-year-old was referred to EHS by the state in an eleventh-hour effort to save him from becoming part of the adult prison population. On the face of it, the effort was costly, even foolhardy.

The youth, from a ghetto family, had been diagnosed early as violent, slightly retarded, and brain damaged from lead poisoning. Such damage is not uncommon. Lead from gasoline exhaust seeps into children's brains from the city streets where they play.

At five, brutalized by his father, he was taken from his home by the city and put in an emergency care facility for a while. At six, he was back home severely mauling other children, sometimes murderously beating them on the head with toys.

Before he was ten, his father had raped him repeatedly and shortly thereafter began forcing him to perform oral sex on visiting male cronies. At ten, the child went berserk and was confined in a mental hospital. By then, he was having schizophrenic and paranoid episodes. Nevetherless, he was sent back into the community.

From ten to seventeen, he was in the classic cycle of violence and confinement. His attacks on others now sometimes had savage sexual overtones. He was in two more hospitals, five group homes, three restrictive institutions. Nothing worked.

As soon as EHS got him, they put him in a home with six others and began one-to-one teaching and counseling. It lasted two months at a cost to the state of $125 a day. For some, the fee approaches $200.

When he had "stabilized," in the argot of the sociologists, he was put in one of EHS's 22 "therapeutic homes" with another youth. Its surrogate parents are highly trained, strict, determined, and caring, not an inexpensive combination. Later a third youth was sent to the home.

After ninety days, EHS decided he was ready to be tried out in a public school. They picked a predominantly white, middle-class school in one of the state's best school districts. At school, the young man came to see he could make it in the community without violence. He concentrated on his vocational studies.

EHS got him an apartment, paid the rent, found him a job as a short-order cook, and has been able to reduce the costs of counseling and monitoring to $160 a week with hopes at this writing of cutting that in half.

Everybody's fingers are crossed. Every institution and every community treatment facility has had its golden boys who suddenly, often unaccountably, went haywire. But a seeming turnaround had occurred after a year and a half of EHS's, and the youth's, hard work.

The costs are high, no doubt about it. The costs of doing nothing, or of confining the boy for the rest of his life, would likely be far, far higher. The problem, clearly, is to find the money.

Finding money, oddly enough, is part of the solution for a spate of new antidelinquency programs. These are profit-making corrections projects, plus private, nonprofit operations that, although not strictly speaking free enterprise, pay their managers on the basis of their success rate, or at least what appears to be the success rate.

As a businessman, I like the idea and see substantial promise here.

Perhaps the best-publicized of these profit-making organizations is VisionQuest, headquartered in Tucson.[27] It has a multimillion-dollar budget, a staff of hundreds, and contracts with dozens of agencies to provide services for delinquent children.

Besides children on the brink of going to state institutions on charges of assault, robbery, and even worse crimes against the person, it also takes "status offenders": truants, runaways, kids with behavioral problems. Its innovative style might very well work with even the most vicious juveniles.

Like the better-known Outward Bound programs, VisionQuest is based on adventurous living. It operates wilderness camps, ranches, wagon trains that go thousands of miles across rough country, sailing projects, and a vigorous, competitive sports program. It has a ratio of staff to residents of about one-to-one, including nurses, psychologists, teachers, and counselors of all kinds. At $32,000 to $37,000 per year per youngster, it does not come cheap.

Generally, youths stay with VisionQuest for twelve to eighteen months. The therapy side is familial and confrontational: shouting, open displays of emotions, even physical restraint when necessary.

But as one "graduate" commented, it was nothing compared to the treatment he had gotten at a reform school where he had been before VisionQuest. Along with school and therapy, there is a good deal of hard work, such as doing chores, caring for horses and mules, fixing meals, and cleaning.

The proof of the pudding is in the recidivism rate. It is by all accounts low. VisionQuest's management points out that the cost of putting one of its wards in a government funded institution can be as high as $80,000 a year.

Looked at that way, VisionQuest has a right to a profit. It does not come easy. The organization has been under serious scrutiny by Arizona and other government inspectors, who in general, and sometimes with criticism, have given it approval. This kind of monitoring, it seems to me, is useful. If a for-profit organization is to make money out of handling juvenile offenders, the government has the obligation to make sure the profits are made from humane activities.

The few profit-making organizations in the sixties that were interested in juvenile crime limited themselves, in the main, to conducting vocational training. Even as late as 1980, the Justice Department found profit corporations—like VisionQuest and Elan, in Maine—"so rare as to be almost non-existent." Now there are many of them, operating all over the country. Elan, one of the pioneers in the field, has about 150 residents. It takes mostly nonviolent juveniles, but some who are violent, as well as people in their twenties. Its techniques are intriguing, based on the principles of hard work.[28]

For example, the residents advance through labor toward self-esteem. They start as workers, become foremen, and finally "executives" by doing various jobs at the center with promotions as they succeed.

There is a good deal of physical release through vigorous swimming, biking, and sports competition. For years, Elan maintained a boxing ring for bullies, who could punch it out under tight supervision. This worthy experiment was ended because the bureaucrats in the state government thought it was too unorthodox. Confrontational therapy, however, still figures in the program.

Its costs are $23,000 per year and are generally paid by some state or local government body, however, which recognizes that Elan can do a more efficient job with certain juveniles than the state can do itself.

The proof of how well Elan's fifteen-year-old concept works is in its records. Although it is true that many of the Elan kids have high IQs, it is nevetherless impressive that thirty-two of the thirty-seven graduates in 1983 went on to college.[29]

In general, the going is rough for profit-making and private, non-profit organizations. When federal funds run out, and when state and local funds are scarce, the juvenile correctional bureaucracy, understandably, protects its flanks. The first cuts come in contract work handled outside the government system, often a foolish policy in the long run—the bureaucratic equivalent of financing a corporation with short-term, high-interest borrowing.[30]

An exception is the private but nonprofit Jack and Ruth Eckerd Foundation in Florida, which runs wilderness camps for juveniles. It had an $8.5 million contract from the state to operate an educational and therapeutical facility for boys in Okeechobee. The staff is enthusiastic, and my guess is that it performs more efficiently than a state body could. Competition between government-run and industry-run enterprises generally works in corrections as it does elsewhere.

A review of the alternatives open to antidelinquency fighters would not be complete without touching on the most controversial of all such ideas. In the 1960s, during the War on Poverty, some youth gangs were federally subsidized. The theory was that you could pay gangs to do constructive things. But the funding got out of control. Taxpayers were paying for the guns used in their own robberies, and for fancy cars for convicted and vicious gang leaders.

The idea has died hard. In some cities, even recently gang leaders have been paid with federal or local funds to serve as "consultants."[31] The theory, again, is that the gang leaders will parley with the leaders of other gangs to solve problems between them so that murderous gang wars do not erupt.

Some statistics, notably in Los Angeles, indicate that gang murders have been reduced. But others show that violent crimes against ordinary citizens have remained the same, or even increased. My own feeling is that the taxpayer should either run with the hunters or with the fox. In the absence of compelling proof that hiring gang leaders works out overwhelmingly in the black on the criminal balance sheet, I believe we should lock up gang leaders rather than put them on the payroll.

As an aid in putting the most vicious of the gang leaders in jail— and in Los Angeles, it is worth noting—a federal grant has been used to develop a program called Operation Hardcore.[32]

The grant allows a district attorney to take on a particularly vicious gang case from the moment of arraignment and carry it through to its final disposition. The money also can be used for protection of victims and witnesses, including their housing and transportation.

Operation Hardcore is in line with a law-enforcement technique called "gang-breaking" in which police concentrate on the gang leaders and the most vicious gang members to crack the cohesion of gangs.[33]

On the one hand, police make the youth gangs aware that they are under surveillance. They may even infiltrate the gang with police informers. At the same time, they let rank-and-file members know that police are available to protect them against outside gangs or criminal activity against them by their fellow gang members. When money is to be spent, I believe, let it be spent on hiring more "gang-breakers," not on turning unreformed gang leaders into federal civil service employees.

All this is not to say that alternative means of handling juvenile delinquents—whether by getting tougher or by getting more lenient, are always better than institutions.

In a "model" wilderness school recently, several twelve- to fourteen-year-olds ran away and told a story of maltreatment to the local newspaper.[34] They said they had been made to sleep in tents on the coldest nights of winter without fires, and when it was warm enough to take them, were denied showers.

Welfare officials found the boys and sent them back to camp. The next day, the boys again fled, appearing at the newspaper with bruises, which they said staff members had given them for talking to reporters. They said they had had no food, although the management said it was because they raided the pantry.

In a more serious case, two staffers and seven young residents of VisionQuest drowned when a boat capsized during an outing off Baja, California. The Coast Guard found no negligence, misconduct, or willful law violations, but said the persons on board the vessels were lacking in experience.[35]

On an individual basis, the management of an institution once pleaded with the state not to cut loose a young criminal to an innovative group home. The youth's juvenile career was based on solving problems with a knife.[36] But in the institution, he was beginning to make some progress.

However, the state government overruled the institution and the young man was assigned to the group home. There, its staff and inmates busily got to work on him in a confrontational group therapy session. The participants, with much verbal fireworks, advised the youth that he stabbed people because he was a homosexual.

The youth demurred, but rather than argue the point, got up from his "hot seat," and excused himself. He found a knife in the kitchen, returned, and "gutted another kid, like you would a fish," as the institution head described it. Then he sat down, said "I'm a man," and waited for the police. Needless to say, the experimental group home was also "gutted."

Then how do we find the best alternative, the proper formula?

In making an automobile or any other product, it is a matter of looking at all the elements the public wants and putting in as many as one can at a credible cost. It is with an eye to identifying the common elements that I have examined these alternatives.

Almost all of them have a number of common elements:

• They are built around a competent, even charismatic, director.
• They deal not just with the young criminal but invariably with his family.
• They work to turn him into a functional citizen, one who can hold a job, find an apartment, pass a driving test, learn how to go from one place to another, and buy groceries, clothes, and services.

(For information on these aspects of the problem, I highly recommend the publications of the National Youth Work Alliance, 1346 Connecticut Ave., N.W., Washington, D.C. 20036.)

• They often encourage religion, either explicitly or implicitly. They try to build self-esteem. They are staffed for violent offenders on a one-to-one basis, sometimes even more.

• They are located or allied with some community unless, as with VisionQuest, Outward Bound, and other "adventure" programs, they purposely go back to the wilderness to build self-reliance and pioneer values.

• They are not large. VisionQuest with 570 kids in its Eastern and Western camps seems large, but the youths are in different locations. The range for other enterprises is more often from four to forty.

• They are tough-minded and honest with their charges. Not one successful operation was run by a "do-gooder." All that have worked are run by well-paid pros who instill in the residents an understanding that life is no rose garden.

In addition to these basic rules, I found suggestions that cried out to be put into practice. One was the kind of evaluation built into the Shelby County Violent Offender Project. I sometimes feel that results are made to be confusing on purpose so that we cannot find out what happens to the graduates. We must know which projects have the lowest rates of recidivism if we are to decide how to allocate funds.

Another is put forward by Dr. Jerome Miller, who as one Justice Department critic put it, "casts a long shadow." It is his idea to give even the most vicious offender a certain amount of choice.[37]

If the criminal can choose which of three maximum-security institutions he is going to, or even shift if he feels he has made the wrong choice, there remains for him a sense of options.

If the least of three perceived evils is the inmate's own choice, he may just possibly make some progress toward rethinking his life. In addition, it tends to make the institution more accountable. Avoidance of an institution, or a high transfer record, clearly means *something* is wrong. If a corrections institution could not collect enough clients, it would fold.

Finally, a component left out of most work with juvenile criminals is preparing them for leisure. If they are unemployed, or even if they have jobs, there is a huge amount of time that is vacant. If the confined youth fills spare time with jogging, movies, music, sports, or reading, rather than the mindless watching of television, when he gets out there may be less temptation for him to spend his leisure on the street committing a crime.

Putting aside the effect on the juvenile offenders, since my main interest is the victim, the costs of institutionalizing a juvenile offender are atrocious. For every year we put one in maximum security, according to the Justice Department, we take from some government treasury enough to send two other youths to college for a year. For every day we jail one young criminal, twenty children eat starch instead of protein.[38]

And for every juvenile we put in an institution from which he emerges more vicious than ever, we miss the opportunity of putting him in some other facility that may at least reduce his antisocial hostility and the severity of his crimes.

# Seven

※

# The Adult Criminal

LONG after our children have turned eighteen, we still think we can change them, mold them into the men and women we dreamed they would be when they were very young. Our parents thought they could do the same with us. Even when we are in our twenties and thirties, they keep trying. As we keep trying with our adult children.

But if we can remember honestly, we will recall that we often resented the efforts of our own parents. At best, we tolerated them. In any case, by the time we reached eighteen, we were sure we knew most of the answers.

If, in our hearts, we know we cannot change those we love, cannot persuade those whose minds and emotions we are most familiar with, why do we think we can do so with strangers? And if these strangers are violent criminals, denizens of the streets, and we are ordinary law-abiding citizens, then aren't the odds of transforming them even more astronomical?

Certainly a company that tried year after year to convert an unhappily alcoholic cleaning woman with an uncontrollable record of absences into a vice-president for sales would be regarded as eccentric, if not suicidal. We would do what we could to help her and if it did not help, we would have to let her go.

Yet, it is this chimera, this dream of reforming the unreformable, that still infuses our thinking about criminals. The police know better; the judges, prosecutors, and even the legal defenders know better. And most of all the felons who are the beneficiaries of our foolishness know better.

Indeed, if one of these hoodlums were to examine his feelings about our solicitude, he would probably find himself resentful—at best, tolerant.

The practical side of our misguided good intentions is evidenced by the way the federal and many state governments are obligated to handle young offenders eighteen and over. On the federal side, if an eighteen-year-old, say, is sentenced under the Youth Corrections Act, the Bureau of Prisons is obligated to assign him to a separate institution for young adult criminals.

All well and good, one might say. Under the old "medical" approach to criminality, the criminal would gradually be "cured" of his violent ways and released when he was safe for society. But it hasn't worked that way at all.

First, the young adult prisons have become barrels of TNT. The prisoners, unrestrained by older adults who might temper their hostilities, contest each other in "macho" fashion with clubs, homemade knives, and pipes. Violence has been flagrant, and is increasing.

Second, there are such anomalies as vicious men in their late twenties, serving long terms under the Youth Corrections Act, who may be forty or more before they get out of the "youth centers."

Norman Carlson, the doggedly decent head of the Bureau of Prisons, has tried for years to throw out the Youth Corrections Act.[1] He now has an assortment of prisons to handle everyone from a scared lamb to an enraged lion. A nonvicious youth is far safer at the adult farm camp in Allentown, Pennsylvania, for instance, than at an eruptive youth prison—but Carlson is bound by law to send him to the youth facility.

This is just part of the uncorrected madness that has grown from the idea that an eighteen-year-old with a history of dozens of violent crimes is somehow still a child.

From the raw statistics, here is the kind of "child" he is: Eighteen-year-old criminals lead *all* other ages for violent crimes, with 685 arrests per 100,000. The arrest rate of eighteen-year-olds for rape, for example, is more than 40 per 100,000. For aggravated assault it is 317 per 100,000. For murder, where the nineteen-year-olds lead, the difference is less than 6 arrests per 100,000.

To get a broader perspective on crime by young adults, consider that persons eighteen to twenty-one make up only 8 percent of our population. Yet they account for 23 percent of the arrests for violent crimes.[2]

Before I began this book, when I read in the newspapers about such men with "long records of arrests," I generally thought of drunk and disorderly conduct, a few assaults, and perhaps a robbery. Now, I know better. For those as naively inclined as I was, it may be instructive to cite the actual record of the kind of criminal who is the subject of this chapter.

He was thirteen when he earned his first charge, armed robbery.[3] At fourteen, he was booked for larceny, and within a month for car theft, larceny, and housebreaking. Two months later, it was armed robbery again. Almost on his fifteenth birthday, he was charged with two counts of car theft, another two counts two months later. Juvenile authorities still did not act to put him away. So he went on committing crimes.

At fifteen, he was declared a delinquent child. He stole another car. At sixteen he went on a spree of three armed robberies, two stolen cars and seven different larcenies. That's just what he got *caught* for. Still the courts cut him loose.

Finally, when he was eighteen, he commited assault and battery with a gun, and drew a year's sentence. But he was out early, stole a car, raped a child under sixteen, carried out a stickup and got a six-month sentence.

Again he was on the street. He stole a car, staged his first kidnapping, and committed another rape and an assault with intent to rape. There followed brief periods behind bars, then more robbery, assault with dangerous weapons—and finally murder. He had made the big time.

Between the arrests, there is always a "style," the young criminal adult doing the ordinary things of his life, but in a way that may seem anything but ordinary to those of us whose style is different.

One such nineteen-year-old felon was willing enough to talk about his life.[4] He had little to do *but* talk. I was able to check out the truthfulness of most of what he said from police records and interviews.

On a typical day, he awoke at eleven or twelve. His girlfriend, with whom he had spent the night, made him coffee. When there was any marijuana left from the night before, they smoked it. Because he had some "downers"—barbiturates, in this case—he took a couple.

Woozy, not entirely articulate, but feeling no stress, he went to an uncle's bar with pool hall in back. The city had just closed down the bar. But the uncle still opened it for regulars who wanted a fried hamburger or beer. There the young felon had some food and shot some pool.

In the afternoon, he dropped in on his parole officer, meeting the requirements of the court—he had done time for narcotics after more serious allegations of violence were ignored. He "hung out" on the street during the late afternoon. As dusk fell, he went again to his uncle's, loaded up on beer, and took some more "downers."

While he was in the bar, a friend came in with packets of heroin for one of his uncle's "customers" and gave our hero some spare pills. One or more of these happened to be amphetamines—"uppers." But no matter; in combination with the "downers," they created a giddy mix of ease and jangled nerves.

That night, although not a homosexual, he went to a park just off the ghetto where white homosexuals went to risk trysts with "rough trade"—young, potentially dangerous black men. The nineteen-year-old filled the bill. Shortly he was approached by a heavy-set white man. They made small talk, fondled a bit, and went to the man's car.

The young felon was contradictory on what happened next. From what police said later, the young criminal and his new friend were in the car, about to drive off, when a second black man, an accomplice, jumped into the car. There was a tussle. One of the two blacks pulled a knife, and the homosexual panicked. He drove off so wildly and fast that police—to his relief—followed him and pulled him over.

Breathlessly, he told the police he had been robbed of his watch and cash by the men. But when they pressed him, he said he did not want to file formal charges. The police, helpless without a witness, did not detain the two black men. Having had enough excitement for one night, our protagonist went home to his girlfriend.

The young criminal's sordid story has some elements common to such tales of sad, violent days. Most are cycles of illegal pursuit of money, drugs, and alcohol, with a little sex thrown in when it doesn't interfere with the three main pursuits of his days.

As with the thirteen- to seventeen-year-olds we wrote of earlier, alcohol and drugs are often factors in their crimes. The heaviest criminal drinkers are from eighteen to twenty-five.[5] Whites, American Indians, and Alaskan natives drink more before their crimes, it appears, than blacks.

Two out of every five rapists, assaulters, and burglars drink heavily during the year before going to prison, and the first two types often are drunk or near drunk when they rape or maim.

Among 12,000 prisoners surveyed by the Justice Department, about 50 percent had potent jolts of alcohol every day compared with 10 percent of the general public. Only one out of six convicts called himself a teetotaler.

The same sort of picture applies to drugs.[6] The gaping hole in people's personalities that makes them kill is often filled with drugs just before they pull the trigger. And when it is not the direct emotional catalyst to the crime, it may be the motive.[7] We have described how house breakers enter pharmacies for drugs. In fact, addicts often kill to get them.

Of 1,832 recent homicides in New York City, 393 were related to drugs. In 160 of these, drug traffickers were killed during robberies. In most of the rest of the 393, two or more hustlers or addicts were squabbling over narcotics when tempers flared and someone was murdered.[8]

New York City, it is worth mentioning, is *not* the "murder capital of America." Recent figures show, in order, East St. Louis, Houston, Miami, San Juan, Puerto Rico, and New Orleans all lead New York City in murders per 100,000 residents.[9]

The most violent predators come generally from among men from ages eighteen to twenty-four. Some studies show that 7 percent of the robbers commit 27 percent of all robberies. Others show that the most violent predators commit 135 robberies a year. Means of measurement vary. But all agree that this age group is overrepresented in the violent fraction that commits a disproportionate share of violent crime.[10] And all agree that these criminals begin getting truly vicious at about fifteen and, as suddenly, begin to slack off at twenty-four or twenty-five.

Why the slack off? Part of it is because society begins to lock them up, at last. Also, they are killed off by police, by shopowners, or most often by each other. In addition, psychologists tell us that violence begins to burn out in most men at about that age, although there are notable exceptions.

By the time a man is fifty-five, he is likely to be law-abiding. Only 1 out of every 1,500 men fifty-five or over is arrested annually for a violent crime. But older men remain a bit light-fingered. One out of every 665 gets picked up annually for stealing something.[11]

From birth to death, there is a probability, according to Professor Alfred Blumstein, that 25 percent of American males in large cities will be arrested for a moderate to serious crime, a so-called "index crime." For blacks that figure is 51 percent. For whites it is 14 percent.[12] Nevertheless, once a man is arrested, it is interesting to note that he will get in trouble and be arrested again for an index crime 85 to 90 percent of the time, whether he is black or white.

In the long run, to prevent this mature violent predator from becoming what he is, we must do something early, perhaps while he is still in the cradle. Indeed, in recent months there is some evidence that the past problems I described of trying "potential" criminals as children may be on the way to solutions. I also have told of some success, at high cost, in defusing violent juveniles.

But the real problem is now. The adult criminal who does us most damage in terms of numbers and seriousness is already among us. We have to deal with him as he is, at this moment.

The best means, it seems to me, is for a community to clearly identify the worst of the worst with a "career criminal" checklist and to get these violent men behind bars by the first legal means that comes along.

In New York, for instance, a pilot list of 1,100 criminals was amassed. Each had a minimum of two robberies or a robbery and another major violent crime charged against him in the last three years. These criminals ranged in age from a few sixteen- and seventeen-year-olds up to thirty-five.[13]

Of this select group of felons, the most dangerous were put under surveillance to try to catch them in the act. Whenever any of the 1,100 were arrested, the system was triggered.

Senior detectives and New York City's toughest prosecutors were put on each case. In a short time, 59 percent of these career criminals had been arrested. A study was done of the first 235 completed cases.

Three out of every five had been indicted under the pilot project, compared with one out of every five citywide. Pilot felony convictions totaled 89 percent, compared with 80 percent. Ninety-four percent of the career criminals went to jail, compared with 70 percent overall.

When these most vicious of felons' records were compiled, the average time they had done *before* the project was three months. In fact, although they averaged seven felony arrests and five misdemeanors, 50 percent had never even been to jail at all.

It is still too early to know whether this kind of concentration will substantially reduce crime rates. A problem is that using the elite cops and D.A.'s for the king shark may allow smaller—but more numerous—scavengers to go about untroubled.

Other cities are already using career criminal programs with fascinating variations. Minneapolis's Target Eight effort, for example, picks eight felons and keeps watch on them. Even the men they drink with are noted by the cops.

These principal targets are selected on the basis of nominations by individual police. When the "election" is completed the criminal goes on Minneapolis's version of the FBI's most wanted list. The police then try to nail him.[14]

A public defender has protested that "maybe tomorrow they [police] are going to select the Jews or Lutherans or Scandinavians" for the list, a parallel that, in my mind, does not hold up under scrutiny. We are talking about criminals, not religions or countries of origin.

It is worth recapitulating quickly how we can make sure that the first encounter an eighteen-year-old—with or without "career" status—has with police is an effective one.

We can ensure that the computer system into which the suspect's name is fed works more like San Diego's or New York City's CATCH (when it is at its best) than like those of most cities. If the police are getting bad vibrations on the freshly arrested man's self-identification, the computer should be programmed so his fingerprints will quickly yield up who he is.

We can also properly expect our city's police computer to print out, or flash on the screen, the arrestee's juvenile record, and any present charges against him in the city or elsewhere, since the computer can be tied in with the FBI's crime information computer. The local computer also may have, if only sketchily, criminal, social, and perhaps even school reports on this suspect, if he has been the subject of earlier lengthy juvenile action.

We can fairly expect the policeman handling the report to be competent and trustworthy. In business, we would generally not hire a person whose previous employers said he was a thief and a liar. Yet this kind of commercial hiring protocol is often ignored by police departments, especially small ones.

Florida, for example, set up a decertification program for police and correction officers. It found that some police departments had ignored, or had not made even the most routine checks on, their applicants' past criminal records.[15] Among police and prison guards they found records as bad as those of the men they were arresting or guarding.

The state is now trying to get rid of convicted sex criminals, murderers, narcotics hoodlums, and others who had been taken on as sworn law and corrections personnel.

I would carry this process a step further. It would be no problem for police, under the aegis of one of their own professional bodies, or the federal government, to set up a small, efficient office to check out the background of police and corrections applicants. The computer files of the FBI, the Bureau of Prisons, and those of states where the applicants formerly worked would merely have to be queried. It is evidence of the police and corrections bureaucracy at their worst that they have opposed or stalled on such a simple and important certification procedure up to now.

In another area, greater and more efficient use of foot patrolmen would help apprehend suspects more efficiently, as would more vigorous policing—questioning street loiterers, stopping suspicious cars, eyeballing groups of known hoodlums, and patrolling crime-prone blocks.

Returning to the arrested criminal, the computer information at hand would give prosecutors an idea of whether he can be released on bail or should be held. Computers would save some of the millions spent each year around the country for laborious clerical work by government bail agencies.

Now in many cities, whether a pretrial suspect gets bail is determined by bail agency workers personally interviewing the detainee at length. How much better if a printout were available, supplemented by only a quick, cell block interview of the suspect. Then the magistrate could make the decision—unless a bail hearing were required by the suspect or government.

Washington, D.C.'s Pretrial Services Agency has automated many of its records, cutting down on the manpower needs.[16] On balance, its record of judgment "calls" is good. It released 65 percent of the suspects on their own recognizance, more than most cities, yet in a recent check, only 5.6 percent were failing to show up, compared with 8.2 percent in New York. Some 8 percent of those who were released committed serious crimes while they were out on bail, an indication that more work is needed on systems to spot the compulsive and habitual criminals.

More often, it is magistrates or judges, acting on their own whims, or careless prosecutors or police who are not alert about records who let dangerous pretrial detainees back on the street.

In a recent case, a man charged with killing his common-law wife was released on $3,000 bond. Some seven months later, his trial long delayed, he shotgunned to death the woman he was then living with.[17]

Another man, arrested thirty-five times and with charges of housebreaking, assaults, and various frauds against him, had his bail cut from $15,000 to $1,000—and walked out of court. He was back in the next day on a new arrest and freed on this second charge on a bail of $200. Police protested to the judge but were helpless to act.[18]

In a third case, two men tried to hold up a restaurant, took workers hostage at shotgun and pistol-point, had a shootout with police, and were finally flushed out with tear gas. Bond was set at a mere $1,000 although they had tried to kill two of the policemen.[19]

It is easy enough to draw up "models" for magistrates, many of whom are at the bottom of the judiciary well, to help them set bond. When the computer is properly programmed, one simply enters the main facts of a case and a range of appropriate bonds is provided within seconds. If a magistrate varies from that general range, he should provide a public, written explanation as to why.

There is one problem in tightening bail practices. While the main concern is the protection of society by getting the violent pretrial suspects off the street—even if it means detention—there is a danger, not just to prisoners, but to the community, in overcrowding the jails.

Overcrowding increases the danger of jailbreaks, and of injured guards.[20] Court orders, in some cases, already have forced the cutting loose of violent detainees awaiting trial or serving sentences in jails. The cost of guard overtime, medical treatment, and prosecutions of prisoners for in-jail offenses mounts and mounts.[21]

Federal and local costs are almost a billion dollars a year for building new jails and prisons and repairing old ones. When financing and all overhead costs are factored in, a new cell can cost as much as $200,000,[22] although many cost less.

There are some commonsense solutions here that are not being applied. To make room for suspects in serious crimes, credit cards could be used for bail on minor offenses. Right now, California, Ohio, and Florida have tried the system. It is promising.[23]

Furthermore, it makes no sense to clog jails with drunks, particularly if it means, as in the case of some jails under court order, that violent suspects are going to be freed. Alcoholics are sick, and jails are both an expensive and inhumane place to put them. We can build dormitories, if we must get them off the streets, which are much cheaper than cells.

The same can be said for hundreds of thousands of juveniles and the mentally ill who are annually locked up in jails.[24]

The infuriating thing is that even when such people, along with the nonviolent criminals, are moved out, judges—egged on by a desire to "get tough" in line with what the public desires—just fill up the jail with lesser criminals. I certainly believe in "getting tough," but that does not necessarily mean using a blunderbuss approach.

Strong community and even national efforts are needed. If we want more safety on our streets, we have to build more jails. Some of them should be less secure than others (and thus cheaper) for suspects who do not need strict confinement.

Finally, there are still some states and localities with space in their jails and prisons.[25] Many are in small communities. I think it makes good sense to shift detainees across state lines when laws can be amended to permit it. Certainly this is far better, and cheaper in the long run, than letting murderers, rapists, and robbers out to commit more crimes while they are awaiting trial.

Once those who don't belong in jail are placed in less secure facilities or in the community, the best way to clean up jail overcrowding is to clear up court calendars. Speedy trials, as required by the Constitution, have a wonderful way of getting people out of jails—and on the way to prison, if that is where they belong.

By swift justice, I do not mean unconstitutional justice. But it is a fact that nine of every ten of us feel our courts are not harsh enough on criminals, and eight of ten believe our law enforcement does not discourage criminals.[26]

Even granting exculpatory circumstances, it is hard to see why only seventeen arrests for rape (and five for all felonies) out of every 100 end with a prison term of more than a year—with time off for good behavior.[27]

One almost unexplored area is how the flood of more than thirteen million *civil* cases filed in state courts slows the criminal justice process.[28]

The judges working these civil dockets could be diverted to criminal courts with ease, and legally. In California, Connecticut, and Pennsylvania, compulsory arbitration experiments have been set up for federal cases with claims of less than $50,000. In such cases, a mutually agreed-on arbiter sits down with the two parties and lays down the law. State courts should immediately start trying similar ideas.

There are other conciliation services for domestic relations, labor disputes, and commercial squabbles—many of them, I am glad to say, profit-making services—to whom judges could forcefully direct the two civil parties. The judges might not scare off all civil litigations, but they would convince a large number.[29]

Judges may not like the grubby work of clearing up criminal dockets, but the gentlemen of the bench have long or life tenures, a good life. And increasingly they have become as much a part of the criminal problem as its solution. They need to work harder.

Another reform, one that business made years ago in its contract and subcontract practices, is cutting down on predecision foot-dragging. By that I mean that we put in our bids, make our pitches, and expect a fast contract decision. The jury system is a perfect field for just such a principle.

At present, the predecision processes in the courts are dismally stuck in the past. The jury selection process can take days, even weeks. While its purpose is to ensure a nonbiased jury, both defense and prosecution rumble along with endless questioning, challenges, and dismissals of jury panelists by whim and emotional reactions. Putting much more of the selection process in the hands of the judges, as is done in federal courts, would save money now expended on jurors, court personnel, stenographic records, marshals, and so on. The greater rapidity with which suspects would go to prison—or to exoneration—would put some meaning back in the Constitution's guarantees of a speedy trial.

In a related field, the Constitution provides that *all* criminal defendants get a jury trial if they want it. In practice, this has often been construed to mean in criminal cases involving imprisonment for more than six months. Those who might get more than six months can tie up the courts for almost as long as they want by asking for jury trials. In many states, minor crimes with penalties of a year could be relegislated to make the penalty six months, since most of those convicted of them now get six months or less.

I have spoken briefly of plea bargaining. It is an ugly fact of life. The prosecutor, defense lawyer, and judge stage a little extrajudicial ritual to set a penalty without a trial. The defense lawyer asks for freedom, the prosecutor for a longer sentence than he could realistically get, and they strike a bargain somewhere in between.

In the classic *Newsweek* issue I mentioned in the beginning of the book, a young Chicago public defender got to the heart of this plea-bargaining darkness.[30] He started out as an idealist, gathering evidence painstakingly in violence-racked slums in order to establish his clients' innocence. But gradually he recognized that his clients were lying to him. They were guilty as hell.

He came to prefer the killer who said frankly, "I killed the (expletive). Now get me off," to the liar who gave him a thousand phony alibis.

He saw that to get along, you had to go along. You gave small gifts to the judges, buddied around with the prosecutors, and dragged out cases as long as you could because it always benefited the defendant, your client.

"I was very liberal when I first started," he said. But he rapidly learned that the whole system was acutely color conscious, even among the judges, prosecutors, and other court personnel who were themselves black, but middle-class black.

A "nigger disorderly," the public defender found, meant anything up to murder as long as it was a lower-class black murder. If a black man raped a black woman, he might get off with four or five years. If it was a "zebra" rape—a black man raping a white woman—then the sentence would be a long one.

To help his criminal clients, he stalled and stalled, knowing that the demoralized victims would finally give up coming to court, knowing that witnesses would evaporate, knowing, even, that threats by the defendant's allies might drive them away.

He knew the character of his clients. In the sixties, a robbery was only that. In the seventies, when violence came of age, he saw that his clients killed as they robbed, simply for the sport of it or to avoid being identified. They didn't even wear a mask to disguise themselves but murdered the victim as casually as a person would cut a piece of steak.

Exposed to violence every day, the defense lawyer began to carry a pistol so that he could protect himself if he had to stop in the city on the way to his home in the suburbs. He understood the irony: the man who murdered him as he changed a tire might be someone he had gotten off in criminal court.

At last, after years in his job, transformed from idealist to realist to cynic, he said:

> We got probation for some kids who got on a bus and stuck the people up. *Probation.* It's just like Jesse James. Well, they didn't get on my bus, so (expletive) 'em. . . . Me letting ten or twenty guys out on the street isn't going to change that. . . . This violence—it's like Niagara Falls. You can't stop it.

Only the most naive individuals talk nowadays about wiping out plea bargaining. Without drastic changes costing incalculable amounts of money, our courts could not handle all the trials, our prisons all the increased prisoners. Still, plea bargaining need not be handled in its present outrageous, inhumane way. The victim, the most important figure in the case, is almost never even consulted.[31]

While plea bargaining has made the courts more efficient, it is doing the job only partway. Many courts still require a probation report, even for plea-bargaining cases. This can slow things down for a week and cost a huge amount of money while the probation officer examines background, recommendations pro and con, and medical and psychological reports, all theoretically to help the judge determine a sentence. But the plea bargaining, in its crude way, is already taking care of the sentence.

A check of the computerized background of the criminal to make sure his lawyer is not putting one over on the prosecutor, victim, and judge is generally enough, if the computer is set up at all well. Then, with at least money having been saved, the unsavory business should be completed and the felon sent to jail, most often for less time than he deserves.

In the trial itself, many of my fellow "hardliners" would like to drastically limit the "exclusionary rule" that presently prevents the prosecution from using illegally obtained evidence to convict defendants. The Supreme Court recently has defined what is illegal and what is not in a way that gives police a little more leeway. I think we have now achieved a proper balance.[32]

Police, both federal and local, often zealously but dangerously go too far when they smell a conviction. I side with the Constitutionalists in wanting convictions to stand up without use of evidence gathered by unlawful means.

Nothing outrages the public more than a lenient judge. I can understand why. While some of them are merely former defense lawyers inclined to be soft on criminals, there are some who suggest hopeless incompetence.

What is one to think of a judge who, while trying the case of a twenty-four-year-old woman charged with killing and cutting up her three-year-old daughter, invited her to spend the night in his guest bedroom; who decided the length of a sentence with a coin flip; or who asked courtroom spectators to vote on witnesses' credibility?[33]

Or the judge who put a twenty-six-year-old, drug-popping robber out on the street after giving him a new trial? The man had been convicted of raping a twelve-year-old girl on her way home from school, but the judge said the jury had no right to know he was once convicted of robbery.[34]

Or the judge who sentenced a twenty-four-year-old man convicted of first-degree sexual assault to only 90 days in jail with work-release privileges because, said the judge, his victim, a five-year-old girl, had been making "advances" to the defendant? The man could have gotten 20 years.[35]

Sometimes, it seems, the court system almost masochistically works against itself. A man convicted of slugging a witness against his brother in a murder trial got off with probation.[36] What greater corruption of justice is the beating of a prosecution witness?

An appeals court cut a thirty-year-old janitor's life sentence for murder to four years although it did not dispute that he tried to rape a twenty-two-year-old woman, then stabbed her 130 times when she tried to fight him off, then burglarized her apartment.[37]

To be sure, there are enormities on the other side, too. Quirky judges have sent first offenders in minor cases to jail for years seemingly on a whim. In the recent past, the sale of two marijuana cigarettes brought a sentence of ten years. These examples horrify my sense of justice as much as lenient judges do.

The answer for both extremes lies so near at hand. In industry we call it "quality control": automated or man-made ways of ensuring that there is a consistent quality to merchandise. In sentencing, there is no quality control.

In a single state, one man got six years for robbing a gas station; another with a similar record got twenty-five. Even with parole, the disparity will still be two years for one, eight for the other.[38]

A survey of 264 judges was conducted in which each one was given the same sixteen hypothetical cases. In only three of them did the judges even agree on whether the convicted man should be put in prison.[39] In another study, fifty federal judges were given twenty identical files. In an extortion case, the range of sentences was from twenty years and a $65,000 fine to three years and no fine. In a bank robbery, the spread was from eighteen years and $5,000 to five years.[40]

While it is dubious whether this wildly unfair system directly affects the safety of the ordinary citizen—for all the talk of how such inequities embitter prisoners—it is a situation that should cease.

Winston Churchill put it well when he said, "The mood and temper of the public with regard to the treatment of crime and criminals is one of the most unfailing tests of the civilization of any country."[41]

We are not Malaysia executing a man for owning a single bullet or Saudi Arabia beheading people for unarmed robbery. The Attorney General's Task Force on Violent Crime has a worthwhile suggestion, and although it does not go far enough in my view, it is a start.[42] It would set up a sentencing commission in the judicial branch of government, which would establish clear sentencing guidelines.[43]

If a judge sentences longer than the guidelines, then the defendant could appeal. If shorter, then the prosecutor could. Minnesota already has a sophisticated version of this idea, requiring judges who deviate to explain fully why they do.[44] Judges, of course, always think twice when they are held to public, written account or faced with appeals.

My own preference would be for a more complex system, based on past record, national averages, and a weighted factor based on the viciousness of the crime, among other factors. Setting up such a "model" would take time, but would be worth it in fairness, consistency, and protection of the public. I would give consideration to the "incapacitation" studies of the Rand Corporation and others, letting the judge assess elements like past employment, drug and alcohol abuse, and other personal background factors that almost always go into the making of the vicious habitual criminal.

The Attorney General's report also recommends abolition of parole. This would be useful so long as some alternative such as gubernatorial or presidential clemency were available for a prisoner so exemplary that he could prove he has come to terms with society.[45]

This implies, as I mean it to, an end to the indeterminate sentences now used by many judges. The prisoner and society should know, with some allowances for "good time" in prison, just how long he is going to serve.

Mandatory sentences are more questionable. It has been shown, as I mentioned earlier, that publicity about them tends to trim the crimes they are directed against, most generally gun, drug, and multiple violent offenses.

But the evidence is unclear as to whether such sentences actually reduce crime. Meanwhile, they load up the prisons, so much so that judges tend to look for ways around them. My feelings are that they are appropriate for only the most heinous crimes.

An alternative, and one the Justice Department seems to be pursuing at this time, is to "jawbone" judges and parole boards into long, quasi-mandatory sentences and see how they work out—with the caveat that the system can be changed if the longer sentences don't seem to do any good.

When all is said and done, we will still need more prisons if we are going to get the violent, unrelenting criminals out of our cities, suburbs, towns, and countryside. How costly and what "kind" of prisons are the questions.

# *Eight*

✳

# Prisons and Other Options

O<small>NE</small> out of every ninety Americans is under some form of correctional supervision—in jail or in prison, on probation or on parole. Some penologists call this vast agglomeration "the Criminal Nation."[1]

At its core are those in prison, half a million as I write this. And like any other criminal subgroup, they are as various as America.[2]

Typically the prisoner is a young adult—the median age is twenty-seven. He is serving an 8.5-year sentence, has been imprisoned before, first as a juvenile. He has a history, as we have found in all our earlier looks at criminality, of serious drug and alcohol abuse.

He is behind bars for burglary or a crime of violence, or both, and, again not surprisingly from our look at crime, he was himself often violently abused as a child. He is white by a few percentage points. By a fourteen to one margin he is in a state, not a federal, prison.

Before his incarceration, he averaged 11.2 years of schooling. He had a job when he was imprisoned (although 30 percent did not and half of these weren't looking) but he wasn't making much money.[3]

When he gets out, he will have a job (only about a quarter have no job promises). A year later, if he is white he will be making better than $10,000 a year, if black somewhat less. By then, if he is white, there is only a one in five chance he will be jobless, if black a three in ten chance. If he went through a halfway house on the way back to the community, the odds are he will do better on employment, particularly if he is black.[4]

So much for the averages; the variations within them tell us how diverse are the citizens of this Criminal Nation.

In New York, for instance, only about 25 percent of the inmates are nonviolent.[5] Indeed, in New York City, auto thieves and burglars are a vanishing breed on the buses bound for prisons. Overall, 47 percent of prison inmates were convicted of murder, rape, robbery, assault, and other violent crimes, although only about a third of the federal prisoners are there for violence.[6]

A figure that is important to remember is that 42 percent of the prisoners are confined to maximum-security penitentiaries—ranging from 94 percent in Texas to 10 percent in New Hampshire, North Carolina, and Wyoming. In fourteen states, more than 50 percent of the inmate population is in maximum-security prisons.

The significance of these statistics, of course, is that such prisons have extraordinarily high operating costs. They should be kept open only to the most violent predators, the most dangerous of the Criminal Nation, and the most dedicated escape artists.

Demographically, it is illuminating to note that the "bubble" of the population made up of twenty- to twenty-nine-year-olds—the group most likely to go to prison—has been expanding up to now. By 1990, it will have deflated and some experts say that prison overcrowding, therefore, will partially take care of itself because of fewer prisoners.[7]

In my reading, I came across assorted unreported or underreported data that helped with my comprehension of what prison is all about. For instance, there are some 9,000 escapes each year, a clear indication that someone guessed wrong on where to put whom.[8]

I found that only 1 percent of the prison population is under eighteen (young criminals have not yet been held to account for their violence) and 4 percent is over fifty (older felons burn out, and once released, seldom show up again).

I discovered prisoners file some 30,000 federal suits each year, 10,000 of them *habeas corpus* actions seeking immediate release. All but a tiny number fail.

I was also interested to find that prison inmate wages are creeping up. A recent tabulation shows they range from a low of zero to $5.00 an hour for some model cons. The average low in states that do pay wages is 20 cents an hour, the average high 76 cents.

I cannot resist pointing out two facts of marginal importance, perhaps, to anyone but prison buffs. Correction officers are union members in twenty-nine states; and it costs more to run prisons in Canada than in the United States.

This brief overview on prisons does not, of course, even hint at the problems inside. It is true that not enough criminals ever get there (only 10 percent of violent crimes result in confinement, 31 percent of murders, 12 percent of rapes). But those who do enter our prisons find a world of horror there.[10]

The murder and maiming of criminals by other criminals in prison is on the rise. In California, prison gangs carry out formal warfare with homemade weapons and military-type organizations.[11]

Rape, homosexuality, drug rings, corrupt guards—all are endemic in prisons. Those guards who do survive the incredible turnover are often themselves victims. Assaults on correctional officers rose from 337 to 431 in a single recent year in New York.

That is not the only shame of our prisons. A known firebug killed twenty-nine of his fellow inmates when he torched a jail.[12] A compulsive and acute schizophrenic, clearly known to be sick, hanged himself. In a nondangerous but pathetic epitome of prisoner self-disgust, two male homosexuals, both psychotic, dressed up as caricatures of women, and lay twenty-four hours a day in a single bed, weeping and weeping.[13] It was easier for the prison to control them that way than to separate them or to take the legal steps necessary to put them into a mental hospital.

The shame of overcrowding exists in 60 percent of our prisons. It is getting worse now that almost every state uses mandatory sentencing.[14] Without parole, the populations grow unrelievedly. Clogged with criminals, stifled by lack of funds, the prisons are decaying. Prisoners jam up air vents to cut off the spread of dust and roaches.[15] There are court orders in twenty-eight states telling them to clean up prisons or in some cases cut loose the prisoners.

Reminiscent of Revolutionary times when felons were confined in abandoned mines, we now use tents, house trailers, boiler rooms, bathrooms, old mental hospitals, gymnasiums, and old army barracks.[16] Yet still the busloads of felons arrive; judges know that in the present climate, even a whiff of leniency guarantees nonreappointment or defeat at the polls.

It is not my purpose to write at length on prison reform. Others have done it infinitely better. But the businessman in me cries out at some of the things that could be easily—or not so easily—done to improve the lot of the prisoner, to make prisons safer for staff, and to cut down on the staggering costs.

For one thing, as I suggested earlier, computerizing the available cells is one way to slightly reduce overcrowding.[17] For another, the federal government can help by turning over more rapidly to the states (and the states can work faster to make it possible) surplus federal land and buildings.[18] Congress, in certain cases, must first act, but it will not move swiftly unless the administration pushes it.

Right now the states cannot expect much money from the federal treasury to build new prisons, but build they must. The now famous rejection of a $500 million prison construction bond issue in New York by voters in 1981 illustrates how a good idea to slow over-crowding came a cropper.[19]

The coalition that beat the bond issue was made up of die-hard budgetary tightwads and die-hard antiprison crusaders. They made a monkey of a usually sophisticated governor. By leaks, by use of care-fully selected statistics, and by playing on the fear of greater taxes, the antibond forces played the media like masters. Those backing bonds could hardly have been more inept.

Then-Governor Hugh Carey had a good product to sell. He simply failed to sell it.

In terms of customers, there were plenty of solid middle-class cit-izens and solid middle-class organizations who could have been mo-bilized to help promote the bond issue.

All the facts were on the governor's side: violent crime was spreading into the upstate cities; the mandatory sentences were clogging the prisons; a backlog of felons in the courts would either have to be sent somewhere, or cut loose. A corporation with a product-item like that could convert it into a fortune.

Just across the Hudson, New Jersey was able to find the money and get the acquiescence of its citizens.[20] It did so by organizing nat-ural allies, getting strong, sometimes even strident messages into the media as to what would happen on the cities' streets without the pris-ons, and treating the whole package as if it were a bandwagon for a good political candidate, or a sales pitch for a quality consumer prod-uct.

A little more of the carrot-and-stick approach could have put across the New York bond issue. Its defeat was a defeat for prison bond issues everywhere and one we are just now recovering from.

When the next "sales program" comes along, a good deal of straight talk will be needed, of the kind chief executive officers give to their faltering division heads, or the kind Associate Attorney General Rudolph Giuliani gave to the nation's correction establishment.[21]

People who retreat from building more prisons on the defeatist idea that judges will fill them unwisely, Giuliani said, "are hiding their heads in the sand. They are ignoring the harsh reality of crime."

To say that new prisons are coddling criminals is equally foolish, he continued. It "is not coddling the criminal by any means. Rather it is a shrewd investment in the safety and welfare of every law-abiding citizen." That kind of talk is guaranteed to sell prisons.

But we are going to have to come up with $4.5 billion a year even to begin the job.[22] And to do so, we'll have to market the idea with the ingenuity and appeal that made the Japanese compact car and diet cola drinks so popular.

Building the prisons won't do the job unless we staff them with experts. Police salaries, just in my adulthood, have doubled in real money. One result has been better-educated law enforcers.[23] We need the same effort in corrections.

All too often guards are "good ol' boys" from the countryside around a rural prison. They have grandfather rights on the jobs and often they are more poorly educated than the most ignorant of their wards. There is a National Corrections Academy at Boulder, Colorado, but we need the same kind of massive federal effort to upgrade our corrections officials that the FBI Academy has done for our police forces.[24]

The Justice Department has taken some steps, but much more must be done. And rapidly. There is no time to wait while guards stand by as prisoners are raped and as correction officers smuggle heroin and even guns to inmates. It smacks of London in the 1700s, when guards sold gin by the barrel to prisoners to ease the pain of confinement.[25]

Our existing prisons are not only inhumane but costly. There are always lawyers ready, and properly so, to represent prisoners when they sue cities, counties, and states for negligence. A recent suit in Maryland seeks $425,000 from a county on behalf of a gang-raped prisoner.[26] If sustained, it is not the bestial and impoverished rapists who will pay. It will be the taxpayers of Maryland.

Chief Justice Warren Burger can hardly be accused of being anti–

law enforcement. Yet he has pointed out how "poorly trained" many corrections attendants and guards are.[27]

"I venture to say," Burger observed, "that there is a correlation between the low salary, the rapid turnover (of guards) and the amount of training."

Burger compared our system with corrections in northern Europe, where guards are carefully screened and highly trained. He might as accurately have compared it with the kind of training industry gives to workers who handle sensitive chemicals, delicate equipment, or dangerous explosives. Industry knows that not training these technicians can mean costly accidents, terrible law suits, and diminished profits.

Simply because prisons are not in business to make money does not mean that they should inefficiently expose the sensitive, delicate, and explosive men under their care to guards who have little or no training or sensitivity in handling them. It defies decency as well as common sense.

A more direct business approach is also needed in prison medical care. In one prison, a physician convicted of murder was doing the work of the regular prison doctor, a drunk and an incompetent. I am sure there are fine prison doctors. There are also, considering the depressing work and the low wages, a large number of prison doctors who could not make it in private practice.

Alabama, Arkansas, Delaware, and Maryland are innovators in a wise switch from government to private doctors, many of them members of for-profit medical companies. In Alabama, the state saved $4.6 million in what it had expected to spend on medical care. Time-and-money-consuming lawsuits on medical care there have dropped from thirty-eight to two.

Even when contracted-out medical services initially cost more, they are worth it if they avert one successful prisoner lawsuit.[28] My only caveat is that, like contract services for juvenile alternatives to youth prisons, the programs must be carefully monitored.

I cited for-profit medical services because they already are in place and are working. There are also a number of other private services that have either been experimented with or should be replacements for government services.

These include food services, educational and vocational teaching, recreational training, psychological counseling, and even in some circumstances, guard services. We already have seen that some high-security facilities have been contracted out for juveniles. I see no problem ethically, certainly in terms of cost efficiency, in trying in a limited way the contracting out of entire penal facilities. Based on the conditions in some of them, private enterprise could hardly do a worse job.[29]

If such experiments can be shown to work more humanely than what we now have, then it does not seem to me wrong for a businessman to expect to make a profit from them. In such cases especially, the state or federal government would have to monitor the operation to ensure it does not merely duplicate the governmental awfulness we now have.

In terms of prisoner handling, there is also much that should be done based on commercial models. There is, for instance, a great deal of trial and error in business. It has caused our Three Mile Islands, it is true. And that is frightening. But it has also created our computer and aircraft industries, envied the world over.

In this context I am intrigued by some remarks a few years ago by Norman Carlson, the federal prisons director.[30] He said that based on an idea of the University of Chicago Law School penology philosopher, Norval Morris, a program for violent offenders was set up in a federal prison.

The pilot offenders had an average of twelve arrests, three major commitments, and an average maximum sentence of eighty-four years. All were potentially violent. Instead of tight security, they were treated in a more relaxed way. They were no more problem than a "control" group of strictly supervised prisoners, and they seemed to take more interest in programs aimed at civilian life.

This kind of original program ought to be experimented with in all its variations. At present *nothing* traditional is working. And prisoners with eighty-four years facing them have nothing but time to devote to the science of penology.

The "good time" concept should also be tested. At present "good time" lets a prisoner out early. It becomes an obsession with him not to lose it. Perhaps "good time" should be given once a year on a nonrevocable basis. To supplement it, such rewards and incentives as furloughs, transfers to less secure institutions, and even modest cash bonuses might be used and could eventually replace the old "good time" idea.

Another excellent idea which should be considered by all systems is the classification method experimentally employed by Vermont, Kentucky, Virginia, and New Jersey.[31] The method determines who should go to what prison. It keeps the most dangerous prisoners in maximum-security prisons with their high walls and high costs. Other prisoners, even if on the basis of their present crime they *look* dangerous, may be sent to far less secure sites with the consequent savings in tax funds.

The National Institute of Corrections, on whose model these four states are testing the new classification, suggests that the "whole" prisoner be considered.

For example, an inmate would get six negative points if he were in prison for multiple armed robbery; if he assaulted and injured someone while in prison, he would get three negative points; an escape from a minimum-security prison would get him one. If he was a major abuser of drugs or alcohol, he would get three, and there would be others for outstanding detainers, prior felony convictions, and so on. There would be "positive" points for being twenty-six or older, for having a high school diploma or a good record of employment or solid school attendance, and so on.

The prisoner's points, plus and minus, would be added up and if he had six or less, he would be sent to a minimum-custody institution; seven to nine would get him medium security. Ten or more would put him in a maximum-security prison.

Other factors such as violence proneness, suicide potential, and willingness to submit to authority are also being used to classify prisoners in a number of states.

These new classification systems have cut down prison violence, particularly rapes. They have also decreased suicides and escapes. By refining the standards further, those who are particularly vulnerable or violent or borderline retarded can be assigned to separate units.

To be sure, this tends to concentrate the worst—and best—prisoners in one institution or another. But that problem can be solved in part by shifting prison personnel.

In considering the internal workings of prisons, there is another area that remains unexploited. I am talking about prisoners' rights. Although my emphasis has been on the citizen on the street, not the inmate in the jail, a few things must be said about fairness.

Being a prisoner is a form of unmanning, a forced regression to an infantile state where someone else tells the inmate what he can and cannot do, a condition where guards do the yea-ing and nay-ing. But the fact is, more than 90 percent of these inmates are going to be out on the street again. And it makes sense that they go out with some sense of reality, and of dignity.

With that in mind, I believe that a longtime and useful industry and labor theory can be more widely used in prisons: the grievance procedures that grew from unions and other worker organizations.[32] I have not said much about the accountability of prison officials, but they, like their wards, are also out of public view.

In a company, the grievance committees of the workers, whether part of union contracts or not, don't just serve as machinery to let off steam. They hold the company accountable. They often lead to personnel reforms—things that we as management simply haven't seen or haven't wanted to see.

Suggestion boxes, a time-honored corporate efficiency-improver, with bonuses for good ideas, are almost as old as the Industrial Revolution. And joint worker-management production improvement committees, while they sometimes break down in wrangles, are often the matrix from which real profit-making ideas come, to everyone's benefit.

Ideally in prisons, there should be a consultative council made up of a strong minority of prisoners, an equal number of corrections people, and perhaps a judge, a prosecutor, a civil libertarian, a businessman, and other community representatives—among them "hardliners" and even a "do-gooder" or two.

This would provide an outlet for legitimate inmate gripes, a means for the press to find out what is going on in the local prison, and an avenue for improving procedures and conditions. It has problems, the main one being the hostility and often recalcitrance of the prisoner and prison representatives. Another problem is the "power trip" of some inmate council members, leading to abuse by the inmate of his position for corrupt purposes. But the councils do defuse tensions, and they do tend to cut down on costly lawsuits.

All fifty states have some minimal procedures now, if only a "grievance officer" who is a corrections official. In my view, without some prisoner participation, there is always going to be a lack of weight and credibility to the procedures.

One significant improvement from grievance procedures is the upgrading of food in prisons. Fresh vegetables—often from the prison farm—are now common. The grievances have led indirectly to cooking classes which also help train inmates for outside jobs—although I am told that prison administrators order the prisoner cooks to go light on calories and starches to keep down the energy of inmates.

In a similar vein, a prisoner "bill of rights" has been proposed by the Quakers, among others.[34] In reviewing their suggestions, I am struck by the practicality of some of them—decent food, medical care and sanitation, freedom of worship, freedom from physical abuse. I do not think the "bill" would make the streets safer, and I am not so naive as to think it would, by itself, vastly improve prisons. But it would serve as a reference point and basis for prisoners' appeals when conditions are intolerable.

Prison industries are another area that cries out for the commercial touch. They bring in a little money to the prison system. But, the unions and management have been reluctant to see prison-subsidized work competing with the free market. That is a false economy. In the long term, letting prison goods compete is good for business. The convicts will become accustomed to doing the kind of work needed for a job on the outside.

Once employed, an ex-con is less likely to rob and injure, to burglarize, to steal cars, or to vandalize. That savings to the community, along with the reduction of welfare and other support for ex-prisoners and their families, would be large, much more than the temporary losses in wages to labor and in profits for industry.

Besides, skills like welding, auto mechanics, computer programming, dental technology, and masonry are often in short supply "on the outside."

A corollary to this in Texas is worth adapting by other states. There, some prisons are built by their own inmates, and prisoners grow 70 percent of their own food. The on-the-job training potential is great, and has a justice to it as well. The savings are huge. Ironically, overcrowding in Texas has recently forced the state to build prisons with civilian labor to speed up construction. Using prison labor, Texas was paying under $4,000 a year at a time when Delaware, for example, was paying an average cost of $30,000 per maximum-security bed.[35]

When labor is performed in prison, it is vital for it to have the same aspects as outside work. Industry can seldom hire a man as a machine operator whose training is on a sixty-year-old machine. By the same token, a convict foreman on a construction or other job should have some hiring and firing powers and disciplinary power over workers under him. It is not just important to let inmates train to do outside jobs, but to let them train to rise within a company to foreman, supervisor, or vice-president or president, for that matter.

Before leaving the question of prisons, there are a few things I have come across which have little to do with business, but which any objective person would wonder about in the course of reading about prisons.

We talk constantly of the problems of homosexuality. Most prisoners are not homosexual when they go in, and they are not when they go out. But inside, they practice it. Without judging the question of gay rights, those who are not homosexual but take it up out of desperation have often found when they come out that they are obsessed with shame, crippled, in a sense, as men.

Given sex's role in our life, does it not make sense for a prisoner whose behavior warrants it to be allowed conjugal visits, or visits by a girlfriend? We use cash bonuses, better quarters, and dozens of other incentives—why not a most basic human need? Professor Norval Morris says "sexual deprivation and disintegration of family were never intended to be part of the punishment."[36] Although it may get me in trouble with the bluestockings, I agree. California, Mississippi, and seven other states experimented with such visits, and it makes sense for more states to do so. I am, however, strongly opposed to bringing prostitutes in for prisoners as is sometimes done by venal guards.

In some California prisons, a prisoner who has a good record of behavior is allowed to invite his wife to spend a weekend with him in a trailer on the prison grounds. In other cases, a brief furlough home is allowed—with severe punishments for those who do not come back.

Another nonbusiness consideration is religion in prisons. For years, prison officials refused to sanction Black Muslims' diets and observances. Yet now they acknowledge the Muslims are generally a stabilizing influence in prisons.[37] Missions to prisons have also been undertaken by traditionalist churches like the Episcopalians, but in fact, it is often the more fundamentalist religions that have greatest appeal for prisoners.

One corrections official complained that the Pentecostal missionaries turn prisoners into religious fanatics. My answer is to ask whether he prefers the alternative kind of fanatics—fanatics of violence—in his penal institutions.

My view is that the government should do all it can to promote and encourage religion in the prisons. Certainly, merely bringing any kind of new, positive outlook before prisoners does not run counter to the Constitution. The problem is not one of civil liberties or rights, but that of emphasis. The corrections officials must promote religion in such a way that the clergy can work independently with the inmates. If the prisoners see a corrections "plot" to brainwash them, they will reject even the most frequent religious overture.

No chapter on prisons is ever complete without some mention of capital punishment. The country is perennially fascinated by the subject. Not too long ago, *Time* magazine did a cover story on Death Row.[38] But most people do not realize we are talking about only 1,400 people.[39]

The debate on what to do with them centers on two issues: Does execution deter other potential murders? Is it moral?[40]

To the first question, there is no answer. Adjoining states with and without the death penalty show similar murder rates. But there are conflicting statistics and studies aplenty. In a word, there is no certain answer on deterrence.

On the moral question, some points should be made. We are not talking about Joan of Arc at the stake. One Death Row inmate, for instance, kidnapped and murdered five teenage girls. Before they died, he and a sidekick sodomized four of them, for days, at times recording this on film. They mashed their breasts with pliers, stuck ice-picks in their ears, strangled one with a coat hanger after mutilating her genitals. As they screamed, the murderer tape-recorded them so he could enjoy their anguish at leisure later. Many others among the Death Row residents are equally vile. I am sorry, but I am not disposed to feel any guilt about wanting them executed. No doubt should be left in the jury's mind that they are guilty; every appeal should be handled by competent defense lawyers. Then the justice that they denied their victims should be done.[41]

The death penalty does not consist of elephants stepping on their heads, or stonings to death, or burying alive, or slow slicing to death, or other ghastly executions of the past. We are talking about a reasonably painless execution of a few hundred terrible criminals—in a world where we daily ignore the innocent hundreds dead in wars, in earthquakes, and in other natural and man-made disasters.[42]

A less dramatic, but equally gnawing, issue is the release of convicted felons who belong in jail. No one can feel good about freeing before his time a man whose company has left toxic chemicals to poison, perhaps even kill, people in some unsuspecting village; or a convicted traitor; a cabinet minister who has betrayed the public trust; or a defrauder of a confused elderly widow; or many other nonviolent criminals who richly deserve to be in prison.

But penalizing them with long prison terms is a luxury which we are not willing to afford ourselves. To build all the prisons necessary to house the entire Criminal Nation would cost us something like $100 billion.[43]

So, already, without really acknowledging it to ourselves, we are cutting them loose. The primary means is early parole.

Parole boards are made up most often of corrections experts but sometimes of political hacks or other nonexperts. They look at the behavior of prisoners in jail and their past record and decide whether they can safely be released into the community before their term is up.[44] They cannot deal with those who have mandatory sentences—ones calling for a fixed number of years.

My personal feeling about parole is that it should be eliminated and replaced with a cut-and-dried term, which would lift the anxieties of the public, the correction officials, and the criminal himself. This reform has been called for by most government and nongovernment specialists, against, however, a determined and substantial minority of experts.[45]

If parole is to continue, I feel it should be decided not by whim, but by a sophisticated computer model such as I recommended earlier for sentencing, one based on background and other factors. Even then, there will be mistakes, but nowhere near the problems we have now where a minimum of 24 percent of parolees are back in prison in three years, many more according to some studies.[46]

As it stands now, once on parole, the newly released prisoner is supposed to report to a parole officer who counsels him, helps him find a job, and contradictorily, recommends he be put back in jail if he violates society's norms.[47] It is an impossible task.[48]

For all its faults, the parole concept does open up options. These are various forms of work-release jobs, even subsidized jobs, halfway houses, community service, part-time jailings, restitution, and restriction to residences. Combined with actual sentencing to some of these options, plus prison farms, prison road and forestry projects, there now exists a multitude of possibilities and options for punishment besides maximum-security jailings.

In Chapter 7, I dealt with some of these alternatives. Indeed, some of the juvenile programs that seem to be working are being expanded for adults.

In North Carolina, juvenile criminals have been put to work plowing fields, chopping wood, and doing other farm work.[49] As long as they are working, they get $3.35 an hour. Of this, $2.85 goes to the victim of the crime and 50 cents goes into a fund that the offender gets if he fulfills his entire sentence. If he falls away, he goes into an institution. The same program, undergoing testing, is now being set up for young adults.

A different kind of work program is being used in Florida.[50] There, prison inmates collect garbage; do road and bridge repair; build baseball fields, playgrounds, bicycle paths, and basketball courts; and participate in other state and community projects. They remain confined at night. But they get time off their sentence for the work.

There are armed guards only for the most dangerous felons. If a prisoner escapes, a bulletin is put on a statewide communications network. If he is recaptured, he may be "docked" for the good time he had already earned. The state's corrections department estimates that the money saved by the state and local governments for whom the work is done is between $500,000 and a million dollars a month.

Florida has also been innovative in turning over its prison industries to a nonprofit corporation. Under a lease agreement, the corporation runs the industries, pays the prison inmates and sells some $30 million in goods a year. The activities range from canning to making shoes and eyeglasses and repairing autos. The state has found this private enterprise move is far more efficient than running the industries itself.

In New York, a citizens' group is pushing for a similar program to use prisoners—even ones sent to jail originally for violent crimes if they can be shown to have given up violent ways—for repair of parks, for cleaning subways, and the like.

The city tried such a plan with youngsters who had been involved in lesser crime, having them clean up graffiti in the subways in lieu of confinement. By all reports, it worked well.

Individual judges, in order to leave space free in prisons for violent predators, have sentenced prisoners who are not violent (or who do not seem to be violent) in many original ways. A seventy-one-year-old criminal art dealer was ordered to set up a scholarship fund and an art-appreciation program for students in high school.[51] A twenty-seven-year-old alcoholic woman, accused of assaulting her husband, was sentenced to attend college for five years, get psychological counseling, maintain a C average, and give up alcohol.[52] An eighteen-year-old girl was given thirty months in a Roman Catholic home for women even though, in a distressed state, she had doused her home with gasoline and mistakenly burned up her nine-year-old brother.[53]

Ira Lowe, a modern advocate of alternative forms of punishment, once tried to get John Ehrlichman, a convicted Nixon aide, sentenced to do community service for Indians.[54] Instead, Ehrlichman was sent to prison. In my view, a short term in jail for Ehrlichman and long hours helping Native Americans would have served justice far better.

Lowe is full of alternative ideas: he would still put the rapist, the murderer, and the habitually violent in jail, and even make those on restitution programs pay back more than they took. But that said, he would use carefully screened offenders to counsel other offenders and do other jobs that are largely unexplored by corrections officials.

Professor Elliott Currie, who has taught at Yale and the University of California, recommends "supported work" for some ex-offenders. His premise is that the costs to the state of paying part of an ex-con's salary for a few months until he gets started is far less than the cost of crimes he will commit if he has no job.[55]

In Massachusetts, nonviolent criminals have been "sentenced" to read to the blind and to work on maintenance in hospitals, mental institutions, and homes for the retarded. The guiding principle for such alternatives, however, is strict supervision and hard work—or a long stay in jail.

One intriguing possibility is to let minor criminals—in order to keep a bed in jail clear—go home in the evenings. An electronic "handcuff"—a device that feeds signals into the wearer's telephone to a central monitoring point—is being used experimentally. If the criminal wanders more than 1,000 feet from his telephone, the signal tells a computer he is violating the terms of his sentence and he can be locked up. The probationer himself pays $70 a month for the equipment, thus making the idea self-sustaining.[56]

Returning to the subject of religion, aware that most writers on crime ignore it, I have found a good deal of useful work being done by religious organizations.

The Quakers in their long treatise on crime and punishment in America take a somewhat more humanitarian view of criminals than I am able to endorse. Nevertheless, it is fresh and challenging, although it was written in 1971. Its title is *Struggle for Justice*. It is full of ideas for work with inmates.[57]

An example of what can be done is also provided by a "born again" group called Prison Fellowship, which was founded by Charles Colson, another imprisoned Watergate aide to Richard Nixon.[58]

The fellowship sends its workers, many of them reformed ex-cons like Colson, around to speak to prisoners. The fellowship workers appoint in-prison prayer leaders and recruit prisoners for weekend seminars out of prison on how to spread the fellowship's religious—and law-abiding—message.

Nonprisoner members of the fellowship have inmates out for Sunday dinner or for a weekend. Fellowship birthday parties and prayer sessions are held both inside and outside prisons.

Some fellowship families on the outside provide halfway residences for prisoners on the way back into society. Other fellowship families throw Christmas parties for relatives of inmates.

Prisoners are also given furloughs under fellowship auspices to go out and repair the homes of the needy. An eighty-two-year-old woman in Raleigh, North Carolina, can thank six federal prisoners for winterizing her house, with an assist from Carolina Power and Light.[59] The specially furloughed inmates also fixed her plumbing and even built an insulated doghouse for her dog, "Pooch," during their three days of labor.

It all sounds very folksy, and it *is* very folksy. But it works. Those prisoners who have joined Prison Fellowship while they are behind bars make better adjustments once they are out. Critics say they were ready to change anyway. Perhaps. But religious organizations around the country can be thanked for a great deal of unsung work—with little reward expected—at least, in this life.

Earlier, I mentioned Robert Woodson, the black self-help philosopher of the conservative American Enterprise Institute. Woodson is as interesting a thinker on adult alternatives for released convicts as he is on ghetto community services for juveniles.[60]

Woodson points to such groups as Jeff-Vander-Lou in St. Louis, which, under the leadership of a clergyman, a shop owner, and a retired teacher, set up a rehabilitation service for slum housing units. Supported in part by grants, the group built a shopping mall, using indigenous labor.

In Chester, Pennsylvania, Hartford, Connecticut, and Brooklyn, New York, Woodson has found other groups that have sprung up from ghetto leadership. He cites studies showing that when neighborhood residents get in real trouble, they turn more readily to ministers, friends, hairdressers, their local barber shop, or neighbors than to professionals.

Woodson's important free enterprise ideas for placing people about to go into prison, about to come out, or already on the streets need government funding and support. It is true that the programs he describes have a good deal of "here today gone tomorrow" risk. But it does not cost much to try them out, and when they work the return is enormous.

More costly and more disastrously hit by budget cuts of the last years have been the halfway houses and the employment centers that have been the workhorses of the "alternative treatment."[61]

Halfway houses, whose sizes range from a half-dozen inmates to chains of houses handling hundreds, have most often been private, nonprofit enterprises, and this tradition goes back to the first half of the nineteenth century. The federal and state governments have also set up halfway houses (and given the bureaucracy's penchant for protecting their own, they are in less economic danger).

A nagging problem, even in good times, is that the attainments of the halfway houses vary widely. And the effectiveness of the several thousand now extant has never been properly measured. Two studies, in fact, say they are no better in preventing recidivism than nothing. Yet another shows they are a useful aid to ex-con employment and reduce recidivism in blacks, but not in whites.

The best of them have strong arguments favoring their continuance. Talbert House in Cincinnati is an example of one of the best, and what can happen nevetherless.[62]

Until the budget woes struck, it had 111 beds in six different locations and ran drug programs, a hotline, and an employment service. When a $290,000 federal grant fell through, an aid-for-offenders program that had served 1,400 had to be shut down.

Federal funds also ran out on twenty-two ex-offenders, then county support for fifty prisoners who were serving alternate time there was discontinued. Finally, along with all these blows, the Ohio state corrections department cut the number of offenders in Talbert House's care from seventy to forty-eight and reduced per diem from $32 to $24.

Within a few months, the once busy enterprise was down to a $1.4 million budget, fifty-five beds, and one house. Happily, the economic recovery has also recovered Talbert House. Its budget has climbed to $1.7 million, and it is running eight programs out of seven different facilities.

Equally important, it is exploring new areas. A small Victims Service Center has been set up in cooperation with the Cincinnati chapter of the National Council of Jewish Women, the police, and the city, which is funding it at $47,000. Selected victims of crime will be counseled and otherwise assisted, part of a growing movement I describe more fully in Chapter 11.

By comparison, well-funded enterprises like those run by the Salvation Army and the Volunteers of America and some large foundations can survive economic doldrums with services pretty much undiminished. It is important that they do.

For in the halfway houses, drug treatment centers, and similar operations, private enterprise operations can do the job of acclimating offenders to the community, and providing cheaper alternatives to prisons far better than government.

The same is true for offender employment agencies often used by parole officers to help place parolees who might otherwise have to be housed in prisons at a cost of $20,000 and up a year.

Such ongoing operations as the Safer Foundation, set up by two ex-Passionist priests in Chicago, have proved not just humane but cost-effective. With a budget of $5 million in fiscal 1985, the foundation will find jobs for 3,000 ex-cons and will put another 1,500 in educational and counseling programs.

Recently, it has branched out into Rock Island and Moline, Illinois and Des Moines and Davenport, Iowa. Its newest programs include a work release center in Chicago which oversees 150 prisoners on the way back into the community, and a Cook County jail enterprise that provides prisoners with educational and vocational training.

A third of its own workers are ex-offenders, and it does not just refer those released from prison to jobs. It teaches them how to read and add well enough to seek, get, and hold jobs.[63]

During the 1980–83 recession, jobs were difficult for such agencies to locate. Now, it is somewhat easier, but it will always be hard to find jobs for ex-cons.

Job counselors at the nonprofit groups often find sympathy but no tea. Corporations are troubled about convicts reverting to type, and personnel officers ask why, when they can get laid-off workers, they should fill positions with ex-offenders.

For their first jobs outside the walls, former prisoners must settle in as gas station attendants or short-order cooks and consider themselves lucky at that.

My own feeling is that the states and the federal government will have to come back to these private programs. There simply are not enough government programs to do the job and, in general, they are less efficient when they try.

The alternative of closing down all these programs is to build new prisons. Legislatures and citizens, torn between funding halfway houses and intensive job programs on the one hand and new prisons at $50,000 to $200,000 on the other, will, I am sure, eventually choose the less expensive, private enterprise way of doing things.

# Nine

*

# Women and Violent Crime

## MOTHERS, FATHERS, AND DELINQUENCY

THERE is a school of thought that says genes play a major role in future criminality. Its most recent support comes from a survey of 862 men in Sweden who were raised by adoptive parents.[1]

Those whose biological fathers were criminals turned out to be criminal themselves in such large numbers that it cannot be accounted for by chance. The internationally respected British medical journal *The Lancet* has cautiously endorsed this genetic theory. It is but one of many.

Certainly, the theory carries more weight than such early posits that shoemakers were so often sex criminals because of the positions of their genitals while they worked, or that murderers could be spotted early by dividing their foreheads into horizontal lines, assigning zodiac signs to them and interpreting the signs—a "science" called metoposcopy.[2]

But genetics is also a long way from offering the answer to why some individuals become criminals and others do not. What can be shown, so far, is only that the reasons for criminality begin one step away: shortly after birth.

In the last few years, solid, repeated, and responsible research—with only a few dissents—has placed the inception of criminality back

144

to the battering a potential delinquent gets in his infancy and early childhood.

If we are to head it off before it costs $100 billion a year to control it, we must understand how it happens. We must find ways to limit the abuse of infants, and remove from their early life the chance that they will see their father or some other man battering their mother until she collapses—or kills her attacker.[3]

Many of those who later become delinquents are the product of unwanted pregnancies, resented even before they are born.[4] In this regard, if there is one thing that the excellent work of the National Center on Child Abuse and Neglect and the National Institute of Mental Health indicates, it is that without a mother's—or surrogate "mother's," female or male—early, attentive, and loving care, a child is at risk.[5]

Studies begun within a hour after birth show that babies whose mothers nurse them, gaze into their faces, and indulge in "skin-to-skin contact" are crying less and smiling more when rechecked at three months. Other studies confirm these findings.

Emotionally healthy kids "by three weeks of age" have strong and positive "mother-infant interactions," unlike infants who are in danger of growing up disturbed.

"Chronic depression in mother," "problems in mother's life history," "abusive mothers," "psychotic tendencies among . . . mothers," "mothers [who were] product of an unhappy traumatic childhood". . . these are common presagers of delinquency I found among more than a hundred research projects on the subject.[6]

These mothers and their similarly distressed spouses or other male partners are the same kind of adults we met earlier in the chapter on child criminals: poor, disorganized, often alcoholic or drug-stupored, sometimes even psychotic, with IQs below normal, with few friends and low self-esteem. Failures in almost everything they have done, they are themselves the children of the same kind of problem-beset parents.[7]

The average age of the abused, sexually molested, and neglected child is seven—lower than that for boys, higher for girls. The more serious the abuse, the more likelihood of a delinquent career.[8] The principle holds as true for girls as for boys. A research project on sixty delinquent girls found more than half had been assaulted by one or both parents with "belts, pots, sticks, cords, and knives."[9]

Indeed, many children never get that far. From birth through two years old, adults murder as many as 5,000 of their children a year. At least a million cases of serious child abuse occur annually.[10]

One typical case history illuminates the enormity of the problem. A fifteen-year-old, as a young child, was chained by his mother to his bed when she went out at night. To "teach" him obedience, he was beaten with an electric cord (and still bears the scars of his beatings). His mother scalded his younger brother to death in a full bathtub. One foster home and juvenile institution after another failed with him. And before he was sixteen, our subject murdered another youngster.[11]

The National Center of Child Abuse and Neglect explains:

> Having learned violence at home, abused children may act out their lessons against their own children or against society in general. Among the more infamous adults who were mistreated as children are Charles Manson, Sirhan Sirhan, James Earl Ray, and Lee Harvey Oswald.[12]

Despite all these studies, the war against child abuse is badly fragmented. Every state has its own reporting system and its own standards for defining and acting against child abuse. Each case brings in a team—often coequal—of police, doctors, social workers, guardians *ad litem*, lawyers, and so on. They are, by and large, splendid, caring professional people. But they are all too often incredibly disorganized.

As a result, before they can act, the situation is often already out of hand. The child is seriously injured because the hospital or police didn't tell the social worker about an earlier case. Or the assaulter has fled the locality. Or the police want to prosecute and the social workers don't. Or vice versa.

Meanwhile, the violence accelerates. And more and more kids are put on a treadmill toward delinquency and adult crime.

A major part of this cycle of violence is the battered spouse, most particularly the battered mother, for battered fathers are in a minority of ninety-nine to one. It is not just the violence of the crime itself, but the effect it has on the child who sees it, the impetus it gives to his own criminality later.

For children are often at home to witness the two million instances a year in which a woman is seriously battered by the man in the house.[13] Worse, they are on hand for many of the 5,200 domestic murders a year, a figure arrived at by the Police Foundation, which has emphasized the relationship between violence in the home and the evolution of criminality. In half of these murders, it is one spouse killing the other, with wives the victims 59 percent of the time.[14]

The child in such a family is not just physically abused, but emotionally detonated. The threat of death hangs over his home like a terrible storm cloud. The Police Foundation discovered that during the two years preceding a domestic homicide or major assault with a weapon, the police had already answered a call there in 85 percent of the cases. In 50 percent of the violent family eruptions, the police had been called at least five times.

When the Foundation examined the families carefully, violent threats had been made in the home prior to more than half the murders. Indeed, when police hazards are checked, a high proportion of assaults and homicides on police occur when they are answering domestic violence calls. The mothers who are battered, as a Yale study reports, suffer from "severe trauma . . . medical and psychological problems that escalate over time" and put women "at increased risk for attempted suicide, alcoholism, drug addiction, child abuse, rape and mental illness."[15]

Men who batter are the same men-in-the-home we identified earlier as child abusers. Failures in everything they attempt, they take it out on their mates, one wife beating every eighteen seconds, more than 5,000 a day.[16]

In hard economic times, the problem is exacerbated. These inadequate men are always the first to be fired. They hang around the house; fights blow up over money.

The triggering words flash out: ". . . and you call yourself a man!" Or "What kind of mother are you?" The data, in fact, show that 60 percent of all domestic murders originate "from conflicts related to perception of sex roles."[17]

Often the fighting words come when one or both spouses have been drinking. In Minnesota, of 100 beaten wives who called a community hotline, 87 said their mates had been drinking. And 71 percent of the women confessed they, too, were frequent drinkers.[18]

One of the most moving pieces of research I found in the tens of thousands of pages I have gone through is a simple drawing by a twelve-year-old.[19] It is by "Tommy, age 12," in a class for children of alcoholic parents.

It shows a man, arms raised angrily, saying to a woman, "I'll smack you anytime I want." The woman, a knife in her crudely drawn hand, replies, "Oh know [sic] you won't." Between them, his hair on end, his mouth a jagged frown, is a child figure saying, "I'm scared."

In the kind of family warfare we are looking at, women often do not call the police. In general, they fear what their mates will do, or they would rather have even a brute than no one. Besides, battered women pray that their mates, who are remorseful, even loving after wife beatings, will reform—all too often a vain hope.

When battered women do leave, it is often with their children. A steady stream has come in recently to such women's shelters as Baltimore's House of Ruth. Similarly, in Illinois, a run on shelter beds occurred after layoffs at plants sent men home for long periods of unemployment. In other states, admissions of battered women to shelters doubled. Many women were turned away for lack of beds.[20]

Instead of waiting until madness or wild temper leads them to stab or shoot their husbands, women increasingly are walking out or prosecuting them—a healthier role model for their kids than that of a doormat or a Fury.

"The right of a man to discipline and physically punish his wife, permitted under colonial laws, and even state laws until the last century, has been rejected," observes the Police Executive Research Forum, another police group attuned to the link between violence in the home and violence on the streets.[21]

Congresswoman Barbara Mikulski of Maryland and Massachusetts Senator Edward Kennedy—two politicians with whom I would disagree on a number of issues—are admirably out front in their support of battered wives.

Mikulski has come up with a Domestic Violence Prevention and Services Act, supported by Kennedy, which would establish a small federal office to assist local shelters and generally to act as a focus for efforts to curb wife beating. The office would, as she says, only cost two one-hundred-thousandths of the total budget.[22]

In explaining what prompted her outrage, Mikulski told of a talk with a woman who, after eight years of beatings by her husband, finally saw her eight-year-old son pounding his five-year-old sister. The child wouldn't turn on the television when he commanded her to.

"What disturbed the mother," said Mikulski, "was that her son's face was innocent and self-righteous and her daughter's stricken with guilt. Neither child thought that he/she had done anything out of the ordinary."[23]

As a businessman, I can see immediate ways to fund Mikulski's modest request. The research going on about child abuse and battered wives is now flooding us with redundancy. One government report tells of more than 250 recent or ongoing studies in the field of child abuse and neglect. Another federal summary mentions a single study costing the taxpayers $250,000, which will tell us still more about family counseling and crime.[24]

All well and good. But don't we have almost all the studies we need on child abuse already? We *know* that abuse ruins families, and leads to crime and other hideous mutilations of the mind and soul. *If* we need more government-funded research, it is a few specific how-to-do-it works on preventing violent domestic crime.

That $250,000 alone would have at least gotten a federal program for battered wives off the ground. I have come across dozens of other useful but nonessential studies that could have kept the federal anti-battering effort going for years if their funds had been diverted. After all, when industry finds out what it wants to know from research, it moves on to production and promotion. Simply to spin out studies is to invite bankruptcy—why should the federal government look at spending in any other way?

The government confusion and waste in combatting child abuse and wife battering is not without a solution. When dealing with it intrastate, the kind of investigation-and-management team I recommended for cleaning up the courts is ideally suited for improving the disorganized services fighting domestic violence.

It is not that much more money needs to be spent, but that waste should be cut, and the whole system reorganized. For instance, the social agencies are handling one phase while the police and criminal justice system are handling another.

The two systems cannot and should not be combined. But liaison must be streamlined; duplicatory functions cut out; failed programs weeded out; and a forceful leader with authority picked for each team. Already, all fifty states have anti–child abuse programs. Closely related battered wife programs should be integrated with them. The federal reporting system for maltreated children data should be tied in by computer with a wife abuse network.[25]

Then in both the state and federal government, we need decisive programs to restructure violent homes when this can be done. And we must get the wives and kids out of them to safer places when it cannot, with taxpayers funding shelters if necessary. It cannot be accomplished 100 percent, of course, but where it is possible, such efforts will cut down substantially on violent street crimes that inevitably will come a few years down the road.

The domestic violence scene should be easier to recast than most because its bureaucracy is less deeply ensconced. For those interested in such an effort, there is authoritative material available from the National Center on Child Abuse and Neglect.[26] Any reformer looking for a sturdy political horse to ride could start with these groups—and travel a long, long way.

To me it seems like administrative Alice in Wonderlandism for both parties to talk so much about violent crime in the streets and to do so little about its proven roots.

## WOMEN CRIMINALS

Although women commit only 11 percent of all violent crimes, and these are generally less serious than those of men, they excite in all of us, men and women alike, a peculiar interest.[27]

In modern times, we have our fascination with school principal Jean Harris and the murder of her diet doctor lover, Herman Tarnower; child-slayer Alice Crimmins; "Candy" Mossler, accused and acquitted of murdering her husband; and Bonnie Parker of Bonnie and Clyde notoriety.

In history, we still are intrigued with Lucrezia Borgia; Salome, with Saint John's head on a plate; heroic Judith whose beheading of Holofernes is so celebrated by artists. In myth, there is Medea, Medusa, and the cannibalistic Sphinx.

Feminists like Dr. Ann Jones find men's interest in female crime sexual, even prurient.[28] Male writers, perhaps with more than a little hypocrisy, say it's not that at all, merely the idea of the weaker vessel, the tender sex, commiting mayhem.

Indeed, prudish magistrates in medieval times consigned women criminals and witches to the stake rather than to dismemberment because it was unseemly for their limbs to be seen in public. Softhearted Englishmen of the eighteenth century, continuing the tradition, garroted women before the flames got to them. This was considered more modest than drawing or quartering them or hanging them from the gibbet.[29]

While there is a consensus that women criminals, sometimes for better, sometimes for worse, are treated differently than men, there is no consensus on why women commit so much less crime.

Some say it is that they are innately less violent, or that society has made them less violent. Others point out that women are generally smaller than men and thus less able to enforce their will on victims. They are, one writer insists, inured to being victims rather than criminals by the physical dominance of their fathers, brothers, and husbands. Why would they turn to violent crime when they can make money by prostitution, rhetorically asks another criminologist. Or they are too busy having and raising children, staying at home, while the criminal breadwinner is out eight hours a day with his pistol, knife, or club. One expert even argues that they do not commit crimes involving money because they are smart enough to get men to go out and take the risks.

Whatever the combination of reasons, women are not, at present, the central problem in violent urban crime. Nor have they ever been. For decades, they have made up about 10 percent of the violent criminals, although since 1960 they have risen from 10 percent to 21 percent in property crimes. Yet even there they approach men's rates only because of shoplifting.

The typical young woman criminal is far less explosive than her male counterpart. She is about sixteen when she begins to get in serious trouble with the law. Her mother likely has been married two or three times—her father not being one of her mother's husbands.[30]

One of the husbands of her mother beat her badly when she was young, and she does not get along well with the present one. In fact, she has just moved in with her boyfriend, himself a street hoodlum.

She has dropped out of school, although she has an average intelligence, somewhat higher than her boyfriend. She dreams of becoming an airline stewardess, but more likely will drift into cheap robberies or prostitution, or both.

Her mother would prefer that she come home, but the girl feels her mother tries to tell her what to do. The mother probably will not make much fuss. The girl has been more or less out of control since she was fourteen.

The statistics show, as in the case of males, that she is black out of proportion to blacks in the population. Black female teenagers are twice as likely to be delinquent and three times as likely to be chronic offenders as white females.[31]

In terms of violence, young black women commit more robberies, assaults with weapons, murders, and simple assaults. White female teenager rates are close to blacks in narcotics use and burglary. However, white girls start their criminal careers earlier—at fourteen for serious crime, compared to sixteen for blacks.

A girl is less likely to become a chronic offender than a boy. She often will commit one serious crime, then stop. But once she gets started, she keeps going. A girl who commits a fourth crime, for example, is almost as likely to commit a fifth, sixth, and so on as the most active young male predator.

As a result, young female criminals are getting more numerous.[32] Since 1970 the arrests for violent crimes by women fifteen through twenty-four has increased by more than 60 percent, for men by more than 20 percent. For property crimes, the rate has increased by some 35 percent for women, 12 for men.

It is both sad and interesting that the increases in property crime arrests for women over fifty-five has gone up more than any category since 1970. These older women's shoplifting, larceny, burglary, and the like has increased 100 percent compared with 60 percent for men over fifty-five and only 9 percent for boys under eighteen. On a slightly more positive note, *violent* crime by older criminals has shown only minor increases.

Women, when they murder, use guns far more often than any other weapon. But as young murderers, they use knives more often than men, and even as they get older, they employ knives in a greater percentage of their homicides than men. They drown their victims—presumably children—at a far higher rate than do male murderers.

As for murder victims, in every age group they are more often male than female except for seven-, eight-, ten-, and thirteen-year-old girls, and for some reason, 81-year-old women.

To combat violent crime by women, all the principles that apply to men would seem appropriate. Indeed, many Equal Rights Amendment supporters make a point of saying they do not want "chivalry" by law enforcement in regard to crimes. They claim that the other edge is that police and judges are doubly tough on women when they do decide to enforce the law against them.

Summing up, it may be true that women's crime does not loom large on the crime tables. But if, as the National Crime Survey reports, there are 6 million violent crimes a year, and if, as the FBI says, 11 percent of all arrests for them are women, then women commit something like 660,000 violent crimes a year.

Not much of a problem? If you are one of the 660,000 victims of homicide, robbery, or assault committed by women, then the problem is plenty serious. A pistol, shotgun, rifle, or knife in the hand of a woman, after all, is still a murderous weapon.

## WOMEN IN PRISON

It says more about women than it does about prisons that in juvenile institutions, the percentage of females to males is far higher than it is in adult prisons.[33]

Overall, the population of women in adult prisons is only 4 percent, while the percentage of females in juvenile institutions is well over 10 percent.

What happens, apparently, is that as they grow into their late teens, young women draw back from the kind of felonies that land them in prison. They might become prostitutes or shoplifters but not, in most cases, armed robbers.

More often, they adopt the traditional roles of homemakers: their mates may be criminals, but they more likely are raising kids, cooking breakfast, and hoping their man will beat his next rap.

Even when they hew to violent criminal ways, it is more often as accomplice than initiator. The justice system recognizes this and generally gives them probation rather than jail, in part, it should be added, so they can take care of their children.

In examining women prison statistics, I found the only consistently high rate for crimes of violence was those women who had killed their boyfriends or husbands.[34] Yet despite the fact that in some states 50 percent of the violent women in prison are murderers, there are only 13 women on Death Row at this time. By comparison, there are 1,383 men awaiting execution.

Most of the women in prison are there for inveterate prostitution, grand larceny, check forging, stolen goods, or narcotics—the classic nonviolent offenses.

Typically, the female prisoner is thirty-one, unmarried, or at any rate single, with two children on the outside.[35] She is black, never finished high school, but has a far higher IQ than her male counterpart. She has a long criminal record.

In more than 50 percent of the cases, she has a drug history; she has abused alcohol far less frequently. There is a strong possibility that when she committed the crime for which she is imprisoned, it was shortly after taking dope or drinking.

While the number of women in prison remains comparatively low, the rate of their confinement is increasing faster than for men. There were only 8,091 in 1974; the figure is now about 20,000.

If there is a trend toward uniformity in the *commission* of crimes by women, and of *sentencing* of women, it has not yet been felt as uniformity of prison *treatment*.

Women's prisons, as one writer has described them, generally look like "low budget junior colleges."[36] They are most often cottages, and although women's institutions have their maximum-security units, those cells are often unfilled. Women behave better in prison than men, and they are treated better.

Their problems, which are very much society's concern in terms of cost as well as sympathy, are also different from those of male inmates. When we imprison a woman, we also take away her children. We must pay for them in a foster home if there is no relative to whom they can go. If she was a good mother, we may be turning a youngster away from a less criminal life when we lock up the mother—a woman who kills a vicious lover is not necessarily a bad mother.

Another difference is the very high rate of homosexuality in women's prisons. It reaches 80, even 90, percent in some prisons. The dominant partner often dons an exaggerated "butch" style of dress. Interestingly, when the nondominant partners are once again released to the community, they almost always revert back to heterosexual liaisons.

Prison administrations, as is often the case in male prisons, ignore the homosexuality—it tends to be a pacifying influence. When the officials are called on to comment on it, they say the practices of adults are not their concern. It is a view that, while it makes me uncomfortable, is hard to argue with.

A more complicated difference in men and women prisoners arises when it comes to conjugal visits. It is clearly unfair to allow men to have conjugal visits in prison and to deny them to women. Yet, suppose the woman becomes pregnant? Should she raise this child in prison? Probably not. Yet it is cruel to take it away.

It may be that an answer to such an unusual but real conundrum lies in a practice of the federal prisons. When a woman is pregnant at the time she enters federal custody, she is referred to an Emergency Shelter Program.[37] After the birth, she may stay there with her child for up to four months. During that time, she can develop placement plans.

A related federal idea, the Children's Center Program, provides teachers who work with inmates and with children who come to visit them. The counselors prepare the prisoners to be better mothers once they get out and resume the raising of their children.

Still another difference between men and women inmates is the women's willingness to take more control of their own lives in prison and to learn while they are there. In women's prisons, such nontraditional but worthwhile trades as auto mechanics, steamfitting, plumbing, electrical jobbing, and housepainting are now being taught—along with more conventional courses in domestic work, keypunching, and clerking.

I have devoted so much space to women in prison because I believe that, while the savings may not be enormous, they are potentially substantial there. When administrators cast around for beds to free up in prisons for violent men, the women's prisons are often overlooked.

For there we have a large number of women whose chances of not commiting violent crimes in the community are often good. Careful screening of women prisoners, I am convinced, would clear out small women's facilities by allowing release of most women and transfer of the hardcore or the violent. In these newly cleared facilities, men still warranting incarceration but only marginally violent and unlikely to escape can be confined. These facilities could be used also for nonviolent criminals serving short, symbolic terms.

The saving, as I suggested earlier, is doubled when these released women take up their mother roles in the community. As expensive as it is, it is still cheaper to have a child with his mother on welfare than it is in most foster homes and in all institutions.

Predetention alternatives to prisons for young women may, in the long run, be cheaper yet. When looking at such costs, though, it is necessary to do a corporate-style cost analysis.

First, there is the money saved by a cheaper form of restriction. Second, there is the money saved from rendering the young criminal less violent. Injuries cost money; so do burglaries. If these crimes are curtailed, money is saved. Then, if the young offender's recidivism is ended or even delayed, money for reimprisonment is also saved. Finally, there is the reward, what a business might call "goodwill," of seeing a young woman turned from crime to a useful life.

In Salt Lake City, a private organization, The Phoenix Institute, for example, has developed a project for treating young women that is regarded by some experts as a model.[38]

Called the Sojourn Project, it was set up after Utah decided to cut back on appropriations for locking up juveniles and ordered its department of youth services to find cheaper ways to handle young criminals, including females.

Sojourn operates around the clock and takes in serious female offenders from twelve to eighteen, although most are from fourteen to sixteen. While the majority of their crimes are larceny and other nonviolent offenses, some are guilty of assault and robbery. Many have already been in state institutions.

The girls, a few at a time, are housed in structured foster homes. "Advocates" in the homes build up one-on-one relationships with the women over months of work, and outside specialists are called in for medical or psychological help when needed.

The girls work toward a high school degree as part of a local school district's "youth in custody" curriculum. In some cases, they attend the school's best precollege classes.

At Sojourn, they get vocational training, psychological counseling, help in getting an outside job, physical exercise, assertiveness training, and classes on how to "make it" on the outside: lessons in filling out forms, finding apartments, getting driving permits, and so on.

The older group—sixteen- and seventeen-year-olds—have, in three-quarters of the cases, been able to move out into independent living in four or six months. Younger children take seven to nine months.

While the girls are in the program, intensive family counseling, an element that seems vital in all these programs, is undertaken. And with these girls it is particularly vital. As many as 80 percent have been exploited sexually by the male in their house, often their own father.

As of this writing, some forty girls have gone through the program and their recidivism rate is about 15 percent. Sojourn's staff estimates that it would be as high as 70 percent without the kind of help they are getting.

The cost is high, from $55 to $77 a day, depending on the kind of program set up for the girls. But it would cost $100 a day in the kind of state facility necessary for these high-risk girls.

As with male juveniles and adult criminals, in every case where these private programs are well set up and function properly, they save vast amounts of money for the taxpayer.

## WOMEN POLICE AND CORRECTIONS OFFICERS

It astonishes me, when we know how good women are as police, that we have so few of them in police work. Among FBI agents and overall on police forces, about 8 percent are women. In big cities it's 7 percent. That's twice as many as there were a few years ago, but not enough.[39]

Women have been doing formal policing at least since 1910, but up until the late 1960s, they worked mainly in juvenile and sex squads, or on clerical duties.[40] Now, they are assigned to all squads, and by all accounts, are as able as men.

Women police range in height from five feet to well over six. Their ages are from the twenties well into the forties. Their education is almost always, as with men, at least a high school diploma, although many have finished college and some have Ph.D.s.

Surveys show that there is no difference between men and women police in sick days or injuries on the job, or on the rate of resignations. One study, however, showed male police were more likely to be picked up for drunk or disorderly conduct while off duty, whereas women were more likely to be late for work.

The practical advantages of women over men—or vice versa—are not great, but worth pointing out. Women are more useful than men on robbery details where decoys are needed, particularly when the quarry are muggers of elderly women.[41]

Assault of the elderly is among the most vicious of crimes, and the effects are among the longest lasting.

The attacks cannot be assessed merely in terms of money lost. An elderly woman's brittle bones and sensitive flesh do not heal as rapidly as a young person's. Nor is she as likely to make a swift and healthy emotional recovery.

When one of these remorseless and ferocious criminals who prey on the old is caught, he often turns out to be one of the habitual predators who are the prime targets of police. His removal from the streets wipes out a one-man crime wave.

A policewoman's work as a decoy, dressed like an old woman, tempting attack, is among the most dangerous forms of police work. These new squads of gallant young women knowingly risking their own life and health are among the bravest police officers.

In surveying how corporate practices can save money in the area of women police, the area that most comes to mind is recruiting. Posters and "help wanted" ads for policewomen, I feel, have been handled well by police departments.

They are no-nonsense, factual, professional. But in the training of these recruits, much more can be done. In an early women police training project in New Jersey, 104 recruits entered the state police training academy, but only 30 graduated. The dropout rate of 70 percent compares with 40 for men.[42]

Apparently many of the women thought it was all going to be like Sergeant Pepper Anderson (Angie Dickinson) in "Police Woman." When they found out it wasn't that way at all, they quit.

Such failures cost money and any city or state gearing up for the recruiting necessary to bring women into the department should forget chivalry, forget pro and con biases, and examine the motives and qualifications of their women candidates every bit as carefully as they examine their males.

The same principles apply in selecting corrections officers. Here, the employment record is better. About 10 percent of the 82,000 on-the-line correction officers are women. Many, of course, are in all-women facilities.[43]

But those in male facilities present a special problem. In police work, only one call in a thousand may result in violence. In corrections work, the possibilities of physical contact with a prisoner are quite another thing. A policewoman generally has her male partner to back her up. Corrections guards do not ordinarily operate in pairs.

A Justice Department study said:

> In what may be a surprising finding, both male correctional officers and male inmates objected vigorously to female correctional officers.

Male officers' feelings toward their female counterparts were especially intense.

Women were considered vulnerable to sexual attack and a liability when confronting a dangerous situation, officers reported. Male inmates expressed similar views but also disliked women having greater power and authority.[44]

This is not to say that women should be forbidden to work in male prisons, only that reflection is needed about assigning them full duties in the toughest tiers. My suspicion is that even the roughest assignments would work out, perhaps to everyone's benefit. But like a new radical product, it should not be fully launched without forethought.

# *Ten*

✳

# Victims and Restitution

OF all the stories which I heard in the course of working on this book, none continues to trouble me more than that of a seventeen-year-old girl. Life most often is a mix of good and bad. But in the case of N.K., decency and consummate evil stand out in razor-sharp terms.[1]

N.K., newly graduated from high school, was working as a day-camp aide while she waited for college to begin. Tired, she came home one afternoon to her suburban home.

"When I walked in, the house looked the same," she said in an interview. "There was some silverware on the dining room counter, but I thought my mother had just been polishing it and had left it there when she went out. I didn't think twice about it.

"I was going to the bedroom for a nap when I heard someone running and turned, but he grabbed my head before I could see and put a washcloth over my face.

" 'Don't say nothin',' he said. He held me up against his body so I couldn't fight. He put me down on my stomach on my bed and asked me when my mother was coming home and how old she and my sister were. I exaggerated their ages, afraid he'd try to rape them and hoping I could turn him away."

The man was six-four, and weighed 180 pounds. He tore her undergarments off, pressed down with his hands on her shoulders, and brutally committed sodomy on her.

"While this was happening," she said, her voice hurried but firm, "a trillion things were going through my head. I thought I'd grab his genitals and put him in shock. But I knew he would hurt me. My biggest fear was not death, because he didn't have a weapon, and he didn't threaten me, but that he would remove my virginity in this meaningless, this vulgar way."

" 'Just enjoy it, just enjoy it,' he kept saying. When he was done, it was just a few minutes, he turned me over and I began to cry and get upset and started to pray, 'Jesus, please Jesus, don't let him do this.' "

The man seemed about to rape her, but stopped before he began and forced her to commit oral sodomy on him.

"It was so gross," she said. "I prayed so hard. I began to feel I was being lifted up away from all this." Her attacker then threw her on her stomach and raped her again anally, brutalizing her in that fashion for five minutes.

"I felt anger more than anything," she said. "I thought, 'There has got to be something good that can come out of this.' And then, it was as if my mind and body were being taken away from it all again and I thought, 'I am going to help other people, make something positive come out of this horrible thing that is happening to me.' "

At last, he pulled down her skirt, yanked the cord from a telephone jack and tied her arms, then used a curling iron cord to tie her legs and hands together in a rocking chair position.

"I heard someone at the door, heard him call my name," N.K. went on. "It was my boyfriend and I thought, 'Oh, my God, he's going to kill Jimmy.' " But she sensed her attacker was afraid. He tried to hide behind the door. Although her friend was six inches shorter and somewhat lighter, he fought the man until he fled, then untied her. "Are you okay?" he asked.

"I felt embarrassed," N.K. said, a common thread in the feelings of raped women. "I couldn't bring myself to say I was raped. I went and showered while he called the police."

The county police were exemplary, the men and, particularly, the women officers treating her with concern and sympathy. But a doctor at the hospital to which she was taken "was so cold. I was so worried I had a venereal disease. But he made me feel I deserved to be raped. I was appalled. I cried and cried. And the nurse wasn't any better.

"When a woman friend, like my second mother, got to the hospital she asked the nurse what she was giving me and the nurse yelled at her, 'The doctor gave me this. Why are you interfering?' The prosecutor, though, was wonderful. So honest and caring."

The twenty-four-year-old man who had attacked her was caught three days later when he dropped a gym bag in the course of a robbery. In it was the girl's father's credit card, which he had stolen along with her high school ring and some cash. His fingerprints matched ones in her house.

N.K. is now a freshman at college. She is amazingly mature, and astonishingly analytical about what it is to be a victim.

"I don't think I feel the rage my mother and father do. I'm not that kind of person. I'm not a vengeful person. I only want to see justice done. He deserves to be put away. I'm concerned about him hurting other people.

"I've come to the conclusion that when a woman is raped, it is an act of power and forcefulness that a man exerts over a woman. All that has to happen to her is to be touched in a way that is not normal. I don't care where. Her breast, her skin. It's rape. If a strange man touches a woman in a sexual manner, it's rape."

She does not believe that the experience has crippled her.

"I believe that my religion has played the largest part in my recovery. Every time I turned around, people were praying for me. My parents, my aunt, my friends, the people who helped me to grow up the way they did, the people that surrounded me all my life. If I'm going to thank anyone for pulling me out of it, it's them."

The rapist was found guilty of three counts of second-degree sex offense, two counts of battery, one count each of attempted rape, false imprisonment, robbery, theft, daytime burglary, and assault with intent to prevent lawful apprehension. He is the kind of vicious habitual predator I have been describing throughout this book. The judge seemed to agree: the sentence was almost fifty years.

But what justice can be done for N.K.?

Another victim, an acquaintance, tells a second story.[2] His house was burglarized while he was at a dinner party. His wife's silver service for eight, given by him to her piece by piece at birthdays and Christmases over twenty years, was gone, along with a Nikon F camera and his daughter's piggy bank with about two dollars inside.

The feelings of this honorable and articulate man are typical:

"First I was outraged. My home had been violated by unknown persons who had roamed freely through it. 'How dare they!' I felt. Then I thought, 'Will they come back for what they missed the first time?' I nailed the front door closed with four-inch spikes and braced it with a two-by-four against the stairs. We'd use the back door which had sturdy locks.

"For weeks, we found ourselves peering apprehensively out the windows at cars moving slowly, at strangers in the neighborhood. I thought about the piggy bank. Disgusting. The petty bastards.

"Then I thought about the system of neighbors watching out for each other, of law enforcement, of society generally. It doesn't work. We were victims without the slightest opportunity for recourse."

There are more than 40 million victims of crime every year, about the same as the combined populations of New York, Illinois, and California. Of these, 8 million suffer violence.[3]

In addition, there are tens of millions more who are indirect victims of crime: stockholders of embezzled corporations; taxpayers who suffer from public corruption of officeholders, from welfare fraud, and from government contract crimes; consumers who pay through the nose for antitrust offenses. In arson of an apartment, all the residents may suffer loss and some injury. Then insurance rates go up, so all policyholders are indirect victims.[4]

Many victims never become known to authorities. Only 35 percent of all crimes are reported. Violent ones, of course, are more often taken to police than minor offenses.[5]

The victims of crimes are generally the poor, and they know it. The Figgie study, to which I have referred before, found that nearly half of those Americans with incomes under $11,000 a year make sure someone is with them when they go out at night. Once a person is making over $16,000, only 16 percent want a companion.[6]

The most fearful groups are the elderly, although the rates of crimes against those over 65 are low—only 8 per 1,000 for violent and personal larcenies, a fifth of the rate against younger persons.

Yet 43 percent of the elderly are deeply fearful of crime, compared with 30 percent of the most secure group, those between thirty and thirty-nine. Across the board, it is interesting to note that 6 percent of American adults—9 million people—are getting to the point where they are so afraid of crime they want to move.[7]

With all this concern, the wonder is that for so long we emphasized the rights of criminals instead of the rights of victims. President Reagan's Task Force on Victims of Crime could hardly have put it better:

> Somewhere along the way, the system began to serve lawyers and judges and defendants, treating the victim with institutionalized disinterest. . . . When victims come forward . . . to hold criminals accountable, they find little protection. They discover instead that they will be treated as appendages of a system appallingly out of balance.[8]

In trying to find commonsense, businesslike solutions to this quandary, I have drawn heavily on the work of the task force on victims and on the Attorney General's Task Force on Violent Crime, although I am in vigorous disagreement with them on a few points.[9] I have also tried to come up with some new ideas, based more on a corporate executive's approach to individual and administrative problems. Many of my ideas have to do with breakdowns in communications among the different elements of the judicial system—a breakdown that would be fatal to any large business.[10] For example, only rarely does a judge hear from the victim at the time of sentencing, or the parole board hear from the victim at the granting of parole. Why not? Should not N.K. or my acquaintance whose house was burglarized bring their input to such a proceeding, letting their suffering be known so the culprit can be suitably punished?

As a second point, in most jurisdictions, it is difficult if not impossible for a businessman hiring a new employee to check with police on his arrest record. Yet that record was public at the time of arrest. I can recall a friend being told to "go through the blotter; you're not getting it out of the master file." But, of course, to go through years of police records in all fifty states is impossible.

We should have access to those records, with the understanding that the applicant will be given the opportunity to explain his arrests when they did not result in convictions. Frankly, I feel people who are arrested without conviction should find it easier to get those records expunged. In any case businessmen should certainly be allowed to learn from police about convicted thieves; schools should be able to know about those arrested for child molestation.

State and federal laws could clear up such problems along with many more. There should be statutes allowing endangered witnesses and victims to avoid some preliminary hearings; a policeman's or prosecutor's sworn word should be enough in such bail and other hearings prior to trial. Victims' and witnesses' addresses should be kept out of the hands of the defense. Defendants and their friends often threaten these already apprehensive people. They must be protected.

There should be legislation to let prosecutors move as rapidly to appeal granting bail or lowering it as defendants can when it is denied or raised. In the most vicious and serious crimes, the criminal should be required to show he is worthy of bail, not the prosecution required to show that he is unworthy, as it is now. And some penalty stiffer than revocation of bail should be levied against those who commit crimes while on bail or those who do not show up for trials.

Schools sometimes tend to be indulgent toward young criminals. They should be required to report to police instances of teacher assaults, of selling of drugs, and other statutory crimes.

By law and by police regulations, a great deal more simple decency can be accorded victims. Certainly, no victim of a sexual attack should have to pay for her own medical examination as is now often the case, or for the materials used to gather rape evidence.[11] Also, an individual's property needed for trial is often kept for months. In many cases it could be photographed and returned without endangering the prosecution.

Police and prosecutors should keep victims informed of what is going on in a case. When an arrest is made, the victim should know; likewise when bail is granted. In addition, the victim should be informed of plea bargaining and in most cases should be allowed to be present.

When those judged mentally incompetent to stand trial or found guilty by reason of insanity are cut loose, even for furloughs, or when they flee, then their victim should be notified. The same should apply to furloughs, releases, or flights from corrections institutions.

The bar associations, often so willing to dodge their responsibilities to victims in order to protect their members' fees, should show a little more humanity. Besides, even lawyers sometimes get mugged and raped. Nothing so embitters me as the sight of a defense lawyer whiplashing a rape victim in order to confuse her and shatter her confidence. Even some lawyers are disgusted by such performances. But bar associations carefully look the other way when it happens.

At least such morally corrupted defense lawyers could be shunned by their colleagues or given a quiet talking-to by more respectable members of the legal trade. Judges, too, could show a little more alacrity in protecting the rape victims when this sort of behavior erupts.

The task force on victims recommends that a constitutional amendment be passed on victims' rights. I think that the Constitution already has the necessary protections. It is our federal and state laws, our regulations, and our procedures that need reform. Much of the change is a matter of outlook. The task force also recommends abolition of the so-called "exclusionary rule," a viewpoint with which I reluctantly disagree for reasons I explained earlier.

On the whole, though, I think the 144-page final report of the Task Force on Victims of Crime is one of the most useful documents put out by the federal government in years. If enough people read it, it will set the rights of victims off to a new, wise, and just beginning. Not only does it lay out good proposals, but it gives names of victim programs that are working now so that other communities can follow suit. It is available from the Superintendent of Documents, U.S. Government Printing Office, Washington, D.C. 20402, for, at this writing, $7.

One of the recommendations of the task force is that federal funding be provided for state plans to compensate victims of crime. The Attorney General's Report on Violent Crime urges a study of the idea.

More than 35 states have crime victim compensation of one kind or another. Most compensate only for injuries, not for property loss, and most have fixed maximums. Almost all are underfunded.

Here is how they work:

In one case, a seventy-three-year-old woman was attacked by two muggers in the parking lot of a supermarket as she walked toward her car. She was knocked down, and both her arms were broken. For more than a week she was in the hospital. Her insurance covered $1,000, but another $1,200 was not covered. Her state crime compensation board picked up the tab for the $1,200.[12]

In a second case, a twenty-nine-year-old man was shot on a city street by an angry husband whose wife the victim had just been visiting. The victim admitted he was with the woman and said he was fleeing the husband when he was shot. At the time he was shot, he was unemployed. Medicaid paid his medical bills. His state refused to give him any compensation money on the basis that he "was not the innocent victim of a crime. . . . The claimant's conduct immediately prior to the incident contributed to the infliction of the injury."

In a third case, a woman's husband was murdered. The state paid the funeral expenses, agreed to pay her the equivalent of her husband's salary for thirty-four months and gave her a lump sum equivalent to twenty-three more months of his salary.

All these cases make good sense. The two who received payments were under the statutory limits for compensation, and the awards seem fair. But a fourth case illustrates one of the problems that arise when there are maximum limits.

A twenty-two-year-old man had just finished college, had no insurance, and was the victim of a disastrous assault. He was permanently blinded in one eye and spent a long time in a body cast. His initial medical bills totaled $30,000 and he was told he would need months, perhaps years, of treatment and therapy to repair his broken body. But his state crime compensation limit was $10,000. At twenty-two, therefore, he faces a future in which he cannot get the medical help he needs and is saddled with debts it will take him a decade to repay. Ironically, if the crime had occurred a few states away, he could have gotten all the money he needed—there, one young man disabled by an attacker was awarded $400,000.

It is a travesty of justice that the costs of the defense are often paid for by the taxpayer through a legal defender system, no matter what they run to. The victim, in states without any crime compensation program, gets nothing. And even in states with programs, he may get half a loaf—and that only after months of bureaucratic foot dragging. Meanwhile, the victim has to pay for food and heat, for rent, for his home loan interest, and for medical help not covered by insurance.

Here, again, when a businessman steps back and looks at the situation, he can only shake his head. To begin with, why do we not have uniformity within the states? One good conference, one good drafting committee could come up with a workable national code. As it is now, in some states, only a resident can be paid. In others, only a person injured in a state can be paid. Some states have reciprocity. All should.

Even the funding is confused. In one state, general revenues pay the freight; in another it is from fines, yet no one does a proper job of monitoring fine payments. Surely, a full-time monitor would more than earn his salary by forcing criminals to come up with their fines—or go to jail.

Relatedly, it is unthinkable that celebrated murderers or rapists should reap profits from the sale of their stories to filmmakers, publishers, and so on. Laws should be passed, as they have in some few states, putting the proceeds into victim compensation. Only a few hundred should be exempted to encourage the criminal to make this kind of deal, and thus to repay his victims, their families, or the community.[13]

In many cases I have examined, the criminal comes out far better off than the victim. When any criminal is well-to-do, why should he not be fined maximum amounts to fund victim compensation? This should apply not just to violent criminals, who most often are poor, but to rich swindlers, fraud artists, burglars, antitrust felons, and all wealthy white-collar criminals. If fines for these defendants are not high enough now, they should be changed by law. Now they do not even keep step with inflation.

As another example of defendants getting the candy while the victim gets the wrapper, most states are willing to pay for psychological help for criminals. But few are willing to foot the bill for counseling of rape victims, widows of murder victims, and others in postcrime trauma. In fact, some state compensation laws are so complicated that a victim has to hire a lawyer even to file a successful claim.

Every company has a contingency fund for emergencies, and so it should be for state crime compensation funds. For a very old person who is obviously needy, or a pregnant woman whose husband has been killed, we should give a hand and ask detailed questions about eligibility later.

The sticking point in all this, of course, is money. At present every government instrumentality is in a bind. The President's Task Force on Victims of Crime believes that the issue is important enough for federal funds to be used to help the states. After all, the states now often pay victims of federal crimes. And the federal government has traditionally helped the states build prisons for felons. It is equally important, it seems to me, to help build new lives for crime victims.

Although crime victim compensation funds get some attention from the media, an almost equally important aid to the victim, the victim-witness *assistance services*, is almost unknown. But when an ordinary person becomes a *victim*, he becomes a part of a whole new world and needs a guide.

The victim-witness coordinators, as they are sometimes called, help fill out the compensation forms; they explain witness rights—how to protest if they get intimidating calls; how to deal with unfeeling police, prosecutors, judges, and doctors; how to postpone hospital payments if necessary; how to talk to the banks; in a word, how to handle *life after crime*.[14]

The benefits to the victim are enormous. As one victim put it: "I was put in touch with a woman in the victim-witness unit who recently lost a daughter in a brutal homicide. She talked with me, got me out of my shell and gave me strength."

Surely, if we have enough money to help suspects and convicts to arrange their lives while they are in jail or prison—by paying for their legal defenders and other counselors—we can find the money to free those caught, through no fault of their own, in the most vulnerable times of their life.

There is a specific area of compensation that I would like to explore in detail. It is called *restitution*, a paying back in time or money or both by criminals for their crimes. In every *case* where it is practical, it should be required by law. A victim put the argument more eloquently than all the pages of research I have read on the subject:

> The man who murdered my husband is in prison. . . . Taxpayers are paying for his room, board, and medical and psychiatric help. My husband was my only means of support. I'm now destitute, very ill, and have no financial means. Meanwhile, the murderer has 600 acres of valuable property. Why should the man who ruined my life be able to keep and return in a few years to that, while I have nothing?

Are we mad that we do not make it a policy to take everything possible from such violent predators, as well as the worst of the white-collar poisoners of our political and economic systems, our environment? For millennia, at least as far back as Hammurabi, restitution by criminals for their crimes has been the moral way. Why, in recent decades, have we nodded?

The task force on victims says bluntly: "It is unjust that a victim should have to sell his car to pay his bills while the offender drives to his probation appointments. . . . If one of the two must go into debt, the offender should do so."

The problem is that the government has not been willing to get tough with the defendants and their lawyers. While the case goes on, the defendant shifts what money his lawyer doesn't get into some relative's name. Or in the case of patently rich defendants, the prosecutors and judges see them as "one of us" and do not sock blockbuster fines to them. Meanwhile, legislatures, both state and federal, prefer to blink rather than reset maximum fines at realistic scales. Fines are too hard to collect, some say.

There *are* ways to collect heavy fines. One is to contract out the work to professional debt chasers. It is not a savory profession, in my view, but it is often an effective one. Another is to make probation or parole contingent on payment of restitution. If the defendant claims he is a pauper and is proved later to be lying, then the sentence or parole ruling should have built into it a quick return to jail or prison. My view is that *everything* a prisoner has when he goes to the penitentiary—if the crime is vicious or serious enough—should go into a restitution or a compensation fund. If he is allowed probation, then only his most minimal assets should be left him.[15]

True enough, you cannot squeeze blood out of a rock. But some of those rocks have not been squeezed very hard—and some of them may have a seam of gold ore somewhere inside.

Increasingly, some prisons are paying wages to prisoners—not much money, but some. A certain percentage of this should go to pay back victims as restitution, when there is a clear case of the victim's loss in this particular case, or into the general compensation fund. Indeed, release from prison can be made dependent on payments.[16]

Restitution in lieu of prison has worked well in many communities, although, wisely, it is seldom allowed for violent criminals or sex offenders.[17] One credit card fraud artist, for example, was six months pregnant. The judge did not want to send her to jail. Instead he sentenced her to sixty hours at home addressing United Way envelopes.[18]

A well-known amateur boxer, up before a judge for burglary, was sentenced to spend the evenings in jail, but to teach inmates boxing during the day. Gradually he was moved into teaching boxing at boys' clubs. He became a lightweight champion.

In another success story, a burglar of a mobile home company was sentenced, with the owner's approval, to work around the mobile home office to pay for the loss. He got into sales and later became a partner in the mobile home business.[19]

Sometimes the restitution is formalized, under court auspices, by a business contract between the victim and the offender. In many cases, the restitution is several times the loss.[20]

A judge sentenced vandals who had broken school and church windows to fix five times as many windows as they had broken. They worked with a glazier who paid them for their work. In addition to fixing the school and church windows, they paid the church the money they made on the other windows.

There is a problem with restitution programs that has been pointed out by Robert Woodson, the urbanologist I have quoted before. He found that a $15 million government project designed to stimulate restitution initiatives for juvenile criminals went mainly into professional salaries, staff travel, equipment, and supplies.[21] Only a tiny amount of restitution was produced from the juvenile work projects.

One court jurisdiction got well over $800,000 to prime 322 convicted youths into paying restitution over a two-year period. Woodson found that personnel costs were $610,955, travel, equipment, and supplies were $124,537, and overhead was $56,695. Only $74,400 was left to pay the youths' initial salaries so they could begin to make restitution.

As usual when government money is being spent, there are no asset and debit sheets. Some cost accounting is vital in these projects. If government cannot do it, then some of the victim-witnesses services, restitution offices and, perhaps, even compensation fund operations might well be contracted out—by bidding—to private firms.

Lately, another intriguing form of victim compensation has been encouraged by victims' advocate groups. It is a *third-party* suit. Even the Attorney General's Task Force on Violent Crime suggests a study to see whether suits are warranted if injury results from the government cutting loose a prisoner too soon or failing to warn a victim that such a person is now at large.

In such a case, a victim might sue a parole board or the Federal Bureau of Prisons or a mental facility or individual officials if a dangerous prisoner is foolishly sent home on furlough or released. The suit would be particularly valid if the original victim were not warned and the ex-con or mental patient harmed him again. Some such suits succeed; some fail.

One such case involved a former U.S. airman who was sentenced to twenty years for almost beating to death a female Air Force member.[22] While in prison he threatened a female employee. Time and time again, he was diagnosed as being a brutal psychotic. But unaccountably he was freed due to what a psychiatrist said was gross negligence. He went on a rampage, murdering two women and kidnapping, raping, and murdering a third. Their survivors sued the Bureau of Prisons and the parole board.

In the state of Washington, the warden of a maximum-security penitentiary conceived a "Take-a-Lifer-to-Dinner" program. Under the program, he allowed a life termer (incongruously named St. Peter) to leave the prison and have dinner with the prison baker.

St. Peter, who had forty felony convictions and had attempted to escape prison seventeen times, then fled. Within a week, he murdered a man in an armed robbery. The widow of the man sued the warden and the state of Washington. She was awarded $186,000.

In California, the Youth Authority paroled a violently antisocial offender into a foster home, where he was left unsupervised. He soon beat a ten-year-old child almost to death. The child's parents sued the state. The California Court of Appeals ruled that the state was not immune against the suit—for negligent failure to supervise—and the state settled the case for $265,000.

In a third-party suit with a different twist, two bank robbers were chased by county police in Virginia across a state line at speeds up to 80 miles an hour.[23] The suspects' car smashed into another car, spun out of control and pinned a pedestrian to a streetlight, so injuring his legs they had to be amputated.

The victim sued the robber driving the car, the policemen giving chase, and the county. He claimed the police should not have been doing more than 20 miles an hour when they crossed the state line. A jury awarded him and his wife $5 million.

In other cases, only the criminals have been sued.

In Maryland, a rape victim sued her two assailants and won a $365,000 judgment. She was aware of the difficulty she would have in collecting the money, but said the money wasn't the point. "I don't think going to jail is enough punishment," she said. "I mean, how many times can you break a guy for what they did to me? The purpose of this trial wasn't to collect. The purpose was that it's high time somebody got off their tail and did something about rape."

In St. Louis, a doctor whose office was burglarized five times in one year, sued the two men who finally were caught in one of the burglaries. The two had pleaded guilty to a lesser charge, had been fined $50 apiece, and had then been put on two years' probation. The angry doctor sued the two criminals for $200,000 in damages, saying, "I'm out to discourage burglaries in this community." His lawyer said the suit was intended "to put the word out on the street that potential burglars are taking risks not only with the authorities, but also with the people victimized."

In Connecticut, a twenty-year-old student at Yale was bludgeoned to death by her boyfriend after she said she no longer wanted to see him. He was tried, convicted of manslaughter, and sentenced to eight to twenty-five years. The victim's parents, disappointed by the sentence, filed a $3.3 million suit against the prisoner, seeking damages for "wrongful death."

The suits in which the victim sues the perpetrator are often easy to win. For one thing, the police and prosecutor have built the case for the victim's attorney. Of course, the victim obviously has a problem collecting the money that is awarded to him.

But a study by the Vera Institute of New York found that offenders both worked and pursued a life of crime at the same time. In the disorders that followed the blackout in New York in 1977, the police arrested hundreds of looters. Time and again it was found that they had legitimate jobs. More recently, after the 1983 Diana Ross concert in New York ended in tumult, forty-seven persons were arrested on various non-narcotic felonies. Thirty-eight percent were employed; twelve percent were full-time students. This type of person can afford compensation and there is nothing in the law that says a victim cannot obtain the garnishment of a criminal's wages or get a lien on his property.

Criminals may also have some hidden assets—an expensive automobile, for instance. These assets may be difficult to find, but certainly an investigation by a victim's attorney is warranted.

Victims are also lashing out at corporate third parties they blame for their troubles. The family of a Washington, D.C., bank teller who was shot in the head is suing the bank for not having protective devices in place when the gunman came in and killed the teller. The suit also named the union which is the main stockholder in the bank.[24]

Finally, some victims are getting at the heart of the system itself: the judges. One woman tried to get a judge removed from his bench because he freed a criminal who had held up her daughter in front of their home.[25] The man got a suspended sentence and no one even notified the victims.

When the woman sought to talk to the judge, she was turned away by the judge's secretary, who told her to write a letter. She did write, but she never got a reply. Finally she went to the nonprofit Washington Legal Foundation, which keeps watch on the judiciary and conveniently already had a case against the judge before the local judicial commission. Too often such commissions are made up of lawyers who do nothing because they practice before the judges they investigate. They took no action on the Foundation's complaint against the judge for his treatment of the woman. Still, such determined efforts are useful. The publicity may shame judges at least into politeness toward the public they supposedly serve.[26]

The National Organization for Victim Assistance, set up in 1972 by victims and their friends, is now getting some national attention and is lobbying for new laws.[27]

Overall, it is good to see victims standing up to be heard. Sometimes it seems that if victims don't take care of themselves, don't get their thumbs in the eyes of their governments and courts, no one will do anything for them.

# Eleven

※

# Volunteers

VOLUNTARISM is America at its idealistic best. Over half of all American adults do some kind of volunteer work. The dollar value is an enormous $70 billion a year.[1]

The things Americans do free for other people include church and synagogue charity work, educational aid, guiding in art galleries, den mothering, reading to the blind, pushing patients in hospitals—an endless variety.

Perhaps 5 to 10 million are doing volunteer work related to justice and law enforcement.[2] Although that's a lot of people, they spread out pretty thin when one considers all the jobs that need doing.

They are serving as members of crime watch teams, police auxiliaries, and victim assistance counselors, the myriad things ordinary citizens can do to pare down the crime rate and to help those victimized by it.

In crime watches—neighborhood watches, they're often called—several million citizens are involved in more than 30,000 "watches," large and small. Statistics prove they cut crime.

Detroit provides an example of how they work.[3] Of the city's 12,000 blocks, about a third are formally organized into neighborhood watch groups. To be officially recognized by the city as a watch organization, and get the Neighborhood Watch signs for posting, two resident meetings must first be held. More than half the households in the block must be represented at these meetings. And each year, under the same strict standards, the watch must pass police recertification checks. At the opening meetings, a police crime prevention officer explains the four components of Neighborhood Watch. They are self-protection, burglary protection, property identification, and crime reporting.

One of the most successful of these neighborhood watches was set up in a 155-block area called Crary–St. Mary's and is described in the Figgie report. Its population of about 13,000 is 35 percent white, 65 percent nonwhite. A fifth are senior citizens; the median income is $18,000; and 65 percent of the homes are occupied by their owners.

At the time the Neighborhood Watch was organized, the area was changing: more senior citizens, more blacks. The jobless rate was about 20 percent, and crime was increasing. On the positive side, there was a strong, active community organization already in place.

A church provided space for the Neighborhood Watch headquarters. Police came in to help the "watchers" focus on burglary, larceny, and car theft, the main crimes plaguing the area.

The police instructed the participants on what kind of suspicious activity should be called in, how to give concise descriptions of suspects and their cars and on the proper way to spell out street names.

As the program is now set up, police and watch leaders work together to get residents to carry as few valuables as possible, to walk at night in pairs, to trim bushes near windows, to light parts of the house (inside and out) at night, to mark personal property with their driver's license or other identification numbers. Even the engraving tools are provided by the city. Some 240 senior citizens are driven to banks, doctors, and stores by police reservists.

"Business watch" and "apartment watch" programs have also been set up. Almost 10,000 people have attended programs—out of the 13,000 in the area, although this 10,000 includes repeat attendance.

The results have astounded even the police.

In Crary–St. Mary's, robberies dropped 56 percent, compared to a drop of 17 percent in a similar area only beginning to organize neighborhood watches. Housebreakings were down 61 percent, compared with 13 percent; larcenies from autos fell 51 percent compared with 5 percent in the "control" area.

Almost as important were the changes in attitudes of the citizens of Crary-St. Mary's. Before the neighborhood watch was set up 40 percent of the residents were "very fearful" of crime. Afterward only

12 percent were. Sixty percent, compared with 28 percent, took measures such as putting in stronger locks and protected windows. Sixty-two percent—compared with 28 percent earlier—marked their property. Happily for law-enforcement agencies, 75 percent of the residents thought the police were doing a good job compared with 40 percent before the watch was set up.

In recent days, the neighborhood has set up with police help a thirty-person mobile radio patrol. Two or three cars are on the street each night, their drivers trained to spot potential crime. They are tied by radio with their own base radio operator who notifies headquarters when police cars are needed.

As of late 1984, Crary–St. Mary's was reporting only thirty-one burglaries a month compared with 120 in a similar neighborhood a mile away without a well-organized neighborhood watch.

Every neighborhood watch has its own individual features.

After two rapes and a daytime mugging in what previously had been a pleasant neighborhood in Belleville, New Jersey, two dozen residents joined to patrol their streets. They stationed themselves outside the local hospital for the change in nurses' shifts and in parking lots when church bingo games broke up. For the most part, though, they simply walked.

Six months after the group was started, one of its founders said: "This place is getting to be the kind of neighborhood it was 20 years ago, when you could leave a bicycle outside and nobody would touch it. And that's the way we want it."

In the North Asylum Hill section of Hartford, Connecticut, burglaries fell by 45 percent after North Asylum Hill did two things: It instituted block patrols, some by elderly women with walkie-talkies and, with the help of urban planners, it rerouted traffic in some of the streets. Once busy thoroughfares were blocked off or narrowed to form one-way or dead-end streets. The theory behind the redesigning was that it would return the streets to the people who lived there. It did. People even began to sit on their porches. The more people sit on their porches, the less attractive a neighborhood is to burglars and muggers.

The North Asylum Hill concept has spread throughout Hartford, although a more sophisticated style of house watching has superseded the elderly women with walkie-talkies. Meetings twice a week in participating neighborhoods now set formal schedules and pinpoint problem areas.

Not surprisingly, Hartford's crime totals plunged, even beyond the decrease in overall crime throughout the United States, particularly in burglaries, which dropped 17 percent between 1982 and 1983. The Hartford Police Department has set up a Community Response Division whose captain, Arthur Williams, Jr., says there is "absolutely no doubt" that the neighborhood watches are a major factor in the significant decrease in Hartford's crime.[4] In New York City, 100,000 residents take part in crime patrol and related programs. These include ordinary citizens; taxi drivers, truckers, and bus operators with two-way radios; elderly people who sit at their apartment windows looking for suspicious activity; youths who escort the elderly home at night; merchants who will assist victims with direct calls to police dispatchers; and high-rise dwellers who patrol their halls in shifts.

Still more volunteers are needed, but in almost every neighborhood where a program has been begun, the results have been impressive. In the Midwood–Kings Highway section of Brooklyn, felonies dropped by 17 percent and burglaries by 30 percent after a federally funded program was set up.[5]

The area had been infested with thieves who stole anything they found in parked cars, and sometimes the cars themselves. Citizens began patrolling in two-way radio cars twenty-four-hours a day. They made their reports to a base station, which screened them and reported the "live" ones to police. By eliminating the time it would take a citizen to get to a telephone and by streamlining the reporting to police, response time was cut to two or three minutes from the normal ten to fifteen.

New York State and the City of New York provide decals, manuals, posters, and the like for watch efforts. When a program needs supplies and postage, the money is raised by bake sales, garage sales, and block parties. Merchants have been generous and the community thanks the commercial contributors publicly at block parties.

Partly as a result of citizen activists, crime in New York City—at a record high in 1980 and 1981—dropped 5.1 percent in 1982 and 9.6 percent in 1983. Significantly, two of the crimes most susceptible to community watch drives, burglary and robbery, fell far more than the average: 16.8 and 12.4 percent.[6]

In Wilmington, Delaware, police gave police radio monitors to fifteen senior citizens in high rises. When a call goes out in the neighborhood, the elderly stay-at-home nearest the crime can report on suspects who hide or run from the scene. As another part of the city's crime watch, young volunteers escort senior citizens on errands.[7]

An unusual service inaugurated by the National Association of Letter Carriers is taking root around the country. Police give training and lists of stolen cars to mailmen, who keep watch for the tag numbers—their familiarity with their route helps them to spot an out-of-place car in the neighborhood.

Phoenix's "Sheriff's Posses," made up of senior citizens, patrol their neighborhoods on foot, on bicycles, and even in golf carts. They have gone door to door urging citizens to mark their property and enlisting them as neighborhood watchers. By relieving police patrols, they have saved the Arizona city $1 million a year.

In the Kensington section of Philadelphia, urban decline led to an increase in abandoned homes, factories, stores, warehouses, and other buildings.[8] Arsonists—either vandals or owners looking for insurance—set 65 fires in one six-month period.

Real estate value went down, insurance went up, tax revenues were lost. Kensington fought back with its Community Arson Awareness Program, in which residents report vacant and rundown buildings and any suspicious activities around them to Philadelphia's inspection and licensing authorities and to police. They also advise the owners of the empty buildings that their properties are being watched. And the community came up with a plan to program a computer with a list of possible arson targets.

Although the antiarson fight is just getting under way, some thirty-five buildings already have been cleared of combustible trash and sealed. Abandoned residences are being taken over by the community and in some cases rehabilitated and sold for a profit.

In Maryland in 1982, there was a surge in the establishment of crime watch programs, largely due to active work by police and local authorities. Statewide crime dropped 8 percent, with a 6 percent drop in Baltimore, where the recession created pockets of joblessness.[9] State police authorities gave the credit to citizens' programs.

There are important lessons to be learned from successful neighborhood watch programs besides the obvious ones—that they work and reduce crime.[10] For one thing, they work best when backed with local money.

It's true that a big injection of federal money sounds great. But it is not dependable and can dry up from one year to the next. While a city may not have much, it can guarantee what there is for years at a time.[11] The Figgie report observes that "the relative shortage of funds clearly shows the civilian volunteers how necessary their role is. No salaried employee of the law enforcement agency will be appointed to do the job if the volunteers fail to deliver."[12]

As the federal funding dwindles, some states have stepped in. One state legislator has suggested uniform allowances for auxiliary police up to $150 a person, and bulletproof vests. Both the auxiliaries and civilian patrols would get a $150 state tax credit—and death benefits if they were killed in the line of duty.[13]

Another lesson to be learned from review of the citizen endeavors is a corrective one. What publicity is given the neighborhood watches implies that they are made up of eager white college students and vigorous white elderly folk, all middle class, all well educated.

Those who have really looked into the programs agree that while white suburban crime watches are useful and numerous, there are actually more crime watches among urban blacks. In both cities and suburbs, however, the programs are most successful where citizens' organizations are already active, even if they were set up originally to pursue other aims such as civil rights, zoning reform, and better sanitation.

More formalized than the citizens' watch groups are volunteer police auxiliaries.[14] These are police-trained citizens who perform law-enforcement duties, sometimes with pistols. In a few cases they even get some pay.

There are some 400,000 at work throughout the country. Their full-time jobs are as bankers, plumbers, lawyers, waitresses, and so forth, and they may be trained by police as long as 315 hours before they get their badges.

Some do no more than help control ballpark crowds. Others serve on vice squads and take on the most dangerous night patrols. Los Angeles County, as one example, has 1,300 volunteers trained in such duties as mountain rescue and forensic photography as well as in ordinary peace officer functions. Dallas has used the "reserves" in special crackdowns on drunken drivers. Jacksonville, Florida, utilizes a dozen trained senior citizens for logging, filing, and cross-filing criminal information.[15]

The cost of training each reserve is generally less than $400. Another few hundred are spent to equip the reservist with uniform, gun, badge, helmet, and baton. In some cities, the desire to become a part-time policeman is so great that the auxiliaries pay for all their own equipment. Yet in other cases, they may be paid $6 or more an hour. One jurisdiction pays them $1 a year so they can qualify for worker's compensation. Another city allows $10 a month for cleaning the uniform.

To build up the reserves, an ingenious idea has been proposed to give scholarships, as in the military, to young people willing to devote a few years to police work. Once the young men and women were graduated, they would serve for perhaps half of what is paid a regular officer. If they liked police work, they could opt to stay.[16]

Easily the most publicized of the volunteer groups is the Guardian Angels of New York. They are nearly all black or Hispanic, and they have been steeped in controversy since Curtis Sliwa organized them to walk the streets of the Bronx. Their true fame, however, came when they shifted their activities to New York's transit system. For the most part, the Guardian Angels, unmistakable in their red berets, serve as a deterrent.[17]

When they took to the subways, publicly warning would-be criminals of their skills in the martial arts, they drew the wrath of the transit police union, hostility from the transit police high command, and coolness from Mayor Koch, who, at first, called them "vigilantes." Later, he withdrew the epithet, although his relations with the Guardian Angels have been, at best, strained.

Basically what the Guardian Angels do is patrol in groups. When they spot a crime, one runs to call the police, another sticks with the victim, and the rest take off after the criminal, subdue him, detain him, and make a "citizen's arrest"—a legal arrest for a witness to a crime.

Critics have attacked the Angels' competence in making citizens' arrests. Their objection, at least on the surface, has been that the Angels are untrained in the nuances of police work: when and how a suspect should be delayed or detained, and what, exactly, constitutes a reasonable use of force.

Beneath this has been another issue, once raised to the surface by Mario Cuomo, then lieutenant governor, now governor, of New York. "If these were the sons and daughters of doctors from Great Neck or

Jamaica Estates, would people be calling them vigilantes?" he asked rhetorically. "Everyone would be giving them medals." And many subway riders, in their hearts, do just that.

Since their small beginnings, the Guardian Angels have gone national, with chapters in 16 cities.[18]

Increasingly, their leaders have been invited into other cities to train groups that will be similar to the Guardian Angels of New York. These groups will be black or Hispanic, patrolling for the most part black or Hispanic neighborhoods.

The ballots are by no means all in on the Guardian Angels, and certainly not on their storm petrel of a leader, Sliwa. No one can guess where this young man will wind up, but his words are expressive of the outrage that many of the citizen volunteers feel. They have fire to them:

Curtis Sliwa, [he says of himself,] gets up in the morning, ready to go to work. The first thing, as I am drying my hair, coming out of the shower, I look at the six locks on the door. I am depressed.

I look at the bars on my window. I mean, on a sixth-floor apartment in New York I have bars on my window. I am a prisoner.

I turn on the news after coming home late at night from work, and the . . . news commentator is like Julius Caesar recounting the barbarian invasion of Rome—raping, ravaging, stealing. I open up the evening newspaper, more of the same.

I am really depressed now, so I go out with the fellows to a local bar. I find out that Jimmy, my best friend, is in the hospital because last night he got jumped on the way home from work and they robbed him of his paycheck and needlessly, for no reason, put a bullet in back of his head.

Forty or 50 years ago, if somebody had broken into somebody's apartment, the whole building would have been alerted. Old women with broomsticks would have been struggling out of their apartments surrounding the apartment. Men who had just downed two six-packs worth of beer and could barely stand up, would be struggling to get down there.

The young, infirm, everyone would pounce upon that apartment. You needed a police officer to get into that apartment to in essence kidnap and rescue from a hostile crowd that criminal who tried to bring out those valuable possessions.

My grandfather told me many times he actually thought about going out and getting a gun, and holding up a grocery store because he had no social relief, he had no welfare. He had to stand in a bread line for 13 kids.

Do you know what stopped him? Not necessarily his pride, but the knowledge that if he tried to go out and commit the crime, the citizens in that neighborhood sitting out on the porches late at night would have jumped on top of him. If he had been caught, the stigma would have forced him to move out of the neighborhood because the neighborhood would not have tolerated him living there. . . .

Now, I think the time has reversed itself 360 degrees where we expect the police to come into a neighborhood that has grown men, that has young men who are physically capable of dealing with certain situations, and we want the police to rescue whole neighborhoods from three or four thugs who have everyone in fear and in terror.

I am horrified, in New York City, that I will ride a subway train and there will be paid advertisements by the Metropolitan Transit Authority urging people to stay at home, not to ride the trains at night, not to wear their jewelry.

Do you know what that is doing? That is flying the white flag. You are giving up to the criminal. . . . Why does this exist? Well, I am going to tell you.

It is our role models. If I come from an impoverished, criminally infested area and my dad is a janitor, working 6 days a week, making $200 to support a wife and family, and just basically meets the necessities of life, how is my dad going to become my role model when "Big-Time Charlie," the guy on the corner, in an hour makes what my dad makes in 6 days?

Big-Time Charlie is out there dealing his dope, hustling his women, with his fancy cars and his fancy clothes. And yet, nobody seems to be interfering with him. Nobody from the public says anything to Big-Time Charlie. There seems to be no input whatsoever from the police department, from the city officials, right on down to the citizens. I blame the citizens because 40 or 50 years ago the citizens would have never tolerated Big-Time Charlie being on the corner. . .

So, we have to analyze, how do you stop that youngster from initially getting involved, from getting rolling to a point where he cannot get out of it? It has to come from the community, it cannot come from the cops; it cannot come from the lawyers or the judges because we have to nip it at the bud before that youngster gets rolling. . .

As far as I am concerned, the only way to stop the rising crime rate is at the community level by participation of the citizens.[19]

While Sliwa and other watch-type organizations have gotten the attention of the media, there are innumerable other volunteer anticrime programs that have worked in one place. They might well be adapted to another.

In previous chapters, I spoke of the excellent survey that was done on juvenile criminals, assessing them on everything from their intelligence to their sense of morals. It was done with only $15,000. Without volunteer help—for data gathering, interviewing, typing—it would have cost ten times as much.[20]

What a saving if researchers on government grants—instead of throwing their friends and students hourly pay courtesy of the exchequer—would enlist capable volunteers! The savings would be particularly large in projects that require large numbers of interviews. In some of the finest of the studies, a training program has turned nonspecialists into pros in twenty or so hours.[21] The current "incapacitation" studies of prisoners to find out from them their characteristics require a particularly large number of interviews or questionnaires, sometimes in the thousands. These interviews are fascinating to conduct and highly useful. They could be conducted by volunteers if the researchers would but spend a little time organizing them.

New York police, always curious about the criminal mind, wanted to interview criminals themselves about their attitudes toward police. Their own staff was too small to carry out the project, and they turned to academicians. How much better if a volunteer research unit had been available to take on the job for nothing.[22]

Police, perhaps because of the television glorification of them, often have an easier time than most in finding volunteers. Ride-along programs in which police take citizens along in their patrol cars offer a genuine thrill as well as an unbeatable way to understand what street crime is all about. Less adventurous volunteers have learned what police are up against by serving them as translators in Hispanic and other non-English cases.

Volunteers, in many cities, have assisted regularly employed court and even corrections personnel. Several hundred volunteers have worked in the New York probation department, counseling juvenile and adult offenders, tutoring them in reading, and helping them find work or the right agency for help—all generally on a one-on-one basis. There are other volunteers working to aid victims, particularly the elderly, and coaching juveniles who have been "sentenced" to the volunteer as an alternative to confinement. The volunteer teaches the young offender arithmetic, grammar, writing, and reading—and gives him the role model of someone not on the "street."

In other states, similar work is being done with adults and juveniles already inside institutions. In Illinois, as one example, the Junior League set up a program called OPTIONS.[23] Inmates who want help get it from skilled counselors who run individual or group therapy sessions. The focus is on how to make decisions, and how to defend against negative peer pressures.

In New Orleans, citizens' groups hold forums at which police come and explain what they can do—and what they can't—to control crime.[24] The interchanges are credited with defusing a potential riot following a police shooting.

The name of the group is off-putting—New Orleans Neighborhood Police Anti-Crime Council (NONPACC). But the concept seems to be working. In line with what young Sliwa said about neighborhoods, one project is "Sit on Your Stoop Night." Citizens sit outside in the evening as a witness that their community belongs to the law-abiding, not the street hoodlums.

Mayor Ernest Morial of New Orleans, telling of NONPACC, had some words with which I heartily agree: "When most people are asked to identify the components of the criminal justice system, they usually reply with the three 'C's'—Cops, Courts and Corrections. There should be another 'C'. . . Community." The community, he pointed out, can fight crime by means that range from reporting suspicious adults to getting young children out of the city on outings. The community's work starts at cradle side.

Volunteers in the child abuse area work in almost every state.[25] In Maryland, there is an emergency foster-care network which takes abused children for up to thirty days while permanent placements are worked out. In Kansas, there is a similar roster of homes. In New York, volunteers counsel the mother or father, just dropping by, letting them know they have a friend willing to hear them out on their frustrations.[26]

The variation in volunteer work is amazing. A sewing machine company volunteered patterns for hidden pockets so that women would not have to carry purses. Senior citizens made and distributed the pockets.[27]

In Arizona, police sought and found—in excessive numbers—volunteers to buy sexual favors in local massage parlors. The volunteers then testified about the transgressions committed on them. Some thirty-five parlors were shut down. One volunteer, however, used up more than $1,200 in undercover funds for his "purchases."[28]

Less controversially, a national elderly citizens' organization has enlisted lawyers and paralegals to advise and represent the elderly poor. The cost: nothing. Also in the legal area, a coast-to-coast vigil of citizens angered at light sentences sits in on and reports in its publications on trials and sentencing sessions by particularly lenient judges.[29]

And one truly zealous, lone-ranger volunteer wrote a song praising police, paid for it to be made into a record, and promoted it with no pay except the gratitude of police.

He has a point worth making for all groups. When police help, citizens often take it for granted. Yet a little voluntary courtesy goes a long way with law-enforcement people.

Abuse victims helped by police should drop a note not just to the officer involved but to his boss—an industry practice well worth adopting everywhere. Organizations doing voluntary work should invite police officials or officers to serve on their boards of directors. It is a graceful thank-you as well as a way to bring experts into the proceedings.[30]

When more money is needed for police, that's the time for those who have been aided, either individuals or organizations, to come forward and testify before city councils and legislatures. Much the same kind of wise politeness should be shown toward prosecutors.

Besides volunteer work now being done, there are untapped clusters of civic-minded organizations that would help or help even more if they were asked and utilized the right way. Some already have crime-related programs: the Chambers of Commerce, major unions, the American Legion, the Boy Scouts, the Urban League, and many ethnic and fraternal groups.[31]

I think particularly of the black Shriners, Elks, and Masons, the black sororities and fraternities. When the black Shriners met in New York a few years ago, it was estimated that their 30,000 members spent $12 million. These are well-to-do, solid, middle-class black men and women. And when they help causes, it is often with more enthusiasm than their white counterparts.[32]

Yet only rarely do either the government or old-line volunteer organizations call on these splendid groups for help and for counsel. It is national folly not to seek the wisdom and the financial assistance of black groups. They, above all, know what they are talking about. For as I have already demonstrated, the data reveals that it is most often blacks who suffer from violent crime.

Sometimes it takes the starkest kind of tragedy to bring out the volunteer in a person. Senator Orrin Hatch of Utah has told how his state was galvanized by the case of six missing children, all of whom were later found dead.

One three-year-old girl named Rachael Runyan was found in a creek bed. Her hands were tied behind her back, her body all but decomposed. When Rachael was first reported missing, thousands volunteered in the search for her. As Hatch described it:

> Businesses and churches donated money, facilities, and manpower. A committee was formed to organize the search for Rachael, working out of a neighborhood center. The committee began a nationwide distribution of flyers with Rachael's picture. From tips a composite drawing of the suspect was created. The community raised $20,000, to be matched by the Runyans, for a $40,000 reward.

Out of this crisis, a continuing child protection effort evolved. The Utah Parent-Teacher Association was the first to swing into action, dusting off unused child protection programs. They were presented in the schools by local law-enforcement agencies. Mothers reinstated "parent watch," to patrol streets during hours when children are going to and from school. With the assistance of the Utah Association of Women, the PTA promoted "McGruff House" posters to be placed in windows telling a child in trouble that he can enter that house for refuge and help.

Town meetings have been sponsored by law enforcement agencies, county and city governments, PTAs, and the Utah Association of Women to formulate policies and instruct parents in preventative measures and appropriate action to take should the need arise. All Utahans have been instructed to report any suspicious-looking individuals.

In addition, the Utah Association of Women organized a new committee with the sole responsibility of developing, coordinating, and promoting child safety. Volunteers dispersed child identification packets—"Identi-Child Kits"—which were produced by "Friends of Child Find." The kit includes identification instructions, precautionary measures, procedures to take when a child is missing, and guide-lines for identifying a suspect and an automobile. This type of infor-mation, when really available to police, can expedite the speedy location of a missing child.

The Utah Association of Women also organized groups of women to lobby the Utah State Legislature for stronger kidnapping legisla-tion. Partially because of their encouragement, the State Department of Public Safety renewed intensive training of police in kidnap recov-ery procedures and plans for an extensive roadblock and communica-tions system.

Further, the department of public safety, with the active support of the Utah Association of Women and the PTA, began cracking down on "juvenile protection" violators. This law prohibits leaving a child in a situation that could prove harmful to the child.

The Utah initiative cannot bring back Rachael Runyan, or the other five, any more than like efforts in the other forty-nine states could *bring back* any of the 1.3 million kids missing each year. But in those states that react as Utah did, the playgrounds and streets will be safer for the children—whose parents care enough to volunteer.

Business is often faulted for keeping its nose in the balance sheets while worlds fall to pieces. And in the area of crime, there is some justice to this view. Later in this chapter, I will have some sugges-tions for business to help stem violent crime. But I would like to de-liver compliments to commerce, which I hope will not seem self-serving.

The Advertising Council's "Take a Bite Out of Crime" campaign is one of the most imaginative and useful drives the council has un-dertaken in its more than forty years.[33] It is paid for in large part by the advertising agencies who contribute their time to plan and exe-cute it. The agencies, of course, derive the income that makes this gift possible.

The drive was begun on behalf of the Justice Department, which also picked up part of the tab, and is supported by the AFL-CIO, the Jaycees and other businessmen, the Boy Scouts, the NAACP, the Urban League, the national associations of women's clubs, social workers, senior citizens, governors, and mayors—and a formidable coalition of other powerful groups, as well.

The Ad Council, as it is called, has prepared free television and radio spots, newspaper and magazine ads, transit posters, and ten specific guides on how businesses, neighborhoods, organizations, the elderly, and others can prevent crime.

The symbol of this campaign is a self-confident-looking bloodhound named McGruff. For kids, there are McGruff T-shirts, a McGruff doll, and even a McGruff costume that can be worn at parties. For adults, there is some of the slickest and most handsomely done material on crime I have ever seen. It covers the whole horizon, and it is expertly put together.

The booklets, for example, are not fluff, but probing, exact instructions on how to crimeproof your house, right down to what bolts to put in what part of the window; on what, precisely, to do if someone puts a gun on you; on the measurements of the best kind of lock to put in your door. Wisely, one of the booklets is in Spanish, as is a radio spot for use on Spanish-language stations.

The Ad Council campaign has already led to such things as a McGruff Walking Patrol in Texas. Kids take strolls with experts, who tell them how to put identification markings on their bikes and other property, and what to do about school vandalism.

The council is pushing people to have paychecks automatically deposited in banks so they cannot be heisted from mailboxes. In Illinois, homeowners are getting a 3 to 15 percent discount on homeowners' policies if they follow the recommendations in the Ad Council's "How To Crimeproof Your Home." And a million English- and Spanish-language brochures on how to avoid being a victim of crime when you travel are being distributed in Florida.

It is not enough, of course, for business to promulgate information on crime, however ably presented. If ordinary citizens are to be asked to pitch in, then industry must join them and perhaps even help lead the van.[34]

Money is the obvious way we can help, and it should not be thrown out scattershot. Industry, unlike government, has the stockholders to account to. And they must be convinced that when we dip into profits, we dip in both for sound moral and financial reasons. Careful publicity when we make grants will show our stockholders how a gift to an anticrime cause is not just good, but is good business as well.

When we let our stockholders know about the gift, we should make clear to them that it is (up to quite high limits) tax-deductible. And we should consider making grants for two to three years, even if they are less on a per-year basis, so the recipients can do some medium-range planning with them.

Indeed, I believe we should walk the whole mile with our recipients. We might have our public relations office help them prepare the grant request for our board (and perhaps even help them, at the same time, prepare requests for government funds).

My own preference—and I realize others may disagree with me—is to make grants and other cash layouts to local organizations. It is not just that it permits a corporation to monitor how the money is spent, but the money stays in the community and the amount of goodwill is always most pronounced in local giving. Besides, it prevents crime down the road in the locale in which we do business and in which our employees live.

I think we should come up with awards to police who do good work. We should provide scholarships for advanced police training, and for prosecutors' and judges' seminars. We should always participate, as in the Utah case, in rewards offered for apprehension of criminals. Payments for crime "tips" that lead to arrests are also worthwhile investments.

Local industry and small businesses must do everything they can to further citizen crime fighting in neighborhood watch and related programs. We should consider, when we have funds available, supporting religious bodies that are particularly active with juvenile delinquency programs.

With care, we should undertake to hire ex-offenders and perhaps, if we give them a break beyond what we would an ordinary applicant, we should get some tax credit for taking the risk. We should take on more missionary work in the prisons in the style of the Jaycees, particularly if our factories are located near penitentiaries or other institutions.

We should be constantly alert to how our developing technology can be adapted to anticrime uses by the police, courts, and corrections institutions. Incentive awards by industry for particularly useful innovations in the anticrime field are very much in order.

We see police and prosecutors speaking to civic organizations on crime. Our public relations people should be out there, too, describing useful crime-fighting practices we use in our plants and offices which might be modified for homes. And we should explain why, when we are hit by criminality—from pilferage to robbery—prices go up and it hurts everyone.

There are innumerable ways we can help if we merely give a few minutes to thinking about it. For example, instead of a Christmas party, a gift of flak jackets to the police might be in order—or better yet, a party to which we invite police and give them the jackets.

I have found in my reading that many of our crime labs are in deplorable shape. A sample from the scene of the crime of hair or blood or semen has far too great a chance of being mislabeled, misdiagnosed, or simply lost than most people think. This could destroy the prosecutor's case or convict an innocent man.[35]

An industrial chemist, or expert lab man, I can guarantee, can find things in a crime lab, either government or private, that would improve procedures. If all he recommended was a better light source for a microscope, dust removal from sample dishes, the cleaning of a dirty test tube stand, or the modernizing of an outmoded procedure, it could be the making of a criminal case—or cases. The bureaucracy, of course, if we offer our services, must be willing to accept, to *let* us help. That is sometimes a problem.

These little (but important) items are myriad. Let me mention only a few more. Industry has developed batteries that last longer, and work better that anything we have ever known before. Yet many other police forces use five-and-dime stuff. A failed flashlight in a rainstorm could doom an officer.

In electronics, we can now transmit digital material on voice channels. This could be vital in sending in material from the scene of a crime, or in letting an officer know on a screen in his car what data on a suspected criminal are available. Yet most police forces are unaware that business even has these techniques. We should tell our local police what we have and how they can get them. Some are already available in police versions.

We now use advanced cameras for keeping our plants and offices under surveillance that can outdo anything we ever had. Corrections and police agencies using cameras in cells and for walkways should surely contact their nearest modern industry to find out what the state of the art is. If they do not call us, we should offer our help to them.

Big-city police departments are now doing mock hostage liberation drills. Often highly trained officers play the role of hostages.[36] Far better to use ordinary citizens. It saves police officers time and taxpayers money. The citizens' reactions are far more realistic than those of experienced policemen. A call to a local business would produce any number of volunteers. In fact, why should not industry call police and offer to solicit its employees for volunteers for such vital exercises?

As simple a thing as an animal hospital offering to care free for injured police dogs is a volunteer role small business can play. Or when a large company bids for its security cars, the contract officer might invite police to bid with them in order to get a better price for volume. Or perhaps the use of a business computer and the assistance of industry personnel could cut drastically the costs of an important research study.

There is no end to the help industry can provide. It only takes a little vision and a little ingenuity, the kind we daily apply to our own business problems.

At present almost half of all voluntary corporate giving is from fewer than a thousand firms, mostly ones with assets of more than $200 million. Obviously, there are tens of thousands of small firms—along with many other large ones—who are not doing their share.[37]

We businessmen are like everyone else. We need motivation. We need to see that we are the victims as much as the people we read about in the paper. It is poor economy and poor citizenship for us to wait for the corporate equivalent of two little children disappearing before we look up from our conference tables and "Take a Bite Out of Crime." It is time we all took McGruff seriously.

# *Twelve*

✳

# Preventions and Costs

VIOLENT crime has taken America a long, sobering way from that time, not so long ago, when women walked alone in parks, when doors stayed unlocked all night, and when shop windows stayed full of goods, no matter what the hour.

Even when we saw it coming, we could not bear to become prisoners of our fears. We thought if we imprisoned enough robbers, executed enough murderers, put enough police on the streets, and funded enough antipoverty programs, that crime would go away and we could walk, sleep, and do business in freedom.

Now we know better. We know that while we must keep the most vigorous pressure on violent criminals, we must also take precautions—lots of them. In previous chapters, while I touched on precautions, I concentrated mostly on how to fight crime—from the babies' first cries to the incarceration of violent old men.

This chapter is a departure. It deviates from my purpose of analyzing crime as *issues* and prescribing *solutions*. Its first few pages are an amalgam of "home remedies," things we can do to protect ourselves. In that sense, it is a little like the man who runs Chicago's water system trying to describe to friends how he replaced a faucet washer.

But I could not exclude a few pages of plain advice. If I needed a further reason, it was provided by my visit to the home of a long-time crime fighter in an area where crime is increasing—where I found he had left a ladder against the rear of his house after cleaning out his gutters.

My own family and my own employees would have been safer if I had been able to advise them then of what I know now. If I could convince a thousand of my readers to observe the precautions I am about to outline, this book's purpose would have been accomplished: I would have saved my readers from injury or loss of goods or money, or both.

I would like to claim all these good ideas as my own. But they are mainly a result of my inquisitiveness and research. While I base some on my business experience, and what I hope is common sense, most come from police, from prosecutors, from judges, from my practical neighbors, from criminals themselves, and from the Ad Council and other groups.

Most people, all studies show, think first of their families and themselves when they think of crime. They worry about crimeproofing their own homes, then about their offices, then about where they shop or bank or read or study or work.

There is good cause to worry, what with 5.3 million reported burglaries a year[1] with losses of $4 billion.[2] So it's smart when you consider crimeproofing to first look at your home as a burglar would.[3]

Is your door a hollow, flimsy one? Install a metal one, or one of solid wood, or one with a solid wood core. It should be no less than 1¾ inches thick. Don't leave more than ⅛ inch between door and frame, to make it tough for anyone to slip in a crowbar. A metal strip can be bolted (no less than six bolts) to the door to fill the gap. A peephole may be useful, particularly for apartment dwellers.

If a door leads directly into your house, it should not have any glass, which is too easy to smash, permitting the burglar to reach in or use a tool to open it from inside. If you are wedded to the idea of a fancy door, put a grill or break-resistant plastic panel over the glass and bolt it through the door with lockscrews.

See if your sliding glass doors can simply be lifted out of their track. If they can, drive screws in the top track so the door will continue to slide, but won't lift anymore. You probably already know the trick of putting a broomstick in the bottom track so the door won't slide. But have you thought of drilling a hole from inside partway through the track and into the door frame and putting a nail or small metal dowel into the hole? It will keep the door from sliding when you don't want it to. Also, make sure your sliding door locks are solid, not cheap.

If your door hinges are on the outside, make sure the pins can't be taken out. There are "no-remove" pins that will accomplish this. Or you can take out the middle screw on both sides of the hinge and insert in one side a headless screw or a metal pin—an Ad Council idea—so that it fits into the hole opposite, effectively safe-bolting the door against the frame when it is locked.

As for locks: make sure your deadbolt locks have at least inch-long "throws." Use three-inch or longer screws to attach the strike plate to the door and be certain the screws of the lock itself are inside the door, not on the outside. The best cylinders have steel guards around the key section to prevent wrenching by a burglar. Good alternate or supplementary locks are rim-mounted locks with deadbolts, easy ones to install and good protection against crowbars.

Some homeowners or apartment managers put "police locks" in the cellar. These are metal rods braced against the door from the inside and anchored into the door and to the floor. For sheds and garages, an old-time padlock with a well-bolted hasp and hasp plate is often used. It should have a ⅜-inch shackle, be laminated, and be able to withstand multiple smashes.

If you hide keys outside, make sure the hiding place is unconventional. Burglars know all about doormats, window ledges, mailboxes, rain spouts. One athletic houseowner puts his on a finishing nail well up in a climbable backyard tree. Don't hook anything on a key ring that will give your address or identify you. And never give a key to delivery or maintenance people. When you move into a new home, change the locks.

For windows, the convenient, center-located turn locks won't do. A burglar can smash the glass or even turn them with a hook from outside. Key locks are not cheap, but they are worth the price if they are legal in your area. At ground level, metal grills and grates make sense so long as they don't prevent you from leaving your house in case of fire. Sliding glass windows can be thief-treated like sliding doors.

There are also precautions for the yard. Trees should be cut back from second-floor windows, and shrubs trimmed when they hide windows and doors from the neighbors or the street. Ladders should not be left in the yard where burglars can simply put them up against the house. High fences of bamboo, wood, or other opaque materials may be attractive, but they give good visual protection to house-breakers.

If arson is a threat to your neighborhood, make sure gasoline and other combustibles are in a locked shed. And lights should shine on good-sized address numerals so they can be seen from the street by firemen and police answering emergency calls. There should also be lights above doors so intruders can be seen by neighbors and from the street.

There are all sorts of alarms. Some set lights flashing, horns blowing, sirens sounding, and bells ringing. Others sound only in a neighbor's house or at a security agency headquarters. In my own family's case, the security agency was slow getting to the house, so a thorough check should be made before using a security agency system. Some alarms set off an automatic call to police headquarters.

I have mentioned the engraving of driving license numbers on property which makes goods harder for a thief to "fence." Some towns even issue "Operation Identification" decals. Put them on your window *after* you mark your property. Theft insurance is also good business. There is a fine federal program available in some thirty states. Your state insurance commission or your insurance company—perhaps reluctantly—will tell you about it.

With a "burglar's-eye" view of your own house or apartment, you should come up with many individual ideas. Some that may not occur to you are keeping valuables out of sight of windows that front on the sidewalk; making sure you do not give out hazardous information to strangers, particularly those doing "surveys" on the telephone; and keeping your address out of funeral notices, society items, and classified ads. And if a stranger wants to use your phone, tell him you'll make the call for him, and keep him outside.

If you go away on vacation, it is almost second nature now to have someone cut the grass and suspend your newspaper subscription. But you should also install a light-timing device; hide empty garbage cans; turn down the bell on your telephone so a burglar will not hear it ringing and know no one is home; ask a neighbor to park in your driveway from time to time; leave shades or drapes in a normal condition; have someone shovel your sidewalks if it snows; and notify your neighbor and—if your police are beyond reproach—your police or sheriff's office that you are going and tell them where you'll be.

Finally, if you suspect a burglar is in your house, don't go in. Call the police from a neighbor's. Don't try to stop him if he flees; he may be armed and may panic. And don't touch anything inside. Let the police go in first for fingerprints and other evidence.

If a burglar is in the house and you can get out safely, then go. If you cannot, then there is no certain single procedure: sometimes passive acquiescence may be the answer, particularly if he is armed; or a hurried phone call to the operator or emergency police number; or physical resistance.

A gun should be kept in a house *only* if you and any other potential users are trained in its use by an officially approved organization. Even then, I would think twice. Often through mishap or anger, pistols are used on the wrong person. And in some states, incredible as it sounds, it is illegal to use a gun on an intruder.

Yet if burglaries abound, people are going to buy guns to defend themselves and their property. With this in mind, my view is that pistol registration makes sense. It gives police a means of keeping some track of handguns. It also gives prosecutors a handy means of locking up criminals who have an unregistered gun, but who have not yet been caught in a crime with it. The pros and cons have been argued for years. Now it is time to act on a nationwide basis.

Having, I am sure, infuriated my friends in the National Rifle Association, I would like to say something about that group. *If* a person decides he must have a pistol, and after he conforms to all state and federal laws, then the National Rifle Association is the place to go. Their training programs teach the kind of respect for deadly weapons that any owner must have.

In my opinion, whatever gun organization you select, you should deal thoroughly with how a weapon can be used against an intruder in the home, including what the laws are about firing on a housebreaker. If you are going to shoot a bandit or housebreaker, you had better do it right on the first try.

In the streets, there are a whole new set of precautions. I have mentioned the sewing machine company's ingenious "inside purse." Men already have pockets in their clothes, but we put our wallets in the worst of them: the hip pocket. There the wallet bulges temptingly for pickpockets.

We should get in the habit of carrying our wallet in our side pockets, where we can keep a hand on it, or in our coat pockets. Both men and women should keep credit cards, driving licenses, and other vital papers in a place different from wallets. And of course, you should carry as little cash as possible. Women should not keep wallets in open-mouthed shoulder bags. Indeed, when shoulder bags with straps are used, they should be clutched under the elbow, not swinging provocatively from the strap for every passing mugger.

Going into high-crime areas at night is asking for trouble. So is cutting through dark alleys, parking or vacant lots, tunnels, and parks. If a traveler is in a strange town, a call to police may be worthwhile to find out where you should and shouldn't be after dark. And if you have to go where crime rates are high, go with someone else.

There are small compressed-air horns and "shriekers" and mouth whistles, which can be blown in populated areas. But sounding one far from help may merely infuriate the criminal more. It's a matter of judgment.

The same kind of general rule applies to mace, tear gas, and related defenses. If you know what you are doing, and someone is near to help, they can be of value. If you are alone and in a desolate place, watch out. They do not stun; they may just anger. Above all, don't resist a demand for money if the man is armed.

For your children, the old rule of being wary of strangers is still a good one, particularly those who offer candy or other gifts, those offering a ride, or those who hang around play areas or seem to want to touch children. Instruct your kids to tell you about it, then call the police if warranted.

Teach your children to lean on parents, police, teachers—not on strangers. For travel, there are sometimes special buses for the young, and mini-buses for the elderly so they can get to shopping centers and safely home.

If you are being followed, don't go to your residence. Drive to a police station, a hospital, or even a gasoline station or other well-lighted place and seek help. Note the suspicious car's license number if you can do so without endangering yourself. When you are getting your car repaired, leave only the car keys, not your house keys, at the garage. In slum areas, keep your car windows up and your doors locked and drive through briskly. If your car breaks down, turn on the flashers, put up the hood, tie cloth on your antenna and wait in the car unless help is immediately available. If you ask a stranger to make a call for you, roll down the window only enough to get the message across.

Rape is not a frequent crime, but for women it is a fearsome one. A confident walk is one natural defense, but next to the curb, not past dark doorways. Walk facing traffic; never hitchhike or accept rides from strangers; and do not be hesitant about screaming or running if there is an implied threat. Better to be embarrassed than raped. If rape is imminent, any action is warranted: break a window, stop a passing car, drop your packages, and run toward the nearest lighted house.

Single women should keep their first names off letter boxes and phone listings. All women should avoid going alone at night to laundry rooms, storage rooms, or sheds. They should not let unknown "salesmen" or "repairmen" or nonuniformed, unidentified meter checkers in their houses.

If a woman is attacked, there is only one word of advice I found in every bit of research: stay calm. Whether to be passive—remember, it is just as much a rape if there is no resistance—or to fight back can only be determined by the situation.

Some experts advise that passivity is the best course, trying to calm the rapist and talk him out of it, or to tell him you are sick, or pregnant, or have VD. Others say to tell him a friend or relative is on the way home, or to pretend to faint or to get hysterical.

Some say fight back, scream, struggle, learn enough judo or karate or other skills to injure the rapist with a blow to the groin, the Adam's apple, or with a jab in the eye. Still others warn that an active defense may only stimulate the rapist to more violence.

One thing all agree on: If it is clear that you are about to be killed during a rape or any other crime, whether you are a woman or a man, then fight in any way you can, and savagely. Claw, kick, go for the groin, or eyes—and if you can escape, flee.

Immediately after a rape attack, get help from the police. Do not try to wash off the evidence as the otherwise level-headed young woman did in my chapter on victims. If the rapist can be caught, another woman may be spared the agony you have been through.

As one last point on this horrible crime: The Ad Council's booklet on "How to Protect Yourself Against Sexual Assault" is one of the best of the many fine anticrime releases.

Although businessmen can profit by many of the suggestions I have made, they also face other special problems. One is protection of the large perimeters around factories and the like. Bushes and other handsome, thick landscaping may look pretty, but it is a perfect screen for intruders. Chain-link fences along with low hedges—ones with thorns or prickles—are wiser.

Lighting commercial premises all night is costly, but a good investment. When lights are missing, replace them and have police or others watch that light for a night or two. It may be that a burglar broke it in preparation for a raid the next night. A watchdog inside the fence is a good precaution. If your business is small, it may make sense to get together with another firm and to hire a security guard. Don't forget the timer boxes, at which your guards "punch in" to show they are making their rounds.

For a business, a good deal of care is necessary in the placement of fire escapes. They should be too high for anyone on the ground to reach them. When they go past doors or windows, these should be barred but with safety features inside so they do not impede employees from leaving the building in an emergency. Large ventilation ducts and skylights should also be shielded with bars or grates.

An alarm system is also generally wise. Commercial enterprises have the same options as those I described for residences. But costs are higher, so sit down with a reputable security consultant to see how extensive the alarm system should be. It is smart to put up decals and placards announcing you have protection. That alone may fend off housebreakers and other intruders.

Small businesses unable to afford sophisticated equipment may want what are called "buddy buzzers" —alarms that go off in a neighboring store so that police can be unobtrusively summoned.

One warning: If an alarm goes off, do not go in your store, factory, or other building. The burglar may be inside, armed and edgy. Let the police enter. They know what they are doing. If, as in one case with which I am familiar, the police come and are afraid to enter, get some better police. Ones with both guts and dogs.

There are commonsense rules that, all too often, are not followed by businesses. For instance, keep all unused doors locked. If you have not investigated use of a camera system—I prefer exposed ones; they have their own deterrent effect—you should do so.

If you must work alone, keep a radio or television on in the back so it will sound like someone else is with you in the store. Make bank deposits at different times so a robber is not waiting for you at a set time.

Your cash register and counter should be visible from the street. The idea of passersby sounding an alarm may persuade robbers to leave you alone. Some merchants even keep a special packet of money with listed serial numbers and years in their cash register. Such a list can be invaluable for police in making a case against a bandit.

If an armed robber does come in, give the man the money. If he is reckless enough to rob, he is reckless enough to shoot. As soon as he goes, jot down everything you remember about him, and keep everyone away from any object or surface he may have touched.

There is no other way to put the man who made you a victim—and probably many others—in jail without cooperating with police. My own view is that if you are dogged enough to run a business in these times, you must be dogged enough to keep at the case, come delays, come annoyance, come disappointments. And this advice is good for nonbusiness victims as well. Whether the crime is rape or purse snatching, only by getting the criminal off the street can we have either safety—*or* justice.

In this chapter, I have dealt with prevention in its specific meaning—the precautions we can take to prevent crime. And because police work—more than courts or corrections—is most immediately tied to citizen precautions, I want to isolate and report on how a good, citizen-backed, police crime prevention concept works.

Picked by Figgie as a model of how theories of police work can be put into practice is the Texas Crime Prevention Institute.[4] Funded by the state, it has trained 8,000 Texas law-enforcement officers and another 1,000 from other American and Canadian cities in the last ten years.

Its teaching center is at Southwest Texas State University. It has an eighty-hour course, a stripped-down forty-hour course, and a forty-hour advanced course, plus twenty-hour classes in rape and armed robbery, crimes against the elderly, executive protection, security, public information, and crime-stopper programs.

It has distributed brochures in English and in Spanish on crime, decals, kids' books, posters, broadcast spots, and films.

This efficient anticrime center was started up with federal money, and when that dried up, the state kept it going in large part with fines from misdemeanors and felonies. Thus the burden has been lifted from the taxpayer and put on the back of the criminal, where it belongs.

All the evidence—including the pride of its graduates—indicates that a policeman who goes through the institute is likely to be a very good cop.

Garland, a Texas town of some 165,000, is an example. A community in the 100,000 to 1 million range, in a recent survey, it had the third lowest per capita crime rate in America. It is no coincidence that 85 percent of its 170 police officers went to the Texas Crime Prevention Institute.

The city's policy is to make every officer a "generalist," someone who can handle almost anything that comes along. Each policeman writes a crime-risk report on any situation he spots that might breed crime—a building, store, or office with poor precautions, an arson-prone accumulation of trash, persistent loitering at any location, and so forth.

The city's few specialists instruct other officers on such things as antishoplifting techniques, and on how to set up neighborhood watch programs. The city *thinks* prevention, and as a result, it does not have to fear the results of the absence of prevention.

Texas, with its criminal-funded anticrime institute and its policy of having prisoners build some of their own prisons, would seem to be a national model. And yet, even Texas is not without problems, fewer than most populous states, but there.

To build the prisons that it needs, it would have to spend a billion dollars. Its corrections system, with 34,000 inmates, is the largest in the United States. It is exploring more use of halfway houses, alternative sentences, and work-release.

The costs of prevention are staggering.[5] The average national cost for an institution bed is well over $50,000; for maximum security it is more than $100,000. In 1982, construction costs for the nation's corrections facilities were almost $1 billion.[6] In addition, there are 150,000 people working for corrections, with salaries ranging over $70,000 for corrections agency heads.[7] The overall cost of corrections alone is about $8 billion a year. And *Time* magazine estimates that between $6 and $8 billion a year is needed to get enough facilities for humane housing of prisoners.[8]

The courts' and other judicial expenditures are more than $7 billion annually. A single trial costs the taxpayer well over $100 an hour.[9] And there are tens of thousands of court proceedings going on all the time.

Police costs are almost $20 billion a year.[10] The pay of a veteran officer in New York City is $38,000 a year. And the $20 billion estimate does not take into account future costs of pension funds, some of which are almost out of control. In Los Angeles, one recent study showed the unfunded liability for police and firemen was $3.4 billion.[11] In Washington, D.C., it was $2 billion. Even in well-run Colorado it was $431 million.

So for criminal justice alone—not counting those pension liabilities—the spending is around $35 billion a year. This figure, of course, does not include the losses from crime. In terms of property losses a low estimate is $11 billion. But what happens when you include increased insurance, home security costs, loss of wages, and long-term psychological treatment of victims?[12]

A detailed Justice Department study, updated for inflation, shows that in direct costs—that is, medical expenses, earnings loss, and any long-term treatment as a result of the crime—the cost of a murder is $282,000. A rape costs $47,000 when there is serious bodily injury; $24,000 if there is not. A robbery with serious injury is $32,000, not even counting the property lost; a serious aggravated assault the same.[13]

Crimes against business cost $35 billion a year by some estimates. We are talking about vandalism, fraud, arson, shoplifting, commercial burglary, increased insurance, security costs, missed work, embezzlement, and an almost endless number of add-ons. One estimate, which also brings in lost taxes, expenses to treat drug abusers, and costs to build up neighborhoods burned by arsonists, runs as high as $300 billion.[14]

When indirect costs for business and individuals such as welfare payments for crime victims, increased taxes, and prevention outlays are added in, the overall cost of crime losses ranges above *$50 billion* a year, even by the most conservative estimates.

Adding that to our earlier figure for corrections, courts, and police, the figure comes to *$85 billion* a year. I would side with the cautious Justice Department approach: that such figures are subject to so many variables that they are only useful to express magnitude, not exactitude.[15]

In fact, I have approached all the statistics I used with the memory of a "statistic" quoted by two different and reputable authors on the same famous murder, the shooting of novelist David Graham Phillips by a ne'er-do-well Philadelphia socialite.

One author quoted the dying man as saying, "I can fight one bullet, but not five."[16] The second author quoted the dying Phillips as saying, "I can fight two wounds, but not six." Those statistics are off 100 percent or 20 percent or both or somewhere in between, depending on how you look at it. So much for statistics.

The fact is that these awesome losses from crime are like any other financial losses. It is not what they are in themselves, but what they mean to each of us in terms of our own suffering, the loss of loved ones, the diminishment of life's goodness, and the theft of our freedom from anxiety. It is not that crime robs us of our gold, but of our golden hours.

# *Thirteen*

❋

# Closing Arguments

AFTER writing so much on the past and the present, after reading so many words of research and speculation by my criminological betters, I have come to a few conclusions about the future.

Even as I was writing this book, FBI reports indicated that the trend I earlier noted in downward crime rates is continuing. We in business tend to look on the bright side. We all hope that we will develop a fine new product, a fine new market, a good profit picture, and something that will be a boon for our fellow man. So it is with these crime rate harbingers.

If these new figures are more than just a statistical correction, then something exciting is happening. It may be that the "bubble" I talked about—the high-crime ages just before twenty—is passing through the population with more impact than I had expected. It may be that the hundreds of millions poured into the anticrime fight by the federal Law Enforcement Assistance Administration, now out of business, are beginning to bear healthy fruit. It may be the citizens' watch movement is producing better results than one could have hoped. Or it may be that the kind of outrage that lets America reject its potential demagogues and tyrants, a kind of national will and purpose, is in operation.

Just conceivably, our police, courts, prisoners, and most importantly, We, the People are "doing our thing" individually and collectively to diminish crime.

If I am *wrong*, I know from my reading what we face. The apocalyptic pessimists I have quoted gave us a surrealistic taste of what we will see each morning. We will look from our windows and see our cities being pillaged by barbarians.

I do not think this will happen. I think there are too many Americans of good will to let it happen. I am not so vain as to think my book will be more than a useful fragment in this effort. Business, of course, doesn't even have all the answers for *itself*.

But public debate on crime is essential. And those of us who are concerned with our cities, indeed, with the country at large, do America a disservice if we do not do all we can to keep alive issues that directly involve us.

I hope that my ideas will help enliven the debate. I hope they will stir controversy because from heated discussions changes can be forged. It may be that in such a dispute I will, on some points, be proved wrong. But some of my ideas will make us a little safer, a little less likely to succumb to the law of the streets.

And that, of course, brings me full circle. In the beginning of my book I described how my friend said, "Why not write it? It'll be worth it if all you save are four or five lives." My reply was that it will be worth it if *one* life is saved.

# ⁕
# Notes

In the interest of conciseness, I have condensed some newspaper and magazine headlines and titles, and the names of some organizations, to the key phrase. I have retained adequate identification throughout to avoid impeding researchers.

## Introduction

1. (a) "Police and Computers," *Police Magazine*, September 1982. This professionally done publication, a strong journalistic arm in the fight against violent crime, has folded up. The reasons are lack of circulation and, I am sorry to say, a lack of support from corporate advertisers; (b) U.S. Senate Subcommittee on Juvenile Justice, "Career Criminal Life Sentence Act of 1981," statement of K. Conboy, October 26, 1981.

2. *Domestic Violence and the Police*, Police Foundation, Washington, D.C., 1977.

3. "Prisoners in 1983," Bureau of Justice Statistics, U.S. Department of Justice, April 1984.

4. (a) P. W. Greenwood, *Selective Incapacitation*, Santa Monica, Calif.: Rand Corporation, August 1982. Also see his references, p. 119, for further readings; (b) "The Violent Child: Some Patterns Emerge," *The New York Times*, September 27, 1982. This important article is based in part on D.O. Lewis, *et al.* "Violent Juvenile Delinquents," *Journal of the American Academy of Child Psychiatry*, vol. no. 18, 2, Spring 1979; (c) B. Cary and S. Gettinger, *Time to Build?* New York, 1984: Edna McConnell Clark Foundation, contains a succinct rebuttal, among much other valuable capsulized information on corrections.

5. "The Prevention of Serious Delinquency: What to Do," *Reports of the National Juvenile Justice Assessment Centers*, U.S. Department of Justice, December 1981.

6. *The Figgie Report on Fear of Crime*, Willoughby, Ohio: Figgie International; 1979–1983. This data is from Part II, "The Corporate Response to Fear of Crime." I have admired and depended on this and the other three parts of the *Figgie Report*, funded by a corporation that made up its mind to do something to fight violent and other "index" crime.

7. Charles Baudelaire, *Flowers of Evil*, New York: New Directions, 1963.

8. A. Blumstein, "Crime, Punishment and Demographics," *American Demographics*, October 1980.

9. Op. cit. and *Figgie*, Part I, "America Afraid."

10. "Two Months of 'Hell'. . ." and "Charges Dropped . . ." *The Washington Post*, January 24, 1983, and April 6, 1983.

11. *Newsweek.* March 8, 1971.

12. Op. cit., note 4b.

13. *Report to the Nation on Crime and Justice*, U.S. Department of Justice, October 1983. If an encyclopedia can be contained in 108 pages, it is this absolutely invaluable source book. Single copies free from National Criminal Justice Reference Service, Box 6000, Rockville, Md. 20850. Cite NCJ-87068 when ordering.

14. (a)"Arson—How Not To Get Burned," National Crime Prevention Council (undated), one of several useful, concise leaflets available from NCPC, 805 15th Street, NW, Washington, D.C. 20005; (b)"Electronic Fund Transfer and Crime," Bureau of Justice Statistics, U.S. Department of Justice, February 1984. (c) See "Federal Drug Law Violators," Bureau of Justice Statistics, U.S. Department of Justice, February 1984.

15. *Uniform Crime Report*, "1983 Preliminary Annual Release," FBI, April 19, 1984, and full release, September 9, 1984. I have used FBI Uniform Crime Reports *(UCR)* for almost all my arrest and many other crime figures. In some cases, my figures are from FBI analyses, and FBI releases that are based on the *UCR* data. To avoid confusion, I am merely citing *UCR*, FBI, and the year or sometimes the month and year.

16. See "Courting Disaster," review of P.S. Prescott's *The Child Savers*, New York: Knopf, 1981, *Washington Post Book World*, June 14, 1981.

17. Ramsey Clark, *Crime in America*, New York: Simon and Schuster, 1970.

18. Interviews with school children, May 1984.

19. Interviews and personal experience, October 1979.

20. Interview, February 1983.

21. John Donne, "Meditation XVII," *Seventeenth Century Prose and Poetry*, New York: Harcourt, Brace, 1946.

## Chapter One. Crime Today

1. "The Severity of Crime," Bureau of Justice Statistics, U.S. Department of Justice, January 1984.

2. Interview, February 1983.

3. Interview, February 1983.

4. Interviews, May 1984.

5. *UCR*, 1983; FBI, 1984.

6. (a) *Report to the Nation on Crime and Justice*, U.S. Department of Justice, October 1983. (b) "Violent Crime by Strangers," Bureau of Justice Statistics, U.S. Department of Justice, April 1982.

7. (a) "Crime and the Elderly," Bureau of Justice Statistics, U.S. Department of Justice, December 1981; (b) Center for Urban Affairs, Northwestern University, per *Criminal Justice Research, Annual Report*, U.S. Department of Justice, November 1980.

8. See "A Mythical Crime Wave?" *Police Magazine*, September 1982.

9. "The Blue and the Gray," *Police Magazine*, September 1982.

10. (a) Op. cit., note 6a; (b) "Households Touched by Crime 1983," Bureau of Justice Statistics, U.S. Department of Justice, May 1984.

11. *Facts about Violent Juvenile Crime*, National Council on Crime and Delinquency, July 1982.

12. (a) Op. cit., notes 5, 10; (b) "Criminal Victimization in the U.S.," Bureau of Justice Statistics, U.S. Department of Justice, July 1982.

13. Op. cit., note 5.

14. *The Figgie Report on Fear of Crime*, Parts I–IV. Willoughby, Ohio: Figgie International, 1979–1983.

15. See also President Ronald Reagan, address, International Association of Chiefs of Police, New Orleans, September 28, 1981.

16. *Violent Crime in the United States* (briefing book for White House), U.S. Department of Justice, February 1982.

17. Op. cit., note 14, Part I.

18. Ibid.

19. Op. cit., note 7b.

20. (a) Op. cit., note 14, Part II. (b) See also U.S. Senate Subcommitte on Juvenile Justice, testimony of B. Renshaw on "Career Criminal Life Sentence Act of 1981," October 26, 1981.

21. *UCR*, FBI 1980–83 figures.

22. Op. cit., notes 6a, 11, 21.

23. (a) J. M. and M. R. Chaiken, *Varieties of Criminal Behavior*, Santa Monica, Calif.: Rand Corporation, August 1982. Not only its insights into its title matter but its bibliography make this an important resource; (b) Op. cit., note 20b, testimony of K. Conboy and J. C. Ball. See also in relation to Dr. Ball's painstaking work, "Baltimore Study Finds Much Crime by Heroin Users," *The Washington Post*, May 12, 1984; (c) Op. cit., note 16.

24. "Criminals Report Wide Alcohol Use," *The New York Times*, January 31, 1983.

25. A. L. Rhodes, "The 'Religious Factor' and Delinquent Behavior," *Journal of Research in Crime and Delinquency*, January 1970.

26. Op. cit., note 5.

27. A. Blumstein, "Demographically Disaggregated Projections of Prison Populations," *Research in Public Policy Analysis and Management*, vol. I, 1981.

28. See "The American Response to Crime," Bureau of Justice Statistics, U.S. Department of Justice, December 1983.

29. *Mandatory Sentencing: The Experience of Two States* [Massachusetts and New York], National Institute of Justice, U.S. Department of Justice, May 1982.

30. *Time to Build?*, Edna McConnell Clark Foundation, 1984.

31. L. E. Wilkins, "Equity and Republican Justice," *Crime and Justice in America: 1776– 1976*, Philadelphia, Pennsylvania: American Academy of Political and Social Science, 1976.

32. Attorney General William French Smith, address, American Bar Association, San Francisco, Calif., August 10, 1981.

33. "What Are Prisons For?" *Time*, September 13, 1982.

34. (a) "Prisoners in 1983," Bureau of Justice Statistics, U.S. Department of Justice, April 1984; (b) "Violent Crime in the United States," U.S. Department of Justice, February 1982; (c) "The Answer Is Not More Jails," *The Washington Post*, May 6, 1984.

35. Op. cit., notes 6a and 30.

36. NAACP Legal Defense and Education Fund, Inc., "Death Row, U.S.A," New York City, August 1984.

37. "Prisons and Prisoners," Bureau of Justice Statistics, U.S. Department of Justice, January 1982.

38. William F. Buckley, ". . . Why Jail the Non-Violent," *Washington Star*, March 24, 1981.

39. Op. cit., note 20(b), testimony of I. Joyner, ACLU.

40. Op. cit., note 5.

41. "Should This Bullet Be Banned?" *Police Magazine*, January 1983.

42. (a) *Police Use of Deadly Force*, Police Foundation, Washington, D.C., 1982; (b) "Deadly Force," *Police Magazine*, March 1981.

43. (a) Op. cit., note 5. (b) "Urban Crisis Makes Police Vulnerable," *Police Magazine*, prototype issue, 1977; (c) Telephone interviews, New York City law enforcement officials, August 1984.

## Chapter Two. The Business Approach

1. C. Hibbert, *The Roots of Evil*, Boston: Little, Brown, 1963.

2. (a) "Police and Computers," *Police Magazine*, September 1982; (b) "Computers Could Revolutionize Business of Policing," *Police Magazine*, November 1982. (c) Telephone interviews with Sgt. J. C. Mosier, Houston Police Department public information office, and Lt. David Michaud, Denver Police Department, Crimes Against Persons unit, August 1984.

3. (a) U.S. Senate Subcommittee on Juvenile Justice, "Career Criminal Life Sentence Act of 1981," statement of K. Conboy, October 26, 1981; (b) Telephone interviews with New York City law enforcement officials, August 1984.

4. FBI Director William Webster, address, Society of Former Special Agents, Las Vegas, October 30, 1982.

5. (a) FBI Director William Webster, address, Metro Crime Alert, Baltimore, May 11, 1982; (b) Webster, press statement, Washington, D.C., July 7, 1984.

6. See ". . . Sherlock Holmes in Modern Dress," *Police Magazine*, September 1982.

7. Op. cit., note 2a.

8. "In the Computer Age, Corrections . . . " *Corrections Magazine*, April 1983. This excellent magazine, like its sister publication, *Police Magazine*, has ceased publication because of insufficient funding.

9. (a) P. W. Greenwood, *Selective Incapacitation*, Santa Monica, Calif.: Rand Corporation, August 1982, also his testimony, op. cit., note 3; (b) M. E. Wolfgang, "Crime in a Birth Cohort," *Proceedings of the American Philosophical Society*, October 1973, as updated by his testimony, U.S. Senate Subcommittee on Juvenile Justice, "Violent Juvenile Crime," July 9, 1981; (c) J. M. and M. R. Chaiken, *Varieties of Criminal Behavior*, Santa Monica, Calif.: Rand Corporation, August 1982.

10. "The Prevention of Juvenile Delinquency: What to Do," *Reports of the National Juvenile Justice Assessment Centers*, U.S. Department of Justice, December 1981.

11. Op. cit., notes 2, 6.

12. "Evidence Favors Aggressive Patrol," *Police Magazine*, September 1980.

13. "Prisoners in 1983," Bureau of Justice Statistics, U.S. Department of Justice, April 1984.

14. D. Stanley, *Prisoners Among Us*, Washington, D.C.: Brookings Institution 1976.

15. "Probation and Parole," Bureau of Justice Statistics, U.S. Department of Justice, September 1983.

16. "The Polygraph Goes to Court," *Police Magazine*, September 1980.

17. "U.S. to Finance Study in Newark . . . Houston . . . ," *The New York Times*, January 11, 1983.

18. "Crime in Subway Station Rises . . ." *The New York Times*, February 2, 1983.

19. (a) "The Rookie Is a Robot," *Police Magazine*, January 1982; (b) "Robots, Brave Yet Temperamental . . .," *Washington Post*, May 6, 1984.

20. (a)"The Technology Assessment Programs," National Institute of Justice, U.S. Department of Justice, July 1981; (b) "2 Convicted in Slayings," *Washington Post*, January 15, 1983.

21. Ellen Goodman, " 'Citizen, Heal Thyself,' " *Washington Post*, February 5, 1983.

22 (a)"The Jaycees: Tapping Inmate Initiative," *Corrections Magazine*, February 1982. (b) Telephone interviews, Jaycees officials, Tulsa, Oklahoma; Miami, Florida, August 1984.

## Chapter Three. The Subteen Criminal

1. "The Violent Child: Some Patterns Emerge," *The New York Times*, September 27, 1982: D. O. Lewis, et al., "Violent Juvenile Delinquents," *Journal of the American Academy of Child Psychiatry*, 1979.

2. "Courting Disaster," review of P. S. Prescott's *The Child Saver*, New York: Knopf, 1981, *Washington Post Book World*, June 14, 1981.

3. "Do Juvenile Offenders Have Criminal Personalities," *Corrections Magazine*, February 1983, which describes the work of David Berenson. I prefer less radical approaches to the problem.

4. (a) *Time to Build?*, New York: Edna McConnell Clark Foundation, 1984; (b) *The Corrections Handbook*, Criminal Justice Institute, 1982; (c) *Report to the Nation on Crime and Justice*, U.S. Department of Justice, October 1983. (All figures updated for inflation.)

5. (a) A. Kaplan, "The Juvenile Offender Survey Project. A Study of 100 Dade County Juvenile Offenders," William and Tina Rosenberg Foundation, June 1980; (b) "Summaries of Current Research Grants," Washington, D.C.: Center for Studies of Crime and Delinquency, National Institute of Mental Health, November 1982 and January 1983.

6. *1978 Annual Review of Child Abuse and Neglect Research*, U.S. Department of Health, Education and Welfare, September 1978. This and subsequent reviews contain summaries of work being done on child abuse and its effects.

7. *Domestic Violence and the Police*, Washington, D.C.: Police Foundation, 1977.

8. Op. cit., note 1.

9. *Facts About Violent Juvenile Crime*, National Council on Crime and Delinquency, Washington, D.C., July 1982.

10. "Under Siege in an Urban Ghetto," *Police Magazine*, July 1981.

11. "Urban Violence: Liberty City . . .," *Change*, vol. V, no. 1 1981.

12. C. Hibbert, *The Roots of Evil*, Boston: Little, Brown, 1963.

13. "The Intervention of Serious Delinquency. . .," *Reports of the National Juvenile Justice Assessment Centers*, U.S. Department of Justice, December 1981.

14. Op. cit., note 4c.

15. Op. cit., note 5a.

16. Op. cit., note 1.

17. Op. cit., note 5a.

18. J. Mitford, *Kind & Usual Punishment*, New York: Vintage Books, 1974.

19. "Focus on Punishment," *Update*, American Bar Association, 1982; (b) U.S. Senate Subcommittee on Juvenile Justice, "Violent Juvenile Crime, testimony of Chicago Police Chief R. Brzeczek, July 9, 1981; (c) *UCR*, FBI, September 1984.

20. Attorney General's Task Force on Violent Crime, Final Report, August 17, 1981.

21. See "A National Assessment of Serious Juvenile Crime," *Reports of the National Juvenile Justice Assessment Centers*, vol. II, U.S. Department of Justice, April 1980. While specific figures are no longer current, they still approximate present data in most areas. We find such sad curiosities as a handful of rapists and murderers nine years old and younger, along with a few enterprising auto thieves who, also, are not yet ten. The breadth of the centers' study, at this writing, still has not been duplicated.

22. Op. cit., note 18, testimony of New York City Juvenile Justice Commissioner P. Strasburg; (b) Telephone interviews, New York City law enforcement officials, August 1984.

23. "The Prevention of Serious Delinquency: What to Do?" *Reports of the National Juvenile Justice Assessment Centers*, U.S. Department of Justice, December 1981.

24. General Order 305, No. 1, effective March 4, 1973, Metropolitan Police, Washington, D.C.

25. Op. cit., note 20.

26. See also "The Complexities of Juvenile Laws," *The Sun* (Baltimore), March 5, 1983.

27. "Corrections Officials Want Access to Juvenile Records," *Baltimore Afro-American*, March 15, 1983.

28. (a) N. Morris, *Proposals for Prison Reform*, Public Affairs Committee, New York 1974; (b) J. Miller, "The Revolution in Juvenile Justice," *The Future of Childhood and Juvenile Justice*, Charlottesville: University Press of Virginia, 1979.

29. Op. cit., note 19b, testimony of J. Miller.

30. Op. cit., note 13.

31. (a) R. Woodson, *Summons to Life* and *Youth Crime and Urban Policy*, Washington, D.C.: American Enterprise Institute, 1981; (b) "The Justice Department's Fight Against Youth Crime," Committee Print, R. Woodson, House Subcommittee on Crime, December 1978; (c) "Grassroots Activists Meet Conservatives," *Washington Post*, May 12, 1981, dealing with Woodson's theories.

32. K. L. Bradbury, et al, *Urban Decline and the Future of American Cities*, Washington, D.C.: Brookings Institution, 1982.

33. A.L. Rhodes, "The 'Religious Factor' and Delinquent Behavior," *Journal of Research in Crime and Delinquency*, January 1970.

34. "The Violence Factor on TV: New Evidence of Its Effects," *Washington Times*, January 14, 1983.

35. Op. cit., note 20b, testimony of M. E. Wolfgang.

36. *A Research Perspective on Television and Violence*, New York: American Broadcasting Company, 1983.

37. Op. cit., note 34.

38. Congresswoman Barbara Mikulski, "Family Violence: A National Issue," *Vermont Law Review*, Fall 1981.

## Chapter Four. Juvenile Predators: Thirteen to Seventeen Years Old

1. A. Vachss, address, Office of Juvenile Justice and Delinquency Prevention Workshop, Nashville, Tenn., May 26, 1982, later printed as "Serious, Violent and Habitual Juvenile Offenders," *New Designs for Youth Development*, January–February 1983.

2. "Murder Teenage Style," *CBS Reports*, CBS, Inc., September 3, 1981.

3. (a) *UCR*, FBI, 1980–1983; (b) "A National Assessment of Serious Juvenile Crime," *Reports of the National Juvenile Justice Assessment Centers, Vol. II*, U.S. Department of Justice, April 1980; (c) "Suspicious Statistics," *The Progressive*, February 1983; (d) "Are Crime Rates Really Soaring?" *Police Magazine*, January 1981.

4. (a) *Facts About Violent Juvenile Crime*, National Council on Crime and Juvenile Delinquency, July 1982; (b) "Violent Crime by Strangers," Bureau of Justice Statistics, U.S. Department of Justice, April 1982.

5. "Violent Crime in the United States," Bureau of Justice Statistics, U.S. Department of Justice, February 1982.

6. (a) *Report to the Nation on Crime and Justice*, U.S. Department of Justice, October 1983; (b) See "Criminal Victimization in the U.S.," Bureau of Justice Statistics, U.S. Department of Justice, July 1982.

7. (a) P. W. Greenwood, *Criminal Incapacitation*, Santa Monica, California: Rand Corporation, August 1982; (b) J. M. and M. R. Chaiken, *Varieties of Criminal Behavior*, Santa Monica, California: Rand Corporation, August 1982.

8. *Criminal Justice Research*, Biennial Report by the National Institute of Justice, 1980–81, U.S. Department of Justice, April 1982.

9. "Teen Held After Siege," *Washington Times*, January 14, 1983.

10. "Transit Officer Wounds Two . . .," *The New York Times*, February 9, 1983.

11. "8th Grader Kills Youth . . .," *The New York Times*, January 21, 1983.

12. U.S. Senate Subcommittee on Juvenile Justice, "Violent Juvenile Crime," testimony of C. A. Lauer, U.S. Department of Justice, July 9, 1981. Based on *Violent Schools—Safe Schools*, National Institute of Education, Washington, 1978; still the most exhaustive study on the subject; (b) "Trends in Interpersonal Crime in Schools," Dr. Oliver Moles, presented at American Educational Research Association, Montreal, Canada, April 1983; (c) "Criminal Victimization in Urban Schools," Bureau of Justice Statistics, 1979.

13. W. B. Miller, "Youth Gangs: A Look at the Numbers," *Change*, vol. V, no. 1, 1981.

14. (a) Op. cit., note 12, testimony of New York City Juvenile Justice Commissioner P. Strasburg; (b) Telephone interview, New York City law enforcement officials, August 1984; (c) Op. cit., note 3a.

15. *Attorney General's Task Force on Violent Crime, Final Report*, August 17, 1981.

16. Op. cit., note 14a.

17. Op. cit., note 12, testimony of Chicago Police Chief R. Brzeczek.

18. (a) Quoted in W. V. Stapleton, "Response Strategies to Youth Gang Activities," Sacramento, California: American Justice Institute, September 1982; (b) See also W. B. Miller, *Violence by Youth Gangs . . .*, National Institute for Juvenile Justice and Delinquency Prevention, December 1975.

19. Op. cit., note 12.

20. Op. cit., note 3b.

21. Ibid.

## Chapter Five. Juveniles and the Courts

1. *Attorney General's Task Force on Violent Crime, Final Report*, August 17, 1981.

2. See U.S. State Subcommittee on Juvenile Justice, "Violent Juvenile Crime," testimony of New York City Juvenile Justice Commissioner P. Strasburg, July 9, 1981.

3. C. Hibbert, *The Roots of Evil*, Boston: Little, Brown, 1963.

4. "Facts About Youth and Delinquency," U.S. Department of Justice, November 1982.

5. Op. cit., note 2.

6. See op. cit., note 2, testimony of C. A. Lauer, U.S. Department of Justice.

7. Op. cit., note 2, testimony of Chicago Police Chief R. Brzeczek.

8. "Fear and Confusion in Court . . .," *The New York Times*, March 12, 1983.

9. "Justice Hampered . . .," letter to editor, *The New York Times*, December 6, 1982.

10. (a) "What Criminal Justice . . .," *The New York Times*, November 26, 1982; (b) Researcher contacts with courts, New York City, Washington, D.C., February and March, 1983.

11. "Youth Probation Found Inefficient . . .," *Corrections Magazine*, February 1983.

12. For exhaustive data on juveniles in the court system, see *Reports of the National Juvenile Justice Assessment Centers*, U.S. Department of Justice, April 1980.

13. (a) "Children in Jail," *Institutions Etc.*, October 1982; (b) *Report to the Nation on Crime and Justice*, U.S..Department of Justice, October 1983; (c) Op. cit., note 2, testimony of J. Miller.

14. Op. cit. note 2, testimony of R. J. Martin.

15. See *Youth in Adult Courts: Between Two Worlds*, National Institute for Juvenile Justice, and Delinquency Prevention, U.S. Department of Justice 1982.

16. "Is New York's Tough Juvenile Law a 'Charade'?" *Corrections Magazine*, April 1983.

## Chapter Six. Locking Up Juveniles: The Search for Alternatives

1. *Facts About Youth and Delinquency*, U.S. Department of Justice, November 1982.

2. J. Miller, "The Revolution in Juvenile Justice," *The Future of Childhood and Juvenile Justice*, Charlottesville: University of Virginia Press, 1979.

3. Op. cit., note 1.

4. "Children in Jails," *Institutions Etc.*, October 1982.

5. "There Are No Juveniles in Pennsylvania Jails," *Corrections Magazine*, June 1983.

6. "The Need for a Rational Response," *Reports of the National Juvenile Justice Assessment Centers*, vol. I, U.S. Department of Justice, April 1980.

7. *Juvenile Justice Digest*, July 23, 1982.

8. Op. cit., note 2.

9. J. Howell, discussion paper for "Serious and Violent Juvenile Offender," *National Training Institute Manual*, National Alliance for Youth, Washington, D.C., November 1982.

10. "The Prevention of Serious Delinquency: What to Do," *Reports of the National Juvenile Justice Assessment Centers*, U.S. Department of Justice, December 1981.

11. Ibid.

12. J. Miller, "The Serious Juvenile Offender," National Symposium, Office of Juvenile Justice and Delinquency Intervention, September 19–20, 1977.

13. Op. cit., note 6.

14. "South East Secure Treatment Unit," *Institutions Etc.*, May 1982.

15. Telephone interviews with staff, March 1983, August 1984.

16. U.S. Senate Subcommittee on Juvenile Justice, "Violent Juvenile Crime," testimony of F. Fattah, July 9, 1981.

17. Telephone interviews with F. Fattah, March 1983, August 1984.

18. R. Woodson, *A Summons to Life*, American Enterprise Institute, 1981; R. Woodson, "Helping the Poor Help Themselves," *Policy Review*, Summer 1982.

19. (a) Op. cit., note 16, testimony of T. S. James; (b) *Figgie*, Part IV; (c) Telephone interview, Jeanne Granville, New Pride, August 1984.

20. "Juvenile Offenders Receive Services," *Youth Alternatives*, Washington, D.C., January 1983.

21. (a) "The Shelby County Violent Offenders Project," *Youth Alternatives*, December 1982; Telephone interview, Michael Whitaker, project director, August 28, 1984.

22. Op. cit., note 19b.

23. (a) *The Street Law Diversion Program*, Phi Alpha Delta Law Fraternity, Washington, D.C., 1982; (b) "Program Seeks to Nip . . .," *Newark* (N.J.) *Star-Ledger*, August 8, 1982.

24. *Criminal Justice Research*, Biennial Report by the National Institute of Justice, 1980–81, U.S. Department of Justice, April 1982.

25. Ibid.

26. "Environments for Human Services," *Institutions Etc.*, December 1982; (b) Telephone interviews, Byrn Anderson, EHS, August 1984.

27. (a) Telephone interview, Bob Burton, VisionQuest, August 1984; (b) "VisionQuest's Rite of Passage," *Corrections Magazine*, February 1984.

28. "Legislation, Jurisdiction, Program Interventions . . ." *Reports of the National Juvenile Justice Assessment Centers, Vol. III*, U.S. Department of Justice, April 1980.

29. Telephone interviews with staff, March 1983, August 1984.

39. (a) "Survival of the Fittest," *Corrections Magazine*, February 1983; (b) Telephone interview, Samuel Streit, Eckerd Youth Development.

31. "East L.A.'s Gang Project: Prevention or Bribery?" *Police Magazine*, September 1980.

32. Ad Hoc Coalition for Juvenile Justice, report, Washington, D.C., May 1982.

33. W.V. Stapleton, *Response Strategies to Youth Gang Activity*, Sacramento, California: American Justice Institute, September 1982.

34. "Youths Allege Abuse at Wilderness Camp," *Washington Post*, March 4, 1983.

35. Op. cit., note 27.

36. Vachss, chapter 5, op. cit., see note 1.

37. Op. cit., 12, expanded on in telephone interviews March 1983, August 1984.

38. Elliot Currie, "Crime and Ideology," *Working Papers*, May–June 1982.

## Chapter Seven. The Adult Criminal

1. U.S. House Committee on the Judiciary, "Bureau of Prisons and Juvenile Policies," testimony of N. Carlson, October 27, 1978.

2. *UCR*, FBI, September 1984.

3. U.S. Senate Subcommittee on Juvenile Justice, "Career Criminal Life Sentence Act Of 1981," testimony of N. Flanagan, December 10, 1981.

4. (a) Jack Anderson, column, *Washington Post*, April 21, 1981; (b) Researcher interviews with police and suspect, April 1981.

5. "Criminals Report Wide Alcohol Use," *The New York Times*, January 31, 1983.

6. *Criminal Justice Research, Biennial Report of the National Institute of Justice, 1980–81*, U.S. Department of Justice, April 1982.

7. See "Federal Drug Law Violators," Bureau of Justice Statistics, U.S. Department of Justice, February 1984.

8. "Almost 25% of Homicides . . . Tied to Drugs," *The New York Times*, February 18, 1983.

9. Op. cit., note 20.

10. (a) U.S. Senate Subcommittee on Juvenile Justice, "Career Criminal Life Sentence Act of 1981," hearings October 26 and December 10, 1981; (b) J. M. and M. R. Chaiken, *Varieties of Criminal Behavior*. Rand Corporation, August 1982.

11. *UCR*, FBI, 1980–83.

12. A. Blumstein and E. Graddy, "Prevalence and Recidivism in Index Arrests: A Feedback Model," *Law and Society Review*, vol. 16, 1981–82.

13. Op. cit., note 10, testimony of K. Conboy, October 26, 1981.

14. (a) "Minneapolis Crime Watch," *The New York Times*, December 19, 1982. (b) Telephone interview, Minneapolis Police Department, August 1984.

15. (a) *Training Aids Digest*, December 1980; (b) Researcher interviews, Director G. Gallagher, Police Standards and Training, Florida Department of Law Enforcement, May 1983.

16. *The D.C. Pretrial Services Agency—An Exemplary Project*, National Institute of Justice, U.S. Department of Justice. May 1981.

17. "The New Bail Law," *The Washington Post*, January 14, 1983.

18. "Bail Cut Twice . . .," *Charlotte News*, July 28, 1981.

19. "Two Held After Siege at Restaurant," *The Washington Post*, February 22, 1983.

20. "Prison Population Jumps . . .," *Corrections Magazine*, June 1982.

21. *Report to the Nation on Crime and Justice*, U.S. Department of Justice, October 1983.

22. (a) "Crisis in the Jails!" *Corrections Magazine*, April 1982; (b) *Time to Build?* Edna McConnell Clark Foundation, 1984.

23. "Jails Committee Urges . . .," *The New York Times*, March 2, 1983.

24. (a) "The Problems of Mental Illness Are Compounded Behind Bars," *The New York Times*, January 22, 1983; (b) "There Are No Juveniles in Pennsylvania Jails," *Corrections Magazine*, June 1983.

25. "Prisoners in 1983," Bureau of Justice Statistics, U.S. Department of Justice, April 1984.

26. Attorney General William French Smith, address, American Bar Association, August 10, 1982.

27. "Tracking Offenders," Bureau of Justice Statistios, U.S. Department of Justice, November 1983.

28. "State Court Caseload Statistics," Bureau of Justice Statistics, U.S. Department of Justice, February 1983.

29. (a) Op. cit., note 6; (b) "Dispute Resolution," *Corrections Magazine*, August 1982.

30. *Newsweek*, March 8, 1971.

31. (a) See "Witness and Witness Assistance," Bureau of Justice Statistics, U.S. Department of Justice, May 1983; (b) *President's Task Force on Victims of Crime, Final Report*, December 1982. I deal much more fully with this important question in Chapter Eleven, "Victims and Restitution."

32. "Let Facts, Not Faith Guide the Police," *The New York Times*, January 21, 1983. Much has been written on the exclusionary rule. The course suggested by the *Times* editorial cited here seems the wisest of several almost equally unhappy choices.

33. "The Scales of Justice . . .," *The Wall Street Journal*, February 5, 1982.

34. "Man Convicted in Rape of Girl to Get New Trial," *The Washington Post*, February 18, 1983.

35. "Wisconsin Judge's Rape Ruling . . .," *The Washington Post*, January 21, 1983.

36. "Man on Probation . . . ," *Montgomery Journal* (Maryland), February 24, 1983.

37. "Killer to Go Free . . . ," *Independent Journal*, Novato, Calif., March 25, 1982.

38. "The Crime of Sentencing," *The New York Times*, January 29, 1983.

39. U.S. Senate Judiciary Committee, statement of B. Forst, "Reform of the Federal Criminal Laws."

40. See Senator Edward Kennedy, "Toward a New System of Criminal Sentencing," *The American Criminal Law Review*, Spring 1979.

41. M. E. Frankel, *Criminal Sentences: Law Without Order*, New York: Hill and Wang, 1972.

42. Jack Anderson column, *The Washington Post*, February 15, 1983.

43. *Attorney General's Task Force on Violent Crime, Final Report*, August 17, 1981.

44. Op. cit., note 38.

45. Op. cit., note 42.

## Chapter Eight. Prisons and Other Options

1. "Violent Crime in America," February 1982; "Prisons and Prisoners," January 1982; "Prisoners in 1983," April 1984; all of Bureau of Justice Statistics, U.S. Department of Justice. I have drawn largely from these for my data in the prisons section of this chapter.

2. "Crisis in the Jails," April 1982; "The Prison Population Boom: Still No End in Sight," *Corrections Magazine*, June 1983. These two inclusive articles summarize the desperate plight of our prison situation.

3. *Report to the Nation on Crime and Justice*, U.S. Department of Justice, October 1983.

4. "Employment, Community Treatment Center . . .," *Federal Probation Quarterly*, December 1981.

5. "People Who Ought Not to Be in Prison," *The New York Times*, December 6, 1982.

6. *Time to Build?*, Edna McConnell Clark Foundation, 1984.

7. A. Blumstein, J. Cohen, and H.D. Miller, "Demographically Disaggregated Projections of Prison Populations," *Research in Public Policy Analysis and Management, vol. I*, 1981

8. *The Corrections Yearbook*, Criminal Justice Institute, 1982 and 1984.

9. "Habeas Corpus," Bureau of Justice Statistics, U.S. Department of Justice, March 1984.

10. (a) *UCR*, FBI, September 1984; (b) "Tracking Offenders," Bureau of Justice Statistics, U.S. Department of Justice, November 1983. My computations are based on FBI clearances of reported crimes and on confinement rates based on arrests. In fact, except in the case of homicides, where reports and incidents are not far apart, my figures are low. Because many rapes are not reported, the rapist jailings, for example, may be 6 percent or even lower.

11. ". . . The Price of Control," *Corrections Magazine*, December 1982.

12. "In Biloxi, a Ten-Minute Fire Kills 29," *Corrections Magazine*, February 1983.

13. "The Problems of Mental Illness Are Compounded Behind Bars," *The New York Times*, January 22, 1983.

14. See "Setting Prison Terms," Bureau of Justice Statistics, U.S. Department of Justice, August 1983.

15. "U.S. Judge Prohibits . . . " *Corrections Magazine*, February 1982.

16. (a) "Grim Outlook for Prisons . . .," *The New York Times*, January 16, 1983; (b) "In Arizona, Crime Falls But Prisons Fill," *Corrections Magazine*, December 1982.

17. "In the Computer Age, Corrections . . .," *Corrections Magazine*, April 1983.

18. Attorney General William French Smith, address, National District Attorney's Association, July 23, 1981, and subsequent press release, Justice Department, on same subject, September 29, 1981.

19. Op. cit., note 16a.

20. "N.J., California Voters Approve Bond Issues," *Corrections Magazine*, February 1983.

21. Address to American Correctional Association, Miami Beach, Florida, August 16, 1981.

22. "The Inmate Nation," *Time*, September 13, 1982.

23. "College Education for Police," *Police Magazine*, November 1981.

24. Federal Bureau of Prisons Director N. Carlson, address, Iowa Sheriff's Association, Sioux City, Iowa, December 7, 1982.

25. "Former Lorton Guard Is Sentenced," *The Washington Post*, January 29 1983.

26. "ACLU Sues . . .," *The Washington Post*, February 25, 1983.

27. George Washington University School of Law, Washington, D.C., address, May 24, 1981.

28. "Contract Medical Care," *Corrections Magazine*, April 1982.

29. Op. cit., note 6.

30. Attorney General's Task Force on Violent Crime, testimony, April 15, 1981.

31. (a) "Objective Classification . . .," *Corrections Magazine*, June 1982. b) "Missing the Boat on Classification," *Corrections Magazine*, June 1982.

32. ". . . Resolving Grievances," *Corrections Magazine*, October 1982.

33. See U.S. Senate Committee on the Judiciary, "Reform of the Federal Criminal Laws," testimony of J. Cleary, Legal Aid and Defenders Association, September 20, 1979.

34. American Friends Service Committee, *Struggle for Justice*, New York: Hill & Wang, 1971.

35. Op. cit., note 22.

36. N. Morris and J. Jacobs, *Proposals for Prison Reform*, Public Affairs Committee, 1974.

37. Op. cit., note 11.

38. *Time*, January 24, 1983.

39. NAACP Legal Defense and Education Fund Inc., "Death Row, U.S.A," New York City, August 1984.

40. See Ernst van den Haag, *Punishing Criminals*, New York: Basic Books, 1975, and his testimony before House Subcommittee on Criminal Justice, "Sentencing in Capital Cases," July 19, 1978.

41. Op. cit., note 38.

42. Ibid.

43. Attorney General William French Smith, "Criminals Without Bars," *The New York Times*, March 6, 1983.

44. "Probation and Parole, 1982," Bureau of Justice Statistics, U.S. Department of Justice, September 1983.

45. "Abolishing Parole . . .," *Corrections Magazine*, June 1983.

46. Op. cit., note 3.

47. U.S. Senate Committee on the Judiciary, "Reform of the Federal Criminal Laws," General Accounting Office Report on Parole, October 1, 1981.

48. D. T. Stanley, *The Prisoners Among Us*, Washington, D.C.: Brookings Institution, 1976.

49. "Young Offenders in Carolina . . .," *The New York Times*, December 1982.

50. (a) "Florida Inmates Work . . .," *The New York Times*, February 20, 1983; (b) Telephone interviews, John Newman, Governor's office, August 29, 1984.

51. "Innovations to Unclog. . .," *The New York Times*, February 11, 1983.

52. "College Sentence. . .," *The New York Times*, February 13, 1983.

53. "Woman in Killing Sentenced . . .," *The New York Times*, February 5, 1983.

54. U.S. Senate Subcommittee on Administrative Practices . . ., "Trial Judges Conference," October 14, 1978: published by U.S. Senate Committee on the Judiciary, October 5, 1979.

55. "Fighting Crime," *Working Papers*, July–August 1982.

56. (a) ". . . Slave Bracelet," *The Washington Post*, March 8, 1983; (b) "Probation 'Bracelets': The Spiderman Solution," *Corrections Magazine*, June 1983.

57. Op. cit., note 34.

58. P.O. Box 40562, Washington, D.C. 20016.

59. *Jubilee*, Prison Fellowship newsletter, February 1983.

60. R. L. Woodson (ed.), *Youth Crime and Urban Policy*, Washington, D.C.: American Enterprise Institute for Public Policy Research, 1981.

61. "The Fiscal Crisis in Private Corrections," *Corrections Magazine*, December 1982.

62. (a) "At Talbert House . . .," ibid.; (b) Telephone interview, Janet Patterson, Talbert House, August 1984.

63. (a) "The Safer Foundation . . .," *Corrections Magazine*, June 1982; (b) Telephone interview, Gus Wilhelmy, founder, August 1984.

## Chapter Nine. Women and Violent Crime

1. C. R. Cloninger, Washington University School of Medicine, as reported in "Research Links Environment, Genetic . . .," *Montgomery Journal* (Maryland), March 10, 1983.

2. (a) C. Hibbert, *The Roots of Evil*, Boston: Little, Brown, 1963. (b) K. Seligman, *The History of Magic*, New York: Pantheon, 1948.

3. "Family Violence," Bureau of Justice Statistics, U.S. Department of Justice, April 1984.

4. A. Kaplan, "The Juvenile Offender Survey Project. A Study of 100 Dade County Juvenile Offenders," Miami: William and Tina Rosenberg Foundation, June 1980.

5. *1978 Annual Review of Child Abuse and Neglect Research*, U.S. Department of Health, Education and Welfare, 1979.

6. Summaries of "Current Research Grants," Center for Studies of Crime and Delinquency, National Institute of Mental Health, November 1982; January 1983.

7. Op. cit., notes 4 and 5.

8. (a) "Everything You Always Wanted to Know About Child Abuse," fact sheet, National Center on Child Abuse and Neglect, U.S. Department of Health and Human Service; (b) *Abused Children as Adult Parents*, study presented at National Conference for Family Violence Researchers, University of New Hampshire, Durham, July 21–24, 1981; (c) "Summary Report on the Relationship Between Child Abuse and Neglect and Later Socially Deviant Behavior," New York: Select Committee on Child Abuse, New York, March 1978.

9. C. M. Mouzakitis, "An Inquiry into the Problems of Child Abuse and Juvenile Delinquency," Graduate School of Social Work, University of Arkansas, Little Rock.

10. *National Analysis of Official Child Neglect and Abuse Reporting*, U.S. Department of Health and Human Services, November 1981.

11. "Child Abuse: A Ticking Bomb," *Changes*, vol. V, no. 3, 1982.

12. Op. cit., note 8a.

13. *Criminal Justice Research, Biennial Report, 1981–82*, National Institute of Justice, U.S. Department of Justice, 1982.

14. *Domestic Violence and the Police*, Police Foundation, Washington D.C., 1977, uses a formula that, when applied to figures in the April 1984 "Family Violence" survey (see note 3), gives the estimate I have used.

15. Op. cit., note 6.

16. Congresswoman Barbara Mikulski, "Family Violence—A National Issue," *Vermont Law Review*, Fall 1981.

17. (a) Op. cit., note 14; (b) Nancy Loving, *Responding to Spouse Abuse and Wife Beating*, Police Executive Research Forum, 1980.

18. "Family Violence," *Alcohol Health and Research World*, Fall 1979.

19. Reproduced for "Children of Alcoholics," ibid.

20. "Rise in Battered Women . . .," *The Washington Post*, January 16, 1983.

21. Op. cit., note 17.

22. *Congressional Record*, H366, February 4, 1981.

23. Op. cit., note 16.

24. Op. cit., note 5

25. (a) *Criminal Justice Research Annual Report*, National Institute of Justice, U.S. Department of Justice, November 1980; (b) *Resource Material: A Curriculum on Child Abuse and Neglect*, U.S. Department of Health, Education and Welfare, September 1979.

26. NCCAN, P.O. Box 1182, Washington, D.C. 20013.

27. *UCR*, FBI, September 1984.

28. A. Jones, *Women Who Kill*, New York: Holt, Rinehart and Winston, 1980.

29. Op. cit., note 2.

30. Op. cit., note 4.

31. U.S. Senate Subcommittee on Juvenile Justice, "Violent Juvenile Crime," testimony and submitted material by M. E. Wolfgang, July 9, 1981.

32. *UCR*, FBI, October 1982 and March 1981. Also see *UCR*, September 1984.

33. (a) "Prisoners in 1983," Bureau of Justice Statistics, U.S. Department of Justice, April

1984; (b) *Report to the Nation on Crime and Justice*, U.S. Department of Justice, October 1984; (c) *The Corrections Yearbook,* Criminal Justice Institute, 1982. I have depended on the three sources cited in this note for most of the statistics in this section.

34. Op. cit., note 14.

35. U.S. House Subcommittee on Courts . . ., testimony of Federal Bureau of Prisons Director, N. Carlson, October 10, 1979.

36. H. Bagdikian, "The Shame of the Prisons," *The Washington Post,* February 2, 1972.

37. Op. cit., note 35.

38. "The Sojourn Project," *Institutions Etc.,* December 1981, updated by telephone interviews with Sojourn staff and material from Sojourn.

39. (a) Data supplied by the FBI, September 1984; (b) Op. cit., note 27.

40. "Women on Patrol . . .," *Police Magazine,* prototype issue, 1977.

41. "Training Tailored for Women," *Police Magazine,* September 1980.

42. "The Blue and the Gray," *Police Magazine,* September 1982.

43. American Correctional Association, as of July 1983, per telephone interview, May 1984.

44. *Criminal Justice Research Annual Report,* National Institute of Justice, U.S. Department of Justice, November 1980.

## Chapter Ten. Victims and Restitution

1. Researcher interviews with victim, relatives, February, March 1983.

2. Researcher interviews with victim and relatives and written statement from victim, February, March 1983.

3. "Households Touched by Crime," Bureau of Justice Statistics, U.S. Department of Justice, May 1984. I have arrived at this figure by multiplying crimes against households, e.g. 23,621,000 for all crimes, by the average number of persons in a household (2.72), and have then adjusted it downward for those victimized more than once each year. No estimate can be exact, but this one I believe is as accurate as data on hand permit.

4. (a) "The Economic Cost of Crime to Victims," Bureau of Justice Statistics, U.S. Department of Justice, April 1984; (b) *Report to the Nation on Crime and Justice,* U.S. Department of Justice, October 1983;

5. Op. cit., note 3.

6. *Figgie,* Part I.

7. See also "The Severity of Crime," Bureau of Justice Statistics, U.S. Department of Justice, January 1984.

8. President's Task Force on Victims of Crime, Final Report, December 1982.

9. *Attorney General's Task Force on Violent Crime, Final Report,* U.S. Department of Justice, August 17, 1981.

10. See "Victims and Victim Assistance," Bureau of Justice Statistics, U.S. Department of Justice, May 1983.

11. Op. cit., note 8.

12. (a) Op. cit., note 9; (b) "Paying the Price of Crime," *Police Magazine,* July 1979; (c) U.S. House Subcommittee on Criminal Justice, hearings, "Victims of Crime Compensation," March 29, April 22, 25, 27, May 5, 1977; "Compensating Crime Victims," February 28, April 3, 1979. These are particularly rich in case studies of the injustices against victims.

13. Op. cit., note 10.

14. Op. cit., note 8.

15. Attorney General William French Smith, testimony, U.S. Senate Committee on the Judiciary, September 28, 1981.

16. *The Corrections Yearbook,* Pound Ridge, N.Y: Criminal Justice Institute, 1982.

17. "The Work Ethic . . .," *Corrections Magazine,* October 1982.

18. U.S. Senate Subcommittee on Administrative Practices . . ., "Trial Judges Conference," October 14, 1978: published by U.S. Senate Committe on the Judiciary, October 5, 1979.

19. "Criminal Punishment That Pays Off," *Reader's Digest,* July 1980.

20. Op. cit., note 18, statement by Judge Albert Kramer.

21. "The Justice Department's Fight Against Youth Crime," Committee Print, R. Woodson, House Subcommittee on Crime, December 1978.

22. Op. cit., note 9.

23. "$5 Million Awarded . . .," *The Washington Post,* March 2, 1983.

24. "Family of Slain Teller Sues . . .," *The Washington Post,* March 9, 1983.

25. (a)"Legal Group Demands Removal of D.C. Superior Court Judge," *Washington Times,* January 14, 1983.

26. Paul Kamenor, Washington Legal Foundation, August 28, 1984.

27. *Catalyst,* National Crime Prevention Council, February 1983.

## Chapter Eleven. Volunteers

1. White House, Private Sector Initiative Office, May 7, 1984.

2. (a) National Sheriffs' Association, May 10, 1984; (b) "Crime Watch Programs: Making a Difference," *Catalyst,* National Crime Prevention Council, May 1983. This excellent periodical summarizes developments in crime watches and other volunteer anticrime enterprises.

3. (a) *Figgie, Part IV;* (b) Telephone interview, Commander James Humphrey, Detroit Police Department, August 28, 1984.

4. (a) *Criminal Justice Research, Biennial Report to the National Justice Institute 1980–81,* U.S. Department of Justice, 1982; (b) Telephone interview, Captain Arthur Williams, Jr., Hartford Police Department, August 28, 1984; (c) UCR Preliminary Annual Release, FBI, April 19, 1984.

5. (a) *New York City Partnership Task Force for Public Safety, Annual Report,* December 1981; (b) Telephone interviews, New York City law enforcement officials, August 1984.

6. (a) *UCR* for 1983, FBI, September 1984; (b) "New York Police Say Crime Rate Fell . . .," *The New York Times,* March 11, 1983.

7. "Senior Citizens Against Crime," National Crime Prevention Council, (undated), and see also "How Your Organization Can Take Action Against Crime," available from the same group.

8. Op. cit., note 3.

9. "State's Serious Crime . . .," *Baltimore News-American,* March 17, 1983; (b) Op. cit., note 6a.

10. See FBI Director William Webster, press statement, April 19, 1984.

11. Partnership II Conference, Houston, Texas, December 1982, address by Houston Police Chief Lee Brown.

12. Op. cit., note 3.

13. New York State Senator John Calandra, press release, March 2, 1983.

14. "Police Volunteers," *Police Magazine,* prototype issue, 1977; (b) Dr. Lawrence Sherman, Police Foundation, feels even 200,000 as a figure for formally affiliated police auxiliaries

is "substantially too high." He agrees to the need for more of them; telephone interview, August 29, 1984.

15. Op. cit., note 3.

16. "Let's Try a Police Corps," *The New York Times*, January 1983.

17. "Does New York Need the Guardian Angels," *Police Magazine*, May 1981.

18. (a) *Figgie*, Part III; (b) " 'Angels' to Halt Patrols," *The Washington Post*, August 28, 1984.

19. U.S. Senate Subcommittee on Juvenile Justice, "Violent Juvenile Crime," testimony of C. Sliwa, July 9, 1981.

20. A. Kaplan, "The Juvenile Offender Survey Project. A Study of 100 Dade County Juvenile Offenders," Miami: William and Tina Rosenberg Foundation, June 1980.

21. P. W. Greenwood, *Selective Incapacitation*, Santa Monica, California: Rand Corporation, August 1982.

22. "Consorting with the Enemy," *Police Magazine*, September 1980.

23. "Improving Corrections," Law Enforcement Assistance Administration, U.S. Department of Justice, undated.

24. New Orleans Mayor Ernest Morial, address, Urban Crime Panel, U.S. Conference of Mayors, June 21, 1982.

25. Ad Hoc Committee for Juvenile Justice, report, Washington, D.C., May 1982.

26. "Help for Mothers Who Abuse Their Children," *The New York Times*, March 3, 1982.

27. Op. cit., note 5.

28. "Any Volunteers?" *Police Magazine*, March 1981.

29. "The Siren's Song," *Police Magazine*, May 1981.

30. See *Working with Police: A Practical Guide for Battered Women's Advocates*, Washington, D.C.: Police Executive Research Forum, 1982.

31. Op. cit., note 7.

32. "Minorities' Self-Help," *The New York Times*, September 2, 1980.

33. This appealing and useful material is available from the National Crime Prevention Council, 805 15th Street, NW, Washington, D.C. 20005; 202-393-7141.

34. "Fund Raising in the Private Sector," National Committee for Prevention of Child Abuse, 1980.

35. U.S. House Subcommittee on Civil and Constitutional Rights, "FBI Authorization," testimony of W. C. McCrone, March 24, 1981.

36. "Hostage Negotiators," *Police Magazine*, January 1983.

37. "Resource Management," *National Training Institute Manual*, National Youth Work Alliance, November 1982.

## Chapter Twelve. Preventions and Costs

1. "Households Touched by Crime, 1983," Bureau of Justice Statistics, U.S. Department of Justice, May 1984.

2. "The Economic Cost of Crime to Victims," Bureau of Justice Statistics, U.S. Department of Justice, April 1984.

3. National Prevention Council. I have drawn heavily in this chapter from these leaflets, mentioned earlier. They include concise and easily understood data on how to crimeproof homes, neighborhoods, and businesses; how to organize against crime; how senior citizens can participate in the crime fight; how to avoid being conned, sexually attacked, or victimized by arson; how to stave off street assaults; and other subjects. In addition, I have drawn from the Figgie

reports previously cited. Much of the information, however, comes from conversations with other businessmen, with law-enforcement officials, and in a few cases, researcher interviews with convicted criminals.

4. (a) *Figgie,* Part IV; (b) Telephone interview, Leland Wood, Texas Crime Prevention Institute, August 29, 1984; (c) Telephone inteview, staff, chief's office, Garland Police Department, August 29, 1984.

5. (a) *Report to the Nation on Crime and Justice,* U.S. Department of Justice, October 1983; (b) "Economic Impact," *Reports of the National Juvenile Justice Assessment Centers,* U.S. Department of Justice, April 1980.

6. *Time to Build?* New York: Edna McConnell Clark Foundation, 1984.

7. *The Corrections Handbook,* Criminal Justice Institute, 1982.

8. September 13, 1982.

9. A. Blumstein, "Planning Models for Analytical Evaluation," in *Handbook of Criminal Justice Evaluation,* Beverly Hills, Calif: Sage Publications, 1981.

10. Op. cit., note 5a, from which many of these cost figures are drawn, broken down and updated for late 1984.

11. "Hard Times for Police Pensions," *Police Magazine,* November 1982.

12. Op. cit., note 1.

13. "A National Assessment of Serious Juvenile Crime," *Reports of the National Juvenile Justice Assessment Centers,* U.S. Department of Justice, April 1980, updated for inflation, 1984.

14. (a) Op. cit., note 5a; (b) C. P. Simon and A. D. Witte, "Beating the System: The Underground Economy," Boston: Auburn House Publishing, 1982.

15. Chief Justice Warren Burger, address, George Washington University School of Law, Washington, D.C., May 24, 1981. He estimates the figure at $100 billion a year.

16. Jay Robert Nash, *Murder, America,* New York: Simon and Schuster, 1980.

# Selected Bibliography

*Alcohol Health and Research World*. Vol. 4. Washington, D.C.: U.S. Department of Health and Human Services, Fall 1979.

Alfaro, J. D. *Summary Report on the Relationship Between Child Abuse and Neglect and Later Socially Deviant Behavior*. New York: Select Commitee on Child Abuse, March 1978.

American Broadcasting Companies Social Research Unit and the Broadcast Standards and Practices Department. *A Research Perspective on Television and Violence*. New York: American Broadcasting Companies, Inc., 1983.

American Friends Service Committee. *Struggle for Justice—A Report on Crime and Punishment in America*. New York: Hill and Wang, 1971.

Anderson, J. "Fighting Juvenile Crime: Success and Failure." *The Washington Post*, January 7, 1979.

*Attorney General's Task Force on Violent Crime, Final Report*. Washington, D.C.: U.S. Department of Justice, August 1981.

Bagdikian, B. "The Shame of the Prisons." *The Washington Post*, January 30–February 6, 1972.

Beck, J. L. "Employment, Community Treatment Center Placement, and Recidivism: A Study of Released Federal Offenders." *Federal Probation Quarterly*, December 1981.

Blumstein, A. "On the Racial Disproportionality of United States' Prison Populations." *The Journal of Criminal Law & Criminology*, Vol. 73 1982.

——, and J. Cohen. "Estimation of Individual Crime Rates from Arrest Records," The Journal of Criminal Law & Criminology. vol. 70, 1979.

——, J. Cohen, and H.D. Miller. "Crime, Punishment, & Demographics." *American Demographics*, October 1980.

——, J. Cohen, and H. D. Miller. "Demographically Disaggregated Projections of Prison Populations." *Research in Public Policy Analyses*, vol. I, 1981.

——, J. Cohen, and D. Nagin, eds. *Deterrence and Incapacitation: Estimating the*

*Effects of Criminal Sanctions on Crime Rates.* Washington, D.C.: National Academy of Sciences, 1978.

———, and E. Graddy. "Prevalence and Recidivism in Index Arrests: A Feedback Model." *Law & Society Review,* vol. 16, 1981–82.

———, and S. Moitra. "The Identification of 'Career Criminals' from 'Chronic Offenders' in a Cohort." *Law & Policy Quarterly,* vol. 2, July 1980.

———, and D. Nagin. "On the Optimum Use of Incarceration for Crime Control." *Operations Research,* vol. 26, 1978.

Bradbury, K. L., A. Downs, and K. A. Small. *Urban Decline and the Future of American Cities.* The Brookings Institution, Washington, D.C., 1982.

Brown, M.R., ed. *American Violence.* Englewood Cliffs, N.J.: Prentice-Hall, Inc., 1970.

Bureau of Justice Statistics. "The American Response to Crime." *Bulletin,* Washington, D.C.: U.S. Department of Justice, December 1983.

———. "Capital Punishment 1983." Bulletin: Washington, D.C.: U.S. Department of Justice, July 1984.

———. "Career Patterns in Crime." *Special Report,* Washington, D.C.: U.S. Department of Justice, June 1983.

———. "Crime and the Elderly." *Bulletin,* Washington, D.C.: U.S. Department of Justice, December 1981.

———. "Criminal Victimization in the U.S." *Technical Report,* Washington, D.C.: U.S. Department of Justice, July 1982.

———. "Death Row Prisoners 1981." *Bulletin,* Washington, D.C.: U.S. Department of Justice, July 1982.

———. "The Economic Cost of Crime to Victims." *Special Report,* Washington, D.C.: U.S. Department of Justice, April 1984.

———. "Electronic Fund Transfer and Crime." *Special Report,* Washington, D.C.: U.S. Department of Justice, February 1984.

———. "Family Violence." *Special Report,* Washington, D.C.: U.S. Department of Justice, April 1984.

———. "Federal Drug Law Violators." Washington, D.C.: U.S. Department of Justice, February 1984.

———. "Habeas Corpus." *Special Report,* Washington, D.C.: U.S. Department of Justice, March 1984.

———. "Households Touched by Crime, 1981." *Bulletin,* Washington, D.C.: U.S. Department of Justice, September 1982.

———. "Households Touched by Crime, 1982." *Bulletin,* Washington, D.C.: U.S. Department of Justice, June 1983.

———. "Households Touched by Crime, 1983." *Bulletin,* Washington, D.C.: U.S. Department of Justice, May 1984.

———. "Measuring Crime." *Bulletin,* Washington, D.C.: U.S. Department of Justice, February 1981.

———. "The Prevalence of Crime." *Bulletin,* Washington, D.C.: U.S. Department of Justice, March 1981.

———. "Prisoners at Midyear 1982." *Bulletin,* Washington, D.C.: U.S. Department of Justice, October/November 1982.

———. "Prisoners at Midyear 1983." *Bulletin,* Washington, D.C.: U.S. Department of Justice, October 1983.

———. "Prisoners in 1983." *Bulletin,* Washington, D.C.: U.S. Department of Justice, April 1984.

———. "Prisoners 1925—81." *Bulletin,* Washington, D.C.: U.S. Department of Justice, December 1982.

———. "Prisons and Prisoners." *Bulletin,* Washington, D.C.: U.S. Department of Justice, January 1982.

———. "Probation and Parole 1982." *Bulletin,* Washington, D.C.: U.S. Department of Justice, September 1983.

———. *Report to the Nation on Crime and Justice—The Data.* Washington, D.C.: U.S. Department of Justice, October 1983.

———. "Setting Prison Terms." *Bulletin,* Washington, D.C.: U.S. Department of Justice, August 1983.

———. "The Severity of Crime." *Bulletin,* Washington, D.C.: U.S. Department of Justice, January 1984.

———. "State Court Caseload Statistics." *Special Report,* Washington, D.C.: U.S. Department of Justice, February 1983.

———. "Tracking Offenders." *Bulletin,* Washington, D.C.: U.S. Department of Justice, November 1983.

———. "Victim and Witness Assistance." *Bulletin,* Washington, D.C.: U.S. Department of Justice, May 1983.

———. "Victims of Crime." *Bulletin,* Washington, D.C.: U.S. Department of Justice, November 1981.

———. "Violent Crime by Strangers." *Bulletin,* Washington, D.C.: U.S. Department of Justice, April 1982.

———. *Violent Crime in the United States.* NCJ-79741, Washington, D.C.: U.S. Department of Justice, September 1981.

Burger, W. E., Chief Justice of the United States. Remarks at the Commencement Exercises for George Washington University School of Law. Washington, D.C.: May 24, 1981.

CBS News. "CBS Reports," *Murder Teenage Style.* Transcript, September 3, 1981.

———. "60 Minutes," *Come On, He's Only a Kid.* Transcript, October 25, 1981.

———. "60 Minutes," "Cruel and Unusual. . . ?" Transcript, May 17, 1981.

Camp, G., and C. Camp. *The Corrections Yearbook.* Pound Ridge, N.Y.: Criminal Justice Institute, 1982 and 1984.

Carlson, K. "Mandatory Sentencing: The Experience of Two States," *Policy Briefs.* National Institute of Justice, U.S. Department of Justice, May 1982.

Carlson, N. A., Director, Federal Bureau of Prisons. Statement before the Attorney General's Task Force on Violent Crime. Washington, D.C.: April 15, 1981.

———. Statement before the President's Task Force on Victims of Crime. Washington, D.C.: October 13, 1982.

———. Testimony before the U.S. House of Representatives Committee on the Judiciary. Washington, D.C.: October 9, 1979.

———. Testimony before the U.S. House of Representatives Committee on the Judiciary concerning Female Offender Program—Bureau of Prisons. Washington, D.C.: October 10, 1979.

———. Speech at the Centennial, Iowa Sheriffs Association. Sioux City, Iowa, December 7, 1982.

*Catalyst*. Crime Prevention Council, Washington, D.C.: 1982–1984.

Chaiken, J. M., and M. R. Chaiken. *Varieties of Criminal Behavior*. Santa Monica, California: The Rand Corporation, 1982.

*Change: A Juvenile Justice Quarterly*. Alexandria, Virginia: National Office for Social Responsibility, 1981—1982.

Churchill, A. *A Pictorial History of American Crime, 1849—1929*. New York: Holt, Rinehart and Winston, Inc. 1964.

Clark, R. *Crime in America*. New York: Simon and Schuster, 1970.

Cohen, J. *The Incapacitative Effect of Imprisonment: A Critical Review of the Literature*. Paper commissioned by the National Institute of Mental Health, Center for Studies of Crime and Delinquency, undated.

Coleman, M., and Milloy, C. "Lorton: D.C.'s Other Neighborhood." *The Washington Post*, February 13–17, 1983.

Collins, G. "The Violent Child: Some Patterns Emerge." *The New York Times*, September 27, 1982.

"Continuation of the Office of Juvenile Justice and Delinquency Prevention." Ad Hoc Coalition for Juvenile Justice, Washington, D.C.: May 1982.

*Corrections Magazine*. New York: September 1976 to June 1983.

Cory, B., and S. Gettinger. *Time to Build? The Realities of Prison Construction*. New York: Edna McConnell Clark Foundation, 1984.

Couper, D.C. *How to Rate Your Local Police*. Washington, D.C.: Police Executive Research Forum, 1982.

*Court Watch Manual: A Citizen's Guide to Judicial Accountability* Washington, D.C.: Washington Legal Foundation, 1983.

Creative Alternatives to Prison, and The Woodrow Wilson International Center for Scholars. *Summary of Trial Lawyers' Conference*. Playboy Foundation, April 1981.

Curd, M. C. *The Street Law Diversion Program: Teaching Practical Law to Youth Involved in the Juvenile Justice System*. Washington, D.C.: Phi Alpha Delta Law Fraternity, International Juvenile Justice Office, 1982.

Downs, A. *Neighborhoods and Urban Development*. Washington, D. C.: The Brookings Institution, 1981.

"An Eye for an Eye," *Time*, January 24, 1983.

Federal Bureau of Investigation. *Analysis of Violent Crime in the United States*. Report prepared for the Uniform Crime Reporting Program. Washington, D.C.: U.S. Department of Justice, March 1981.

———. *Crime Indicators System: First Semiannual Briefing on Crime*. A report prepared for the FBI Director under the Uniform Crime Reporting Program. Washington, D.C.: U.S. Department of Justice, April 1982.

———. *Crime Indicators System: Second Semiannual Briefing on Crime*. A report prepared for the FBI Director under the Uniform Crime Reporting Program. Washington, D.C.: U.S. Department of Justice, October 1982.

————. "1983 Preliminary Annual Release," *Uniform Crime Reports*, Washington, D.C.: U.S. Department of Justice, September 1984.

Ferry, J., and M. Kravitz. *Publications of the National Institute of Law Enforcement and Criminal Justice: 1979 Supplement*. Washington, D.C.: U.S. Department of Justice, February 1979.

*The Figgie Report on Fear of Crime. Part I: The General Public*. Conducted by Research & Forecasts, Inc. Figgie International, Inc., Willoughby, Ohio, 1980.

*The Figgie Report on Fear of Crime. Part II: The Corporate Response to Fear of Crime*. Conducted by Research & Forecasts, Inc. Figgie International, Inc., Willoughby, Ohio, 1982.

*The Figgie Report on Fear of Crime. Part III: A Fourteen-City Profile*. Conducted by Research & Forecasts, Inc. Figgie International, Inc., Willoughby, Ohio, 1982.

*The Figgie Report on Fear of Crime, Part IV: Reducing Crime in America—Successful Community Efforts*. Conducted by Research & Forecasts, Inc. Figgie International, Inc., Willoughby, Ohio, 1983.

Frankel, M. E. *Criminal Sentences: Law Without Order*. New York: Hill and Wang, 1972.

Fyfe, J. J. ed. *Readings on Police Use of Deadly Force*. Washington, D.C.: Police Foundation, 1982.

Gelles, R. J. *The Violent Home: A Study of Physical Aggression between Husbands and Wives*. Beverly Hills, Inc., California: Sage Publications, Inc., 1972.

Giuliani, R. W., Associate Attorney General. "A New Partnership Against Crime." Keynote Speech before the 11th Congress of the American Correctional Association. Miami Beach, August 16, 1981.

Graham, H. D., and T. R. Gurr, eds. *The History of Violence in America: Historical and Comparative Perspectives*. Report submitted to the National Commission on the Causes and Prevention of Violence. New York: Frederick A. Praeger, 1969.

Greenwood, P. W., and A. Abrahamse. *Selective Incapacitation*. Santa Monica, California: The Rand Corporation, 1982.

Hamparian, D. M., L. K. Estep, S. M. Muntean, R. R. Priestino, R. G. Swisher, P. L. Wallace, and J. L. White. *Major Issues in Juvenile Justice Information and Training; Youth in Adult Courts: Between Two Worlds*. Columbus, Ohio: Academy for Contemporary Problems, 1982.

Hibbert, C. *The Roots of Evil*. Boston: Little, Brown and Co., 1963.

*Institutions, Etc.*, Alexandria, Virginia, November 1981 to December 1982.

Jones, A. *Women Who Kill*. New York: Holt, Rinehart and Winston, 1980.

"Justice on Trial." *Newsweek*, March 8, 1971.

Ketterman, T., V. Green, and M. Kravitz. *Publications of the National Institute of Justice: 1980 Supplement*. Washington, D.C.: U.S. Department of Justice, December 1981.

Klein, C., D. M. Horton, and M. Kravitz. *Bibliographies in Criminal Justice: A Selected Bibliography*. Washington, D.C.: U.S. Department of Justice, December 1979.

Klein, M. W., and K. S. Teilmann, eds. *Handbook of Criminal Justice Evaluation*. Beverly Hills, California: Sage Publications, undated.

Law Enforcement Assistance Administration. *The Cost of Negligence: Losses from Preventable Household Burglaries.* Washington, D.C.: U.S. Department of Justice, 1979.

———. *Improving Corrections.* Washington, D.C.: U.S. Department of Justice, undated.

Ledger, M. "To Watch a Thief." *Pennsylvania Gazette,* April 1983.

Lewis, D. C., S. S. Shanok, J. H. Pincus, and G .H. Glasser. *Violent Juvenile Delinquents; Psychiatric, Neurological, Psychological and Abuse Factors.* Yale University Child Study Center, undated.

Loving, N. *Responding to Spouse Abuse & Wife Beating: A Guide for Police.* Washington, D.C.: Police Executive Research Forum, 1980.

———. *Spouse Abuse: A Curriculum Guide for Police Trainers.* Washington, D.C.: Police Executive Research Forum, 1981.

———. *Working with Police: A Practical Guide for Battered Women's Advocates.* Washington, D.C.: Police Executive Research Forum, 1982.

McDermott, M.J. *Facts About Violent Juvenile Crime.* Hackensack, New Jersey: National Council on Crime and Delinquency, July 1982.

Martindale, D. "Criminal Punishment That Pays Off." *Reader's Digest,* July 1980.

"A Message from the Siskiyous." *The Progressive,* February 18, 1983.

Mikulski, B. "Family Violence—A National Issue," *Vermont Law Review,* vol. 6, Fall 1981.

Miller, D. L., and C. Challas. *Abused Children as Adult Parents: A Twenty-Five Year Longitudinal Study.* San Francisco: Institute for Scientific Analysis, July 1981.

Miller, J. G. *The Serious Juvenile Offender.* Proceedings of a National Symposium held by the Office of Juvenile Justice and Delinquency Prevention, September 19–20, 1977, in Minneapolis, Minn. Washington, D.C.: U.S. Department of Justice, undated.

———. "The Revolution in Juvenile Justice: From Rhetoric to Rhetoric." In *The Future of Childhood and Juvenile Justice,* edited by L. T. Empey. Charlottesville: University Press of Virginia, 1979.

Miller, W. B. *Violence by Youth Gangs and Youth Groups as a Crime Problem in Major American Cities.* National Institute for Juvenile Justice and Delinquency Prevention, Washington, D.C.: U.S. Department of Justice, December 1975.

Mitford, J. *Kind and Usual Punishment—The Prison Business.* New York: Random House, 1971.

Morris, N., and J. Jacobs. *Proposals for Prison Reform.* New York: Public Affairs Committee, Inc., 1974.

Mulvihill, D. J. *Crimes of Violence.* vol. 12. Washington, D.C.: U.S. Government Printing Office, 1969.

Murray, R. F. *Fund Raising in the Private Sector.* Chicago: National Committee for Prevention of Child Abuse, 1980.

Nagler, M. N. *America Without Violence—Why Violence Persists and How You Can Stop It.* Covelo, California: Island Press, 1982.

Nash, J. R. *Murder, America—Homicide in the United States from the Revolution to the Present.* New York: Simon and Schuster, 1980.

National Center on Child Abuse and Neglect. "Everything You Always Wanted to

Know about Child Abuse and Neglect and Asked!" Washington, D.C.: U.S.
    Department of Justice, undated.
National Crime Prevention Council. *Arson—How Not to Get Burned.* Washington,
    D.C.: U.S. Department of Justice, undated.
———. *Got a Minute? You Could Stop a Crime.* Washington, D.C.: U.S. Depart-
    ment of Justice, undated.
———. *How Not to Get Conned.* Washington, D.C.: U.S. Department of Justice,
    undated.
———. *How to Be "Streetwise"—And Safe.* Washington, D.C.: U.S. Department of
    Justice, undated.
———. *How to Crimeproof Your Business.* Washington, D.C.: U.S. Department of
    Justice, undated.
———. *How to Crimeproof Your Home.* Washington, D.C.: U.S. Department of
    Justice, undated.
———. *How to Protect Your Neighborhood.* Washington, D.C.: U.S. Department of
    Justice, undated.
———. *How Your Organization Can Take Action Against Crime.* Washington, D.C.:
    U.S. Department of Justice, undated.
———. *Senior Citizens Against Crime.* Washington, D.C.: U.S. Department of Jus-
    tice, undated.
———. *Take a Bite Out of Crime—Senior Citizens Against Crime.* Washington, D.C.:
    U.S. Department of Justice, undated.
National Institute of Justice. *Criminal Justice Research Annual Report.* Washington,
    D.C.: U.S. Department of Justice, November 1980.
———. *Criminal Justice Research: Biennial Report by the National Institute of Justice
    for Fiscal Years 1980 and 1981.* Washington, D.C.: U.S. Department of Jus-
    tice, April 1982.
———. *The D.C. Pre-trial Services Agency—An Exemplary Project.* Washington, D.C.:
    U.S. Department of Justice, May 1981.
———. *The Technology Assessment Program: Findings from a Decade of Technological
    Research.* Washington, D.C.: U.S. Department of Justice, July 1981.
National Insitute of Law Enforcement and Criminal Justice. *Publications of the Na-
    tional Institute of Law Enforcement and Criminal Justice.* Washington, D.C.:
    U.S. Department of Justice, February 1978.
National Institute of Mental Health. *Television and Behavior.* Washington, D.C.: U.S.
    Department of Health and Human Services, 1982.
National Institute of Mental Health, Center for Studies of Crime and Delinquency.
    "Current Research Grants." Washington, D.C.: January 1983.
———. "Recent and Current Grants in Domestic Violence," November 1982.
National Juvenile Justice Clearinghouse. *Facts About Youth and Delinquency: A Cit-
    izen's Guide to Juvenile Justice.* Washington, D.C.: U.S. Department of Jus-
    tice, November 1982.
National Training Institute on Serious and Violent Juvenile Offenders. *Serious and
    Violent Juvenile Offenders: National Training Institute Manual II.* Washington,
    D.C.: National Youth Work Alliance, 1983.
Newman, G.R., ed. "Crime and Justice in America." *The Annals of the American*

*Academy of Political and Social Science.* Philadelphia, 1976.

Office of Human Development Services, Children's Bureau. *Executive Summary: National Study of the Incidence and Severity of Child Abuse and Neglect.* Washington, D.C.: U.S. Department of Health and Human Services, undated.

————. *National Analysis of Official Child Neglect and Abuse Reporting (1978).* Washington, D.C.: U.S. Department of Health and Human Services, September 1980.

————. *National Analysis of Official Child Neglect and Abuse Reporting (1979).* Washington, D.C.: U.S. Department of Health and Human Services, November 1981.

————. *1978 Annual Review of Child Abuse and Neglect Research.* Washington, D.C.: U.S. Department of Health, Education and Welfare, September 1978.

————. *Resource Materials: A Curriculum on Child Abuse and Neglect.* Washington, D.C.: U.S. Department of Health and Human Services, September 1979.

Office of Justice Assistance, Research, and Statistics. "Justice Assistance News." Washington, D.C.: U.S. Department of Justice, November 1982.

*Police Magazine.* New York: July 1979 to January 1983.

*Policy Positions* 1982–83. Washington D.C.: National Governors' Association, 1982.

*President's Task Force on Victims of Crime, Final Report.* Washington, D.C.: The White House, December 1982.

Raspberry, W. "White Crime, Black Crime." *The Washington Post,* March 31, 1980.

Ray, M. W., R. N. Brenner, and M. Kravitz. *Firearm Use in Violent Crime: A Selected Bibliography.* Washington, D.C.: U.S. Department of Justice, September 1978.

Reagan, Ronald, President. Address to the International Association of Chiefs of Police. New Orleans, September 28, 1981.

*Reports of the National Juvenile Justice Assessment Centers.* "A National Assessment of Case Disposition and Classification in the Juvenile Justice System: Inconsistent Labeling." Washington, D.C.: U.S. Department of Justice, April 1980.

*Reports of the National Juvenile Justice Assessment Centers.* "A National Assessment of Serious Juvenile Crime and the Juvenile Justice System: The Need for a Rational Response. Volume I: Summary." Washington, D.C.: U.S. Department of Justice, April 1980.

*Reports of the National Juvenile Justice Assessment Centers.* "A National Assessment of Serious Juvenile Crime and the Juvenile Justice System: The Need for a Rational Response. Volume II: Definition, Characteristics of Incidents and Individuals, and Relationship to Substance Abuse." Washington, D.C.: U.S. Department of Justice, April 1980.

*Reports of the National Juvenile Justice Assessment Centers.* "A National Assessment of Serious Juvenile Crime and the Juvenile Justice System: The Need for a Rational Response. Volume III: Legislation, Jurisdiction, Program Interventions, and Confidentiality of Juvenile Records." Washington, D.C.: U.S. Department of Justice, April 1980.

*Reports of the National Juvenile Justice Assessment Centers.* "A National Assessment of Serious Juvenile Crime and the Juvenile Justice System: The Need for a

Rational Response. Volume IV: Economic Impact." Washington, D.C.: U.S. Department of Justice, April 1980.

*Reports of the National Juvenile Justice Assessment Centers.* "A Preliminary National Assessment of the Numbers and Characteristics of Juveniles Processed in the Juvenile Justice System." Washington, D.C.: U.S. Department of Justice, June 1981.

*Reports of the National Juvenile Justice Assessment Centers.* "The Prevention of Serious Delinquency: What to Do?" Washington, D.C.: U.S. Department of Justice, December 1981.

Rhodes, A. L., and A. L. Reiss, Jr. "The 'Religious Factor' and Delinquent Behavior." *Journal of Research in Crime and Delinquency,* January 1970.

Roy, M., ed. *Battered Women—A Psychosociological Study of Domestic Violence.* New York: Van Nostrand Reinhold Co., 1977.

*Second Annual Report of the Justice System Improvement Act Agencies.* Washington, D.C.: U.S. Department of Justice, undated.

Sedgwick, J. L. *Deterring Criminals: Policy Making and the American Political Tradition.* Washington, D.C.: American Enterprise Institute for Public Policy Research, 1980.

Seligmann, B. *The History of Magic.* New York: Pantheon Books, Inc., 1948.

Shields, N. M., and C. R. Hanneke. *Violent Husbands: Patterns of Individual Violence.* St. Louis: Policy Research and Planning Group, Inc., undated.

Silberman, C. E. *Criminal Violence, Criminal Justice.* New York: Random House, 1978.

Smith, W. F., Attorney General of the United States. Address before the House of Delegates American Bar Association. San Francisco, August 10, 1982.

———. Address Before the National District Attorneys Association. Lake Buena Vista, Florida, July 23, 1981.

———. Remarks at the Law Day Banquet of University of South Carolina School of Law. Columbia, April 2, 1982.

———. Remarks Before the National Conference of U.S. Attorneys. Washington, D.C., November 16, 1981.

———. Statement on S. 1630 Before the Committee on the Judiciary, United States Senate. Washington, D.C., September 28, 1981.

Sojourn Project. Phoenix Institute, Salt Lake City, undated.

Stanley, D. T. *Prisoners Among Us: The Problems of Parole.* Washington, D.C.: The Brookings Institution, 1976.

Stapleton, W. V., and J. A. Needle. *Response Strategies to Youth Gang Activity.* Prepared by the American Justice Institute for the National Juvenile Justice System Assessment Center. American Justice Institute, Sacramento, California, September 1982.

Steinmetz, S. K., and M. A. Straus, eds. *Violence in the Family.* New York: Dodd, Mead & Company, 1974.

Straus, M. A., R. J. Gelles, and S. K. Steinmetz. *Behind Closed Doors—Violence in the American Family.* Garden City, New York: Anchor Books, Doubleday & Company, 1980.

*Survey of Police Operational and Administrative Practices—1981.* Police Foundation and Police Executive Research Forum. Washington, D.C., 1981.

U.S. House of Representatives, Committee on the Judiciary. *Report to Accompany H. R. 6915; Criminal Code Revision Act of 1980.* 96th Congress, September 25, 1980.

U.S. House of Representatives, Subcommittee on Civil and Constitutional Rights. *Hearings on FBI Authorization.* 97th Congress, March 19, 24, 25; April 2, 8, 1981.

U.S. House of Representatives, Subcommittee on Courts, Civil Liberties and the Administration of Justice. *Hearing on the Bureau of Prisons Youth and Juvenile Policies.* 95th Congress, October 28, 1978.

———. *Hearing on the Bureau of Prisons Pre-trial Detention Program.* 95th Congress, May 4, 5, 1978.

———. *Hearings on General Oversight on Justice Related Agencies.* 96th Congress, April 10, May 2, 16, 1979.

———. *Oversight Hearing on the Bureau of Prisons and the U.S. Parole Commission.* 97th Congress, March 5, 1981.

U.S. House of Representatives, Subcommittee on Crime. *Committee Print on the Justice Department's Fight Against Youth Crime: A Review of the Office of Juvenile Justice and Delinquency Prevention of the Law Enforcement Assistance Administration.* 95th Congress, December 1978.

———. *Hearing on Increasing Violence Against Minorities.* 96th Congress, December 9, 1980.

———. *Hearings on Police and the Use of Deadly Force.* 96th Congress, March 21, 22, 1980.

U.S. House of Representatives, Subcommittee on Criminal Justice. *Hearing on the Victims of Crime Compensation Legislation.* 95th Congress, March 29; April 22, 25, 27; and May 5, 1977.

———. *Hearings on Compensating Crime Victims.* 96th Congress, February 28, April 3, 1979.

———. *Hearings on Sentencing in Capital Cases.* 95th Congress, July 19, 1978.

"U.S. Prisons: Schools for Crime." *Time,* January 18, 1971.

U.S. Senate, Committee on the Judiciary. *Hearings on the Reform of the Federal Criminal Laws.* Part XIV, 96th Congress, September 11, 13, 18, 20; October 5, 1979.

———. *Hearings on the Reform of the Federal Criminal Laws.* Part XV, 96th Congress, September 11, 13, 18, 20, 25; October 5, 1979.

———. *Hearings on the Reform of the Federal Criminal Laws.* Part XVI, 97th Congress, September 28, October 1, 1981.

U.S. Senate, Subcommittee on Administrative Practice and Procedure. *Committee Print on the Trial Judges' Conference.* 95th Congress, October 14, 1978.

U.S. Senate, Subcommittee on Juvenile Justice. *Hearing on Violent Juvenile Crime.* 97th Congress, July 9, 1981.

———. *Hearings on Career Criminal Life Sentence Act of 1981.* 97th Congress, October 26, and December 10, 1981.

van den Haag, E. *Punishing Criminals.* New York: Basic Books, 1975.

Webster, W. H., Director, Federal Bureau of Investigation. Remarks Before FBINA

Section IV Retraining Session. Niagara Falls, June 29, 1982.

———. Remarks Before the International Society of Barristers. Phoenix, March 9, 1982.

———. Remarks Before Metro Crime Alert. Baltimore, May 11, 1982.

———. Speech Before the Society of Former Special Agents. Las Vegas, October 30, 1982.

"What Are Prisons For?" *Time*, September 13, 1982.

Wilt, G. M., J. D. Bannon, R. K. Breedlove, D. M. Sandker, R. K. Sawtell, S. Michaelson, and P. Fox. *Domestic Violence and the Police: Studies in Detroit and Kansas City*. Washington, D.C.: Police Foundation, 1977.

Wolfgang, M. E. "Crime in a Birth Cohort." *Proceedings of the American Philosophical Society*, vol. 117, no. 5, October 1973. (Paper read before the American Philosophical Society, April 20, 1977.)

Wolfgang, M. E., L. Savitz, and N. Johnston. *The Sociology of Crime and Deliquency*. New York: John Wiley & Sons, Inc., undated.

Woodson, R. L. "Helping the Poor Help Themselves." *Policy Review*, Summer 1982.

———. "The Importance of Neighborhood Organizations in Meeting Human Needs." In *Meeting Human Needs: Toward a New Public Philosophy*, undated.

———. *A Summons to Life: Mediating Structures and the Prevention of Youth Crime*. Cambridge, Massachussets: Ballinger Publishing Co., 1981.

Woodson, R. L., ed. *Youth Crime and Urban Policy: A View from the Inner City*. Washington, D.C.: American Enterprise Institute for Public Policy Research, 1981.

*Youth Alternatives*, National Youth Work Alliance, Washington, D.C. November 1982 to January 1983.

Zeisel, H. "The Disposition of Felony Arrests." *American Bar Foundation Research Journal*, Chicago, Spring 1981.

# Index